12/16

THIS IS WHERE I AM

D0063459

This Is Where I Am

A Memoir

ZEKE CALIGIURI

University of Minnesota Press
Minneapolis • London

Published by the University of Minnesota Press
111 Third Avenue South, Suite 290
Minneapolis, MN 55401-2520
http://www.upress.umn.edu

ISBN 978-0-8166-9572-0 (pb)
A Cataloging-in-Publication record for this book is available from the Library of Congress.

Printed in the United States of America on acid-free paper

The University of Minnesota is an equal-opportunity educator and employer.

22 21 20 19 18 17 16   10 9 8 7 6 5 4 3 2 1

Dedicated to Deborah Appleman,
whose faith and commitment to me
and the men in these places
always far surpassed my own.
My life went from a cell to the entire world.
This book is just as much yours as it is mine.

CONTENTS

Prologue

REARRANGING DESTINY

M Y FRIEND TEE got shot in the face. It happened in spring, on the basketball court at Stewart Park by the grade school I used to go to in South Minneapolis. Exact words and most of the exact actions are lost to history. Something that started like the tales you hear that circulate, details that grow like creeping Charlie around the very little we know for sure.

It happened just as the city was getting ready to change us all. It was 1993, and I was fifteen years old then, skipping school and hoping girls would understand my story. Back then I used to say I wasn't afraid to die. I don't know where I got that idea.

THERE WERE MANY THERE, but only three actors mattered: my friend Tee, our own sixteen-year-old version of Heracles dressed in a blue flag; Rock, only fourteen—I had run against Rock in the shuttle run and played basketball alongside him before we learned how to tie our shoes. And the third actor was a shaky .22 caliber pistol pulled from the pocket of Rock's Chicago Bulls starter coat. Everyone else was just a gathering of scarred faces that always seem to see these kinds of slanted scrapes of reality.

Only the three primary actors were left when the gun came out. Even the girl the disagreement seemed to be centered

1

around, whose being was intertwined in the binds that connected the whole event, was gone—invisible when the timetaker came out of that pocket.

I've heard someone say that bullets are really just hardened tears, a manifestation of a person's hurt slung to transfer that hurt into another. I think of bullets more as words: small, incomplete fragments of language speaking in combustion for their hurt. It is language most of us believe we speak, until someone screams it at us. They were the same tears and the same words I was releasing a couple years later when I would go to the park across the street to fire off rounds from a .38 Special. It gave me a vibrating flash of exhilaration before having to go back to an unflexing loneliness. How small my world was then. They were the same tears, but different words without anyone intended to hear them.

With an arm outstretched, Rock curled his fourteen-year-old finger around a trigger that could only speak for itself, connected to a brain that couldn't see the future, maybe only sense a destiny. The weight of the ground shifted from the trample of feet escaping the inevitability of what this small piece of metal was capable of, making the flat park tilt at an angle from a blurred set of moments. Tee, strong and fearless, before this day he seemed built of stone, ran against a wind that had pushed everyone else in another direction, but pushed *him* toward the mouth of that pistol—its words fierce and murderous. He ran as though the bullets couldn't speak to him—as though it were language he could change the shape of with his bare hands. He reached out in front of himself as though to grab the gun and muffle its voice—as though he could catch its words.

But it was a language he didn't understand yet. You can't catch bullets, or rearrange their path, or rearrange a destiny that way. Two of those words caught him; one scraped over his skull and another under his chin. The tears of the bullets transmitted from the body of one man toward the body of another. He laid there slumped over, blood spreading like concentrate gathering in the cracks of the asphalt. While Rock jogged off with his spokesman in his pocket.

I heard the story afterward from Rock's brother while we smoked one at the bus stop at Thirty-second and Cedar. I thought it was my business. He told me, "The dumb mother-fucker tried to catch the bullet!"

||||||||||||||||||||||||||

I HEARD SOMEONE SAY: scars define a life, not the injuries. They are the lives we lead afterward. I was still a child, full of angst. I didn't have any scars yet. Most of the kids I knew were already collecting them.

When I saw Tee, he was at the Children's Hospital only a couple of blocks from where it happened. I had skipped school with a friend who was just as disconnected from Tee at that point as I was. I saw him in the darkened room, blinds closed—the kind of dimness of light where you find dead bodies. But he wasn't dead. He moaned at multiple agonizing frequencies, squirming for a position to rest that didn't hurt so obviously. His head was entirely wrapped in a helmet of gauze, only one eye visible, a mummy, crying constantly. I didn't know what to say to him. I don't think I knew why I came. Maybe it was a way to get closer to death, to see what it looked or felt like.

What I felt was shame, for what I didn't know. For not understanding. For putting too much power into the lifestyle he lived and the persona he played; for not understanding that even with all of that strength and courage, he was still a child. Just as it can be so easy to be afraid of the things you don't know; it can be just as easy for some not to be afraid of the bullets if you haven't felt them yet. As tough as it was to watch, to see the man-child chopped down, it wasn't death to me yet. Death was still something you saw on the news.

It was before everything that mattered happened in my life. It was before Jail, before hustling, before Junior got killed, or Justin got paralyzed. And it was before I lost my virginity or dropped out of high school. It was before Murderapolis in '95. It was before I spent so many hours in meditation with my own gun, staring out the front window of my apartment on Cedar Avenue, looking for answers in my reflection, wondering if the world would end at the turn of the century. It was all before I went away. I thought time was something I could make up; experience I could catch up on as I needed to.

llllllllllllllllllllllllll

YEAH, I USED TO TELL PEOPLE I wasn't afraid to die. So did a lot of kids I knew back then. I don't know why the other kids said it, but I think I thought it made *me* seem dangerous and unaffected. Maybe I was just so depressed and I secretly wanted to die but couldn't express it clearly enough. Bullets flew everywhere then, untimed and often without reason. Bullets whistled by without names etched on their casing, purposes slungshot at faceless young ones—I was just as easily one of them. They wound up in walls, in the dirt, jammed in invisible matter. So many bullets ended up in somebody's leg, somebody's chest, or somebody's head. By not being afraid to die—it whispered how much living scared me.

In the fall after seeing Tee in the hospital, our friend Justin died and came back to life. He got shot, the bullet went through his neck, and he spent months in a hospital bed hooked up to all sorts of machines, and when we saw him again he was in a wheelchair trying to tell us about crossing over. He told his best friend he saw the light. I didn't know what that meant, and he was never able to tell us it showed him anything that would change his life. It seemed like we instantly all wanted to believe the meaning of life had been revealed to him, so we wouldn't have to go on looking for it.

llllllllllllllllllllllllll

NINETEEN NINETY-FOUR was supposed to look different. Justin had survived, and some of the fellas felt like that meant we as a group had come through the worst and were safe now. I didn't. I was just as unsure about living as I ever was. That spring I was with a whole spectrum of personalities one night, most I don't know anymore, standing in a cipher by the railroad tracks on Twenty-ninth and Fifteenth, listening to the guy we called Mr. Excitable rap and exaggerate stories. Justin was there, too, less than a year after seeing the light, balancing himself on his feet by leaning on the shoulders of another standing in the cold that night. It was another night, another one of those moments slipped and lost somewhere from history. Even in the dark, the circular scar from the bullet and the zipper marks from the surgery were obvious on Justin's long neck.

The railroad tracks had always been there; we had been kids dodging vagrants who dwelled down there. They didn't make their intentions known to us then, and we weren't asking. Generations of kids had been ducking the destinies of the men and women on those tracks; we were all trying to dodge that life. But there were other lives out there, just as dangerous, that we were running from, too.

I still remember how I felt then, something too fast to see, too sporadic to understand. A night at the tracks being young, drinking the cheapest beer, and smoking blunts. We lived in a bubble, the bubble of our crew. The kid who rode by on his bike that night wasn't in that bubble. It seems to me now that this was one of *his* moments. He rolled by slow, no grander conception of himself or the world than any of us in that circle, in the high brush surrounding the railroad bridge on Fifteenth Avenue. Mr. Excitable said something to the kid; it was easy later to blame those words, but it might not have mattered—it was the kid's night, hoodie-clad on a BMX bike like so many others from the streets I wouldn't recognize again. I don't remember the pullout, or the hidden hand, or a look in the stranger's eyes. I remember the zing, the subtle brushing of something whistling past my ear—then again. I remember falling lazily to the ground, then the rest of the shots. I rested there in the quiet, my nerves vibrating, listening to my heartbeat. In levels the world started coming back—ears ringing, dogs barking. I kept my eyes closed until I heard voices and realized I was alive. I got up and collectively we made sure *everyone* was still alive, especially Justin, who just couldn't seem to escape this kind of volatility. The confusion over what almost happened turned quickly to confusion over what we were supposed to do next.

For some reason we all thought it would be a good idea

to get in the car and go find this kid, as though he hadn't just ducked into the thick of the city's jungle, as though he couldn't put more bullets into that gun. Maybe we were all just trying to compensate for what we couldn't do about what had happened to Justin the previous fall, hoping to rearrange our destinies somehow. That kid on the bike didn't know about Justin, didn't know about the rehab in the swimming pool, the wheelchairs and the grief, the monotony of learning how to walk again on legs that didn't seem to work, or learning to do everything with his left hand. That kid didn't know Tee or the gauze helmet in the hospital. One day he might, but that night that kid knew only a little more than what we did in crisis: squeeze, run, live, die.

It made sense that we got pulled over less than a block away and laid down face first in cuffs on the cold April pavement, where I was stepped on and kicked and eventually left there. There was a sheen that covered the rest of that night like looking out from a plastic cellophane bubble wrapped tight around the city and the world.

That night stuck with me, just like seeing Tee's face swollen to outer space. There was that jolt still vibrating in my legs, in *me*. I didn't sleep. I watched the sun come up from my bedroom. After that, the vibration was replaced with numbness. So much of me stayed that way. The parts that could still feel became that much more sensitive. I stayed quiet because it was nothing compared to what I'd seen Justin or Tee go through.

The next fall I would sit with my father at Junior's funeral and see what death looked like. Sixteen years after that—and over a decade into a prison sentence—I would sit by myself in the same room with my father's dead body. It was so much easier when it happened to someone else. It was before I knew how I was supposed to feel. I don't know how much of it I manufactured because I thought I was supposed to be affected. I think maybe when the injuries are fresh we act different, without perspective outside of the hurt.

I only saw Tee once after that afternoon in the hospital. Someone pointed him out to me in a crowd. I kept looking at him, not to see if he recognized me, or to ask him if he remembered me visiting him in the hospital. I was trying to see his face; I was trying to see the scars, the proof it was him, the same body, a different life. I wanted to see what those tears turned into, or if there was anything else written in them. He was the same person, but there were chips in his stone. I recognized the words, but they weren't meant for me.

IIIIIIIIIIIIIIIIIIIIIIIIIIII

IN A PRISON CELL, things get put in boxes: books, clothes, and piles of notebooks in with all the ideas you ever had. It is where we put all of the early versions of ourselves and experiences, with all of the injuries, the old friends. And perhaps the largest boxes carry around a lifetime of feelings. It is where you decide who matters, what matters, what you can endure, and what you absolutely can't face in the future or in the past. Regret is the king in those spaces. It is where you decide what you are afraid of. I have spent years trying to write myself out of that fear.

We always told ourselves we died when the doors closed behind us. But there are all kinds of death, all kinds of dying. There was more I put away in a box, while I lived in a slightly larger box. I didn't need to see any of this stuff to tell me I wasn't strong enough to withstand certain kinds of obliteration. I knew I wasn't. I could push it right up to the edge and know I wasn't ready to walk into those kinds of explosions; I had proven it with fear my whole life. I have my own scars now to show for it. There is no shame, though, in coming close and deciding you want to live, no matter how ugly or terrifying it can be.

IIIIIIIIIIIIIIIIIIIIIIIIIIII

I WAS TOLD ONCE I should write a memoir about my childhood—but to me there was nothing about my upbringing so exceptional that needed writing about, except for a swirling melancholy I carried with me forever. Don't a lot of kids grow up with a version of that? So should I write about a kid who was sad for no reason—had good parents who loved him and supported him through all his fuckups but still came away injured? Would I write about a kid who never liked himself—who still doesn't—who still retreats into ideas about dying and spent whole stretches teetering on the romanticisms between light and dark?

What would that memoir say about the kid who grew older and robbed and sold dope like an idiot, carried guns he probably never needed to shoot—went to jail, got out—did things just like all the kids who didn't have any of the opportunities and support he did? The sad kid, who didn't seem sad until one fall it got so bad he locked himself in his apartment in South Minneapolis and waited to die—didn't know *how*, just waited. How he hoped on most nights he just wouldn't wake up the next morning. Wouldn't that memoir make him look spoiled and self-pitying? Wouldn't it? What if the same kid who ran into all the vicious energies he'd played with his whole life finally got thirty years in the penitentiary? Would it make his experience any more credible? Would it make him any less self-pitying?

I was that kid, raw and overwrought.

What would be the angle? The diversifying urban landscape of South Minneapolis and its post-Vietnam baby-boom coming of age at the most violent, most brolic segment of its history? How kids who might've become artists or activists started playing with guns and hanging out on corners on Franklin and Chicago, and how they were thrown into the cycle of the state prison system? Or it could be about how that kid—despite the smile he painted on, the charisma he faked, and the personality he constructed—how this kid knew he was probably not good enough to deserve the good things he had, the support and safety, the freedom and independence. That he was really just a con to begin with, merely waiting for the ugly he felt and the darkness he lived in to overtake him and dominate his life.

This is by no means my life story, but it is about a boy with various pathways to manhood that coincided with all of the volatile components coming into contact all at once in Minneapolis, coming up after the city's first great crack wave and how so many in the generation before us became dope fiends. We were surrounded by a new brand of violence, where guns made dying that much easier, and life that much shorter, and forgotten that much quicker. Some of us were the young kids of parents who were activists who used to gather at Cedar–Riverside and Loring Park to demonstrate against the Vietnam War. Others' parents and uncles were those living in the cells at Stillwater prison, coming and going without understanding how big it would get, or how many of their children would end up there later on in their lives. We were just the latest generation trying to figure out what we really believed in—and to learn how to make a living and craft an identity amidst it all.

〰〰〰〰〰〰〰〰〰〰〰〰

I LIVE IN A CELL NOW, with burn marks nipping at my back trying to run from the blast of my life. It was the explosion that changed my life, changed my family's life and the lives of so many families. It was a blast that I had no idea how powerful it would be, of how it would obliterate and transform me after I got far enough away from it to recognize what had happened. Early on, the flash blinded me and my family, and my friends and their families as well. So many of the young people who were around back then scattered to the different places that became their lives. My explosion became just one of the exponential explosions that occurred so often to so many others in the mid- to late nineties as well. We thought, just as we still do, that we are sheltered, but then they come and we tell ourselves, of course not.

I came up around guys who had bigger sacks and bigger guns than me, girls with bigger dreams and larger ideas than I had. I came up with kids with much rougher childhoods than I had, under poverty and other kinds of adversity. I knew dope fiends who fought their way out of addictions, and I knew dope fiends who couldn't. It was these people who shaped my life, walked me to this point—so my memoir becomes really about them. It is the explosion that we share.

It seems to get forgotten or diminished—the time when our city went crazy. The same city that was always considered a stepchild to all of the other major urban metropolises of the

Midwest. It was the time in our history where local news went nuts and pushed their news vans into the heart of the north and south sides, trying to put a generic human interest onto something they didn't understand—and still don't. They would interview the most smoked-out, dance-for-the-camera motherfuckers they could find, hoping they would say something colorful for their broadcast. Every night there was the body count—the impersonal number in the corner of the screen keeping score. It was the time in our city's history when it was printed on T-shirts: *Murderapolis,* with the image of the Grim Reaper standing over the skyline. Block clubs formed like they were militias that were going to take back their streets, with telephones as guns to call the police whenever they heard gunshots. But that was every day, and their efforts just made what they were doing seem all that more ridiculous. They whispered in secret circles and excluded families from the apartment buildings on the block for fear they would inform the dope dealers of what was happening at their meetings. People were going crazy. We were too, right along with them.

This period of time killed or incarcerated some good kids— kids the police swore were much worse than the generations that came before us. In many cases it gave them an excuse to be as vicious as they ever were. Just about every male we came up with has their own story of abuse or outright brutality. There *were* monsters, too, the deviant elements that have always existed here—while the police were running around chasing after kids who were chasing after other kids themselves.

They filled state and federal prisons to capacity with young people carrying astoundingly long sentences. I was one of these people. I still walk through the hallways alongside a lot of those youngsters who aren't young anymore but are still as trapped as ever, whose kids have grown to the ages we were when we all started getting dirty.

It was never as violent in Minneapolis as it was during those years in the mid-90s. But the prisons stayed full, and more people were still going to jail than ever before. Every once in a while the news will start putting statistics in the corner of the screen, maybe in hopes they can raise the temperature again, and there will be something other than costume pageants and Easter egg hunts to cover every night. Maybe it would make today's story as relevant as yesterday's.

I live in one of those cells, catacombs for the souls of thousands of men who once saw themselves as something different from what was ultimately made of them—ended up with lives written in actual life sentences. They were young and sometimes wild, sometimes hideous and unrelenting—now they are older and less severe, dying or gone crazy.

ııııııııııııııııııııııııı

No, THIS IS NOT MY LIFE STORY—it would leave too much out. Nor is it solely about me or who I am. Rather, it is about a city, a chunk of time, and about individuals with unique idiosyncrasies who were there—saw what I saw, were sometimes braver, more involved, but just as confused. People who played with a deck that held the probability of the same kind of circumstances—people who thought they'd be famous or make revolution. A lot of them took their shot too early, jumped from a point too high, too early, and too severe. A lot of them just took off, shucked the clothing of generation and left to be free of it. Most just got older, had kids, waited for things to settle down, and tried to find purpose in their lives.

This story could be about all those complex social perceptions that have always said what is good and what is bad—and what creates the circumstances for how people turn out or become—the things they'll eventually do—and how most of it is a sham. Charts and statistics only talk about what has already happened, not what was going to. There's not a magic formula that made me or any of the kids from my generation who they are—maybe someone could be wrong and still reemerge. It could be a memoir that says maybe we weren't the only monsters, and that there was another beast that swallowed so many of us up who became the veal stuck in its teeth.

It is a story about teachers and coaches who believed they could inspire the troubles of the world away. And they all had the same uncertainty in their hearts—with different variables, where the violence that struck their city was a different kind, where even the crooks didn't fit in the same as they always had. It was a criminal era whose identity had changed and for a few years went frantic, a whole generation that got its sick off at once. It is about the city I come from—where my father was born, raised a few blocks from where I grew up, next to the same park with all of its many beginnings and endings.

Then there is the part of the story that is about the promises of family, and how the people who deserve things don't always get them; it's about the disproportion of blessings and the thieves in the night. I wrote a memoir as a story about those forces in my own life that protected me when things exploded and fell apart, and it became about loss and recovery. It is about families that hold on to sons and daughters the rest of the world has let go. They will sacrifice their own blessings to protect their families, even as the balance they try to maintain gets altered at every new malady. It is about how tenuous all these bonds really can be, how we can be so lucky and then so unfortunate. These stories are about how kids can start as something that means hope and fulfillment for parents and grandparents, and wind up disappointments, shattered to pieces. These are stories about how people get stuck behind the future with a handgun and seemingly no way out, asking themselves what they're going to do. Sixteen years later I still don't know what to do, how to move on, what I should've done, or what I am going to do now. And it's about how these people get stuck in time warps with only themselves and a pen or a brush, or two empty hands, and trying to do something with them.

I want this to be a book about how we are one and several things at once—how we almost become or do something, and then something else happens and we become something else: something more sinister and ugly, broken and disconnected. It's about how people can be good—a part of healthy families with good intentions—and be bad, part of something evil at the exact same time. And it's about how what became so sinister and ugly can hopefully transform again.

I. The Beginning

I used to ice skate
in my living room
on hardwood floors
with plastic bags on my feet.

Living across the street
from the park and the lake
with that big-ass turtle.
Big like unexplained phenomena,
big like large expanses of time-welded waterway,
and big like long days
of shared enigmatic experience.

Back then
my mother would tell me
that my eyes glowed
like fireflies
and that I was the promise
of new life.

I promised her that new life,
before understanding how heavy a promise is
and before I made a hundred more.

—from "Turtles, Fireflies, and Stars"

One

THE DODGE DUSTER

IT SEEMED SAFE—Dad driving, me sitting in mom's clutches in the passenger's side seat of an old off-white Dodge Duster. I was holding on to my old metal Gene Autry lunchbox with vintage clasps. At three or four I was beginning to learn from my mother about the irritation and angst that often came from short mornings. We were rushing on our way to my preschool, training for an entire childhood of this routine: get up before we were ready, zip out the door with dried little pieces of sleep still in our eyes, and put a smile on to go with the OshKosh emblem on my shirt.

The lazy gray could've meant morning, though it may have just reflected dirty winter: piles of snow that had fallen, melted a little, refrozen, and been buried under more snow. Exhaust and refuse saturated to black in the pile. It was ugly and sad—an entire scene, the dirty streets, the sidewalks with debris resting in its cracks. Green hadn't even begun to think about sprouting from under the dinge. The Duster wore a coat of winter film; words had been finger-tagged all over the body, language not yet wiped away.

There was a right turn that had to be made. People make right turns, they make left turns—it is simply a part of how lives are navigated. During the swooping right turn, curling around a snow-gathered corner, at the end, just as the Duster straightened before it could regain the speed it needed, something happened. A portal in the sky opened; a hole in the protective sheath punched through; and the passenger-side door of the Dodge Duster swung open. The conjecture over what happened next begins here: just as a football squeaks out of a ball-carrier's grip and falls to the field, or the routine ground ball gets botched and ricochets into the outfield, or the baton gets fumbled during the handoff in a relay race—what happened? Something happened; and I went flying through the hole ripped into the universe and fell out on the other side of the world— on the outside of the car, out of the womb, from the hands of the woman I thought was holding on to me, whose grip wasn't now as certain as I previously believed it to be. Something happened, and I flew from the American steel vessel I thought was meant to support me from the world speeding by the windows.

I went tumbling onto the street, my momentum stopped only by the curb and a winter's worth of snow pileup. It took a few seconds for the adults, the life-givers and protectors, to register that something had happened. A door had flung open and a child—their child—had fallen out into the wilderness. I lay in the ditch, still and discombobulated, until my dad could pull the Duster over to the side of the road, and my mom could come running out from the car, my well-being an obvious priority now. Thanks, Mom—you almost lost us the game, the gold medal—she'd say, "The turn was too sharp"—he'd say, "You gotta close the door tighter"—they'd say, "The people at Dodge fucked something up. What kind of door just swings open?" As I walked back to that car—to a spot in the backseat this time—I still had my little miniature baby-hand clutched on to the handle of my Gene Autry lunchbox. I'd somehow held on to it through the chaos. They told me later the look on my face was classic, a stone stare of morning angst laced with mistrust and confrontation. I didn't have the words yet, or the injuries to explain how I felt—just a newly injured faith in the things that were designed to hold on to me.

Two

AN ORPHAN AT CHRISTMAS

I BOLTED FROM MY ROOM before my parents were even awake. I was ten years old and I was still taken by the glow of Christmas. I started rifling through the presents wrapped up in Frosty the Snowman and Santa Claus wrapping paper, taking a minute to plug in the lights of the Christmas tree. There was no need to see who the gifts were from; I had discovered the myth that was Santa Claus years before and the incredible similarities to the handwriting of my parents. Despite that, I knew well the euphoria that came with this one morning of the year.

My parents came downstairs much less exuberant, much less enthralled with the adrenaline of the morning. My dad went to make coffee, my mom found a spot on the couch in her bathrobe. We all came together as I pulled boxes from under the tree, a monument created through several generations from ornaments my mom had accumulated since she was a child. There were crystal and glass icicles blown in so many different shapes, reflecting the tangles of lights, and handfuls of tinsel— half on the tree, the other half on the floor and in loose strands through the house. There were popsicle-stick crafts with school pictures pasted onto red and green construction paper, clay-molded reindeer, and blown-glass bulbs and a sock monkey on the top. There were garlands and plastic pine garnishes hung up and down the staircase and along the wooden trim. My mother would hang little angels from the ceilings, children with wings and little golden halos.

I tore open packages in an exhilarated mania: shirts and hats with the logos of my favorite teams, video games, a remote control car, hockey equipment. I got the hockey equipment from my dad. I was high on euphoria. Dad got his tomato sauce going; the smell of garlic overtook our little space in the world, with meatballs and sausage, homemade noodles and gnocchi on standby for when the rest of the family got there.

Apparently, my dad saw him first. I was upstairs playing Tecmo Bowl, comfortable in the heat and security of our house. Outside was the wilderness. Outside there were trenches carved out of four-foot snow banks and razor-blade winds. There he was, alone outside of our window, his head barely visible above the snow banks at the park across the street. There was a deliberation, three perspectives: my mother weighing things out loud; my father, coolheaded man of action; and me, the observer.

My dad went out and got him, brought him in from the cold, from the tundra into the warmth, into the untouched stillness of our Christmas. He had been shivering on that sidewalk in a jean jacket with only a little bit of flannel insulation, thin stone-washed jeans, and a pair of little pleather shoes with Velcro straps worn down close to the point of bursting at the creases. No hat, no mittens. Just a dark-skinned kid probably four years old a few weeks behind on a haircut, with tears of confusion that ran hard and connected to a flow of snot coming from his nose.

My mom tried to ask him questions—the who's and what's, the how come's—but all she seemed to get was his name, Eric. In a story I wrote later in my life I gave him a scar above his right eye shaped like an asterisk—maybe to denote an architecture of undetermined abuse or neglect, perhaps just to add something distinguishing. In real life, there was no such mark— and other than being an underdressed kid too young to know his last name or a home phone number or any phone number at all, there wasn't anything that stood out about his appearance. He could have been one of dozens of kids running around the playgrounds at Powderhorn in the summer. I think I used the scar as a line that could connect the past to the future— resounding proof that this was indeed the same kid if I ever saw him as an adult. The scar could be the universe's way of explaining the ways people end up. But there wasn't that when I looked at him, a boy hesitant to take his coat off in our living room, a misery-stricken kid in a perplexing new world where there were strange white people looking in his face.

At first he was too shy to smile, no joy in the midst of what was happening. It took him a little while to relax enough to sit down, just enough to rest modestly on the edge of the foot rest. He stared at the glow and the shiny movement of the ornaments on the Christmas tree, standing over all of the freshly torn paper and boxes full of gifts just recently ripped through. That was before a blade had come in and cut the euphoria into a cold chasm of reality. I started throwing a ball around with him, and gradually a little bit of life came into his face. He didn't talk, just nodded his head when I brought out cookies. A weird feeling took over me, different from how I felt earlier when I was opening presents and accumulating new things. I kind of felt sick, like I could cry, like I knew stories like this existed but now they had a face.

My mom had an array of speculations over how this could happen. Was the family just so poor that they couldn't afford to feed him? That maybe in desperation they left him out there for somebody else to find him? Was it just out of plain cruelty, malice toward his innocence? Was he just the newest burden that was too much for someone to carry? Were they out on Christmas morning and forgot him on that sidewalk as they kept moving on with their holiday? There was no way someone would intentionally leave a four-year-old out in the wind-whipping winter of December, would they? What kind of people would do something like that? These were just some of the outwardly verbal conclusions my mom actively jumped to. It was the part of the narrative in life, where nobody wants to think the worst of someone and simultaneously everybody wants to think the worst of someone. It was easy to create an enemy out of someone when there wasn't an actual face with an actual motive. In certain ways it made the offense more obscene, made the monster more hideous and capable.

My parents were in the other room debating over whether to call Social Services or the police or wait to see if someone would come looking for him. The two of them kept going back to the window to see if somebody would come looking for him—but there was no one. My mother has always had this soft spot for children. That's probably why every year during the holidays our house was full of gold-shrouded angel ornaments hanging everywhere. It was probably very hard for her not to think that this child was left out in front of her house for her to protect and take care of. I'm sure something fierce gnawed at her rational self to adopt the kid who had been left in her hands to feed and nurture on Christmas morning.

How could she send him into one of those unimaginable environments that might send him back to the people who left him behind in the winter or might lead to displacement on the foster home circuit? At least here she would know what he'd get. But that wasn't realistic—people can't just keep kids they find on a street corner. They agreed the only feasible option was to call Social Services, which sent over a squad car. I didn't know how I felt, I only knew I felt sick, like I was going to throw up. As a family we watched with that nauseous feeling as little Eric, his fear and trembling renewed, got into the backseat of a blue-and-white, moving with his eyes closed toward whatever his future held. We watched the kid leave in that squad car, then went back to what was going to be a party soon, our insulated home with a fresh layer of disappointment covering it now.

A hazy film now coated itself over the sanctity of our Christmas. It *should* have, though; life could be devastating, and I was realizing that there was plenty of hurt going around while all of the good things we had were manifesting themselves in our lives. It made me ask myself if we even deserved Christmas after that. It added a confusion of sadness and regret, privilege and guilt over not being able to fix something broken beyond what we had the tools to repair. The day started again—the rest of the family came over. We talked about it a little bit, but Christmas still went on as though a little boy hadn't been abandoned in the street outside. It was as though there hadn't been this little messenger who ended up on our doorstep to tell us indirectly about our happiness and security—the apostle with tears frozen to his face.

After that I didn't want to celebrate Christmas anymore. Kids I went to school with at times hardly had shoes to walk them there and back. That next spring, our teacher took us on a field trip to the Waite House on Twenty-sixth Street. Most of us already knew it was a soup kitchen; after all, it was only three blocks from school. When we got there, a kid from our class was there with his family, his poverty on egregious display. I felt sick and nervous to a point of being dizzy. It seemed like every day I saw something new that reinforced these feelings.

Mom still decorated the house in coming years, but as a family we stopped giving each other presents. Instead, we bought toys for toy drives and sponsored families. But it didn't cover any wounds or stop what happened from happening. The angels still hung from the ceiling.

When I came to prison so many years after that Christmas, I created a daydream scenario where as new people came into the joint I would recognize the asterisk-like scar of the young man who I would know, right away, was the same boy from that day. I think maybe in my own narrative about what happened that Christmas morning I was trying to tell myself about the sad places people end up, and trying to make sense out of the strangely recurring cycles that are created when babies get dropped off in the system. But because the scar never really was, I have no idea what happened to that kid. I wouldn't know him if I did run into him. It is conceivable that he could have passed through these walls at some point in my bid, but the real thing here isn't about those cycles or the greed of Christmas or irresponsible parenting—it is just about a little kid who spent one Christmas morning at the house I grew up in. There is an innocence we all depend on to make our lives livable for so long until it is disrupted by something we never expect.

Three

GRANNY IN A YELLOW DRESS

I WAS TEN YEARS OLD and I thought our house was being robbed. That's what it sounded like anyway—like there were people downstairs picking and digging through our things. It was the first summer I could be at the house alone, so I slept in a lot and roamed around the city on my bike trying to find pick-up baseball games. Before I was legally a latchkey kid, I went to my grandma's after school and during summer days. She lived right across a section of the park in the house my dad grew up in, that accumulated all the ghosts and the junk they left behind in boxes stacked to the ceiling. But that morning I woke up to commotion, odd sounds of electricity humming from downstairs. I waited, tried to be still and invisible. But it was just too much; I had to know what was happening and if there was someone downstairs. So I took a few light steps from my room, and the whole house creaked from the hundred-year-old floorboards, so I held myself up with the walls to keep from creating too much pressure with my feet. I took a look down the short half of the staircase, but all I could see was the light from the late-morning sun and a few bees swirling around. That wasn't strange, though, not then. There was a hive of nasty little bees over one of the windows in the dining room, and throughout the summer one or two would slip in through an open window and buzz around. They were kind of a vicious brand, too, stinging unprovoked while we slept or watched TV. In the mornings I walked around with a fly swatter.

I scooted down the top flight one stair at a time, still listening to what sounded like someone watching our TV or digging through things. I hit the landing, where I could curl my head around the corner and see what was happening downstairs. I had to shoo a bee that was hovering around my head just to get into position to see around that corner. I took a one-eyed peek at the bottom floor of the house and saw a haze of swirling movements. Until I could get my focus, it looked like fog, moving in bands of funnels. I finally was able to see that the miniature iridescent tornadoes were actually swarms of bees in innumerable clusters buzzing and knocking things over. It was an unbelievable sight, what seemed like thousands, probably hundreds of thousands of bees in force upon the inside of our house, moving and working in large and small groups, larger swarms absorbing smaller ones, and other smaller ones breaking off onto their own. The bees that had previously only visited in ones or twos had overtaken the entire ground floor of our house. I was stuck. If there was a realistic way out, I would have just run for it, but getting to a door meant an actual confrontation with something I couldn't comprehend, and I couldn't jump out of a window. I was trapped upstairs in my own house.

My parents were at work, and Granny was the only one I could call during the day. So I called her, the little gray-haired old lady who drove an enormous Cadillac Calais but still walked the five blocks to the bank on Lake Street or to get her permanent at the beauty shop on Thirty-sixth and Chicago. Or anywhere her legs would take her really regardless of weather or the not-so-hidden treachery of the neighborhood. I told her on the phone what I saw. I warned her that what was happening wasn't natural, that these bees were different from the bees that pollinated the lilies of the valley alongside her house: they were mean and indifferent. She told me they were "just bees— don't panic." I told her she didn't understand just how many

bees there really were. "Well, where did they come from?" I
didn't know what to tell her then.

She's the woman who, despite what she might have expected for her life, became my grandma, somehow became Granny.
Granny was a peculiar example of compulsions and contradic-
tions that made her just tough and eccentric enough to be the
one I would call in such a situation. She was an unlikely city girl
who set roots down in Minneapolis where she's been for sixty
years. It wasn't where she started; she just kind of ended up
there. It was where she moved from Anoka to wait for the Ital-
ian boy she met in Hibbing to get back from the War. He was a
boy several years younger than her, a woman who had possibly
conceived the notion that she was too old by then to be wed. A
boy who tricked her into showing him how to dance but turned
out to be as smooth as glycerin, a boy it turns out who had finished runner-up in a local jitterbug competition.

He was the boy who outcharmed a Swedish kid who was
also after her, vying to be the one she waited for during the war.
The boy for whom she wrote a letter every day of the two years
he was gone, until he finally came home and they moved into
a house on Twenty-seventh and Lyndale, then to a house on
Twenty-first and Fourteenth that soon after became a slightly
bigger house by Powderhorn in order to make room for the two
boys they would have. And this became her headquarters, from
where she set up a mostly solitary life after the boy who had become her husband died and went into the ground at Fort Snel-
ling before her oldest son could turn thirty-five. Far too many
years before she was ready for it. And it was where the little
gray-haired old lady could be seen after every snowfall shoveling snow on her front sidewalk or the driveway in the alley.
Or in the summer steadily walking that old push mower that
was so antiquated she had to get the blades sharpened at the
antique shop on Thirty-eighth and Cedar.

She was always kind of a loner anyway. She'd say, "After all,
I went down to Mardi Gras by myself." And she had: she'd gotten on a train and met three girls, young just like her and about
to see all the same things for the first time. She was going to

drink mint juleps in Kentucky, but a late freeze ruined the mint crop that year. In the summer after finishing a trade school program in sign painting at Dunwoody, she took a trip by herself to a dude ranch in Wyoming. She had no idea then she would meet my grandfather later. It might have also been something intrinsic that prepared her for all those years alone after he died, the years no one else was going to mow the lawn or shovel her way out of a snowstorm.

She still watched all the CBS soap operas and *The Price Is Right* on an old wood-boxed TV she bought at Sears with a service contract. We asked her many times if she wanted us to get her cable, but she said she had plenty to watch as it was. So she watched *The Young and the Restless* while crocheting hat and mitten sets or snowflake doilies we got from her every year at Christmas. Despite her protests, we got her a microwave, simply by bringing it up and plugging it in. "There, it's yours." It was hard to convince her how easy it was to use when she had been conditioned on the electric stove her and Papa had also bought at Sears with the service contract she would keep for the rest of her life.

Some of us who have known her had always been privy to her natural independence, which came with a certain dominance over nature, likely from her days as a farm girl in Fairbury, Nebraska. The story begins when she got sent home for wearing her overalls to school—something "very unladylike" in those days. She held a bit of a grudge over the demonstration created over that one. That was even before she committed an entire lifetime of votes to the Republican Party because of a bank account she lost during the banking crisis of the Great Depression. She blamed FDR for the collapse of her bank. I would say, "Granny, you're too poor to be a Republican."

"I never asked for no handouts, and I'm not going to start now. That's the problem with people these days; they expect the government to fix all their problems."

"Well, that's very Ayn Rand of you, Granny."

It was probably around the same time that the numerous black-and-white photos of young Granny started to circulate among our family, before she was even close to being a granny, proudly carrying impressive stringers of fish or with a rifle in her arms, hunting with her uncles. Later on, this fearlessness was manifested in the Sisyphean job of capturing the bats in her attic, a deed done one at a time in a plain glass jar with her bare hands—a task undertaken so matter-of-factly and with such a determined indifference as to indicate her innate and almost unfeeling natural fearlessness. In the mornings she'd flick on the light in the attic and there were always more bats.

|||||||||||||||||||||||||||||

REGARDLESS OF MY WARNING, she left her house, didn't take the shortcut across the park, but instead took the long way up Elliot and across Thirty-fifth Street. I could see her coming from a window, an astounding sight, striding at her own leisurely pace in a yellow sundress, in tennis shoes and nylon bobby socks with lace sequins. She was coming to fight a house full of bees in a yellow sundress. She arrived and nonchalantly unlocked the door, just as she had once before to chase out a sparrow that was bounding off the walls of our living room. I peeked around the corner from the landing to see what she thought she'd be able to do about anything at all. She had a can of Raid in each hand—just plain Raid, for flies and cockroaches. I was afraid to leave the steps to help her, so I didn't. She was on her own; I had told her how many bees there were before she came over, and she came over anyway with drugstore bug killer. I guess I didn't know what I was asking of her when I called her, but I didn't expect this old lady with six shooters of bug spray to take on an entire colony.

Without even a pause to register what she was seeing, she systematically started spraying clouds of poison at every individual, every cluster, every swarm. Granny went an inch at a time across the expanse of our ground floor knocking them down, some in midflight, some gathered along windowsills. As she sprayed, the intensity of the bees sped up; agitated and drugged, larger swarms fractured into smaller groups moving faster and more determined in looping motions. She kept spraying, though, ducking and dodging rather sprightly from the chaotic movements of the swarm. It seemed she would be mauled and stung repeatedly, even as she sent struggling bees down writhing to their deaths. And as she covered ground, moved her way through the living room and out of sight, more of them came, and the buzz that was a hum before grew higher and sharper. She called for me to come downstairs; she told me most were taken care of, so I came down reluctantly. I trusted her protection but crept a good distance behind her. The whole house smelled like chemicals, so I had my shirt covering my nose and mouth. When I looked up there were still errant bees circling her, but she had her two cans of spray and was standing over a huge chunk of drywall in our dining room that had fallen from where the wall meets the ceiling. There was a huge gap there, where the hive had expanded its limits and pushed their way into our house. As fast as she killed them, fifteen or twenty more would fly in from the new back door of the hive. It seemed an endless task to fight an army that just kept regenerating, and it seemed stupid for me to be standing anywhere near the hole in that wall. And it seemed stupid that a little old lady in a sundress and bobby socks was walking right into the crescent of the fire.

Sometimes nature just dominates because it is far more savage and indiscriminate than we can prepare for. It was a good fight, and she won huge points for courage, but some forces were just too great. It was time for her to accept that she could have killed bees for hours, but as long as that hole lay untouched and out of reach in our dining room, there would always be more bees, more agitated and confused than the others. She had cleared enough space for me to get downstairs and out the door, and that was enough—she had done her job—so I tried to convince her it was time to leave, it was time to spend the rest of the afternoon at her house. But like when I tried to speak with her ten years later about Reagan's detachment from the poor and lower class, she couldn't hear anything I was saying. Next thing I knew, she had one of the dining room chairs pressed up to the wall and got up on it, spraying bees that had drifted out of reach. Then she maneuvered the chair just under the chasm of wall where the entire problem was coming from and got back up on the chair, her head two feet from the ceiling. I was still in the living room with the fly swatter, whiffing at the stragglers still trying to hold themselves up with all the poison in the air. Granny reached an arm upwards, exposed and unprotected, and started spraying into the hive. Almost immediately there was a gust of escaping bees that blew into the house to avoid their extermination. There was a cloud of commotion around Granny's head. No bee stings, though—instead just more Raid in the hole. When one can was empty, she got down off of the chair and started spraying up into the hive again until bees stopped coming into the house. There were still a few, but the main torrent was over. And I was happy she was finally willing to escape to the front yard with me. I was still a little lightheaded from the cloud of poison I had been walking around in. Granny didn't have much of a response. She just said, "That was really something, wasn't it?" Then she asked me if I was hungry. She said she had Tombstone pizzas in the deep freeze. "They were on special," she said. As nonchalantly as she disregarded her conquest of the bees, she had shown me what I already felt but didn't quite understand: that she was one of the invisible forces in the world, protecting me from the harshness of life, intending to protect me until my skin had hardened to armor.

Four

ON PILGRIMAGE

I WAS THE BABY who was never supposed to be born. Doctors told my parents they could probably never have children. That's the way the story was told to me over the years. So in the summer of 1989, before I turned twelve, my parents decided it was time to bring me back to the place in California where I was born. It had been ten years since either of them had seen most of their old friends, or the terrain high in the mountains of Trinity County. For me, it had been an entire remembered lifetime; all I had were a few scant memories of a basset hound named Murphy and a recurring dream with a waterfall, a suspension bridge, and a bar I stumbled into at two years old— otherwise all other imagery was just folklore to me. Folklore created from names of valleys and creeks, and from stories I had been told about my birth in a one-room house in the town with a population of ninety-two. About the red jumpsuit I wore so that I could be seen running around in the forest by somewhere called Canyon Creek. It was our folklore, anecdotes and names of people I only knew from my parents. They were the things that happened high on the edge of a mountain before I could remember.

My mom always emphasized these places and stories as my home. To me California was the mythical home of Giants and

Raiders, Dodgers and Forty-Niners. To my parents it was the magical place they found while driving around the country in a black van my dad bought with credits from the government after coming back from Vietnam. Somehow, perhaps through divine navigation and just enough serendipity, they found this community that became the place they ran off to when they were told they couldn't have children. And it became the place where they miraculously got that child they weren't supposed to be able to have.

To them it was a creation story, the cosmic birth on the other side of a mountain on the outer edge of the universe. And even though I was well aware of their thinking and liked the idea of coming from somewhere that seemed otherworldly, South Minneapolis was my home. We moved back to Minnesota when I was only two years old. I had my father to thank for that. He was the one who gave me Powderhorn Park in all of its grandiosity, as well as its insidious underbelly. It was where he taught me how to skate holding myself up on the ice with a folding chair. He also gave me Lake Street and Franklin, Elliot, and Chicago Avenues. It was where most of the people I knew lived and where my earliest forms of identity came from. All the rest was just somebody else's history. I was too young then to glean much from it.

And in the summer before I turned twelve they decided it was time for the three of us to rediscover the organic, bandana-and-bell-bottom beginnings of our family. As the plan evolved, the idea was presented to drive there. It was supposed to be like all the times they spent on the highways trying to find themselves, part of the great transitory freedom of the 1970s that helped germinate the creation story. It was before gas skyrocketed and there were dogs waiting at every state border, and before we were a settled American family with a home base. The family car was a gunmetal-colored Buick Century. At the time it was only a couple of years old, and by our family's standards it was kind of luxurious, with air conditioning and electric windows and a tape deck. But there were still doubts it could make such a trip. Regardless, driving was going to be the way to show me where I came from. I think the idea was to make the trip while I was still young enough for them to show these places to me. They expected it would take about three days to get there, with a night or two at hotels. We would spend a week in the mountains and another four days with friends in San Francisco, another vague part of the legend I didn't yet know much about.

My parents were a little worried I wouldn't stop talking for the entire three thousand miles, but the first night I slept all the way through the Hawkeye State, burning through double-A batteries, listening to Public Enemy on my Walkman.

In the morning after the first night of driving, we were on a stretch of Highway 80 that crossed over into one of those never-ending superflat stretches of Nebraska. Once we got through Omaha and Lincoln, it seemed like the plains ran on forever—until off in the distance a glimpse of the Rocky Mountains started to show itself on the Wyoming side. It was the first time I'd seen mountains since I was a baby. We took a detour to drive by Fairbury, Nebraska, the small farming town where Granny was from. There was a road sign with the name but not much town to see—it really just looked like the rest of the state, flat and naked.

Nebraska turned into Wyoming, a mash-up of names I only remembered from playing Oregon Trail as a kid. I slept through most of another long day. Wyoming turned into Utah with the glow of Salt Lake City in the distance. Utah became Nevada: hours in the desert, stopping only to eat in Reno before getting back in the car.

By evening we were being inspected at the California border for produce. It felt like we were entering into a different universe that only really existed on television or in movies.

"Why did we move to Minneapolis, anyway?" I asked, curious at that moment, probably sensing we were so close.

"There weren't jobs. When I got laid off at the lumberyard, there just weren't any other places there to work. And we wanted you to be closer to your grandparents." It was the simple answer that couldn't quite put to words what the late seventies were, especially in small towns where manufacturing was the only engine to prosperity, unless a person worked for the city or the state. There was a somberness to the way my dad said it, like there was a disappointment that hadn't gone away—like maybe everything could've been better than what it became. It sounded like the great adventure that had been his life was over, and he was back in the neighborhood again. But the job thing was enough answer for me, and I let it go.

Soon, Highway 80 became Highway 5, and California became mountains—scenery from two-lane highways that wound around tectonically constructed corners in its ascent into the sky. It was like the Boundary Waters, but with trees and wilderness meant for the dinosaurs towering over us, and without my parents arguing in a canoe for hours about how my mother could only save one of us if the boat tipped over. For the first time on the entire drive, I started to get dizzy. It was probably the altitude, and the winding roads, and the expanding dementia of the land of the giants that completely disrupted my equilibrium. We stopped at a rest stop to help me get my balance. But I couldn't find a comfortable place to escape my motion sickness. I found the best possible place was on the floor behind the seats, seeking out any kind of relief from the polyester interior against my face. It still wasn't enough of an escape to fight the vertigo.

We ended up at another motel, in Redding. The stop brought back more stories and fingers pointed at all the things that had changed or stayed the same. It was kind of like an oasis—the last stop before we could ascend to the top of the universe.

In the morning, as we got closer, the wilderness started becoming more and more recognizable to my parents, pointing out certain bends or bridges they remembered.

"That's where Gretchen, Susan's sister, fell off the road."

"Did she die?" I asked.

"No—just broke some bones—messed the car up, though."

"It's probably still down there."

My dad navigated the slim roads, pushing fifty on the asphalt that turned in acute angles on the edge of rock faces that looked like they dropped off the other side of the earth. There were blind turns that vehicles going in either direction turned into on faith, that the others would see them coming; compact, midsize, pickups, and logging trucks—all borrowing their share of a road that didn't apologize for its severity.

It was late afternoon when we arrived in Weaverville, a town where only one street had stoplights. We pulled into the driveway of a home whose lights went on as soon as the Century's went out. Smiles and embraces came from three people I didn't at all recognize—for whom it might have felt like an entire lifetime had elapsed since my parents packed up their stuff and drove east. The couple that greeted us were a little older than my parents, so there was kind of a paternal familiarity that had probably always been there, and still shown under the thin layers of the years. For me, the reintroduction to these two people and their daughter was brand new and welcoming—they welcomed me like they knew I was connected to this place, or at least part of me was.

I figured out right away it was different there. When we walked across Main Street, a man and his son smiled and asked us how we were doing. I watched them both as they crossed the street and walked off in the other direction. Then I looked at my dad. That didn't happen in the city much. He told me that was the way things were there. It was one of those rare towns that hadn't been infiltrated by fast food joints yet. As we walked around, Dad pointed out what was different and what was the same; only some of it had modernized.

Days were stuffed with reunions and updates on husbands and kids whose ideas of running off only brought them to towns in the nearby valley or on another mountain not so far away. We met up with a woman my mom knew from a New Age woman's group, full of yoga and transcendental meditation. Apparently, her daughter and I ran around in cloth diapers together. Dad brought me to see an old boss of his when he worked for the fire department, who sat drinking beer, watching the hills spread out in different directions. He talked about the wind and what direction the smoke blew that year. And we went to see the family of diehards high up into the mountains, who stayed even when everyone else moved into town. They were once city people who followed the same dream my parents had, only they chose to stay.

The next day my dad brought me on a misty, overcast day to the softball field where he used to play, the one people came to from all the surrounding towns to watch him track down balls in left field. At least that's what my mom says. He didn't quite seem to remember it exactly that way, but he smiled anyway. We pulled out the gloves and played catch—just the two of us, tossing a ball back and forth like we had since before I could remember, a park at the beginning of my universe, thirty yards from a playground and the merry-go-round I fell off of a few times. I fell off of a lot of things back then. On a field that sowed legends in our household, two mountain ranges and a great plain away.

We went as a family to see the house on Buckhorn Mountain. It was the house we moved to after I was born. It was just a house with nothing but slant and wilderness behind it, sitting near the top of Buckhorn. From the road, Mom and Dad agreed it seemed smaller than when we lived there. They told me it was where we had Murphy, the dog I remembered. A wistful bit of fog hit their eyes as part of the past unveiled itself— brought snapshots of youth and hopefulness to the front pages of the photo album. I could envision clotheslines and little kids in bare feet, with banana smeared on their shirts, with messed blond hair and sunflowers in their hands, running around in the boundless yard. We left before anyone who might've lived there started to wonder why a family of strangers was staring at them from outside of a Buick Century.

On our last day in the mountains, the people we were staying with took me and Dad to the top of Buckhorn. Mom urged me to make the trip, along the imbalanced dirt road just wide enough for a pickup truck to keep from falling off the edge of the hill. It was a place high atop the world where she overcame her lifelong fear of heights. There was a fire tower lookout on the very top of the mountain. A clear-cut space at the top of the treacherous path, hardly paved with limestone. We climbed a ladder to the top of this lookout, a small conservatory where someone could see for hundreds of miles, would be able to see the wind push fire through the forest during the driest part of the year.

Just looking down I saw the entire world at my feet. This was the part where I was supposed to see what my mom saw that had changed her life—that made her dream of what she was going to be—and where I'd see who I could be. I think I understood it then, at least a little bit. That little bit that allows me to look back at it and understand its enormity, its carving in stone, the beginning of our family.

Then we went to Junction City—the town, around a mountain and into the old grooves carved out of terrene collisions from before any of this was written, where I was born. The town, with a bar, a few small houses, and hillsides of hidden little houses and their hibernating owners, with a highway sign that told us the population had soared to 416 since we'd left. We pulled off the winding road and my parents showed me this miniature home, one main room, a living room, and kitchen and a bedroom all at once. A bathroom the size of a closet—a toilet and a shower, no sink. I was born on the bed because there wasn't time to make the trip to Weaverville. So that was where the world started, a big bang, the baby born in the hills, just up from Canyon Creek. And while it may have contained the mystical gateway to my incarnation—the beginning of weather beating at our faces for a lifetime, alpha and omega—it just looked like a house, a plain house, a few feet from a plain bar with neon beer signs in the window.

"That's where you were born."

There wasn't a lot to be impressed by—four walls that could've been cardboard—the vessel that created me, the cosmic womb with woods behind it that the sun sent glances through, and the canyon creek at the break in the hill. I took it in. Eleven years old, trying to figure out what it was—overcast with low-lying clouds that looked like fog but was really just the atmosphere for what I came from—the root of why I am here. From where I was standing I felt so much closer to the rest of the universe, like I could reach and grab stars. But eventually, inevitably, the value of staring at a house, and some trees, and a hill diminished to a point where there was nothing left to do but leave.

When we got back, we ate a big meal for our last night there. Together we set the groundwork for another visit we fully intended to make. Someone made a suggestion that they should consider a trip to South Minneapolis. They could come in spring and watch the puppets march down Bloomington Avenue in the May Day Parade, watch all the little kids with flowers painted on their faces at the festival at Powderhorn Park. It might've been cool to show them Minnehaha Falls or Lake Calhoun in the summer. It seemed like a great idea. The daughter liked the idea, but I got the sense that it would never happen. It probably wasn't supposed to.

The next morning we left in the gunmetal-gray Buick Century on our way to the Pacific Coast Highway so I could see the ocean and drive through the Redwood National Forest.

We merged from the Redwood Highway to the Pacific Coast, stopping before it got too dark and too cold to pull up our cuffs and walk around in the ocean for the first time—next to "Beware of Sharks" and "Strong Undercurrents" signs. It was my first experience with the ocean. I was mesmerized by the ebb and flow of the tides, while off in the distance the sun went down slow and calculated over the horizon. I was a kid with frozen feet and wet cuffs on my jeans, trying to stay in the water as long as I could.

We drove the rest of the way to San Francisco—the other half of the pilgrimage. It was another mythic place my parents came through to see friends during the great hippie migration of the late sixties before deciding they wanted to live in the mountains. Old friends of my parents welcomed us in and talked about the coincidences that had brought the friends together. There were stories with dimensions I couldn't completely understand at the time but that had somehow added members to our family.

We went to baseball games at both Candlestick and Oakland–Alameda, just months before the great earthquake struck in the middle of the World Series between the two Bay Area teams. We sat along the first-base line at the first game so we could cheer for Darryl Strawberry. I was such a fanatic I had my face painted blue and orange to match my Mets jersey with an 18 etched in the artwork. It was ridiculous, and every time I stood up Giants fans booed the shit out of me. The wind blew like crazy, cold and nasty. It was one of the only times I ever got to see baseball outdoors, with grass, and not under the plastic baggy of the Metrodome. It made me somehow feel cheated out of my childhood baseball experience.

Going through Oakland, we ate at a KFC and bought food from behind bulletproof glass. Across the street vendors sold bean pies and Malcolm X T-shirts—it was like a Too $hort video.

The entire pilgrimage may have been unconsciously leading up to the ferry trip to the random mound of stone and decaying concrete structure sitting in the San Francisco Bay. From the first mention I was enamored with Alcatraz. I walked into a prison for the first time, right into the cell blocks, fortresses of tiers rising to the ceiling—rows and rows of bars—each cage representative of human souls once held inside of them. One after another, counting days off of primitive calendars in the plaster and concrete, daydreaming about girlfriends and kids and worlds separate from themselves. Hands holding on to bars looking out at nothing but reflections of themselves and at how small their worlds had become.

We went on the headphone tour and listened to a severe voice tell the narrative that walked us from place to place: the chow hall, the medical unit where the Birdman lived, the cell where Al Capone allegedly stayed. There was the cell with bullet holes from one of the most violent insurrections over the years, where the inmates got into the gun lockers and held the prison captive for days. There was a cell with displayed dummy heads made of papier-mâché, and holes in the back of the cells where Frank Morris and the Anglin brothers chipped their way out and escaped—to where exactly and how far, of course, who knows? There was a peculiar familiarity for me with the place for some reason, maybe premonition, maybe association with something shared and cultural with all the generations of people thrown in cages and dungeons through the history of humanity. My mom and dad were mostly just amused by the B-movie music and overly dramatic voices on the Walkman. I felt something different, maybe foreboding.

The narration brought us along painted lines on the concrete floors to solitary confinement. There were cells and within the cells there was a second door that shut and locked out any possible light, a pitch-black experience that could only drive someone crazy. I got an odd chill when the door closed behind me, a panic at being shut in, choice being stolen away, and an unavoidable claustrophobia. One of the voices on the tape said he would play a game where he took a button off of his shirt and tossed it randomly in the dark. Then he would spin himself dizzy and try to find the button in the spinning void. It planted a fear in me that made me gag every time I would ever have to shut myself into such a space again.

When we came out, there were open cells we could walk into, feel the space and the seclusion. There is a picture somewhere in my mother's possession, intentionally hidden somewhere out of even accidental sight, of me standing in a cardigan sweater and a Georgetown Hoyas turtleneck, with my fingers clenched around the solidity of those cell bars, looking out from behind them as though it were a peculiar bit of memorabilia and not a prophetic talisman. Eyes looking out unsuspectingly at a world that would never see him as the accidental tourist in one of these places again.

The next day we started the drive back home. This time there was nothing new about the places we drove through. Nevada just seemed hot, and for long stretches it seemed like we were chasing giant slabs of bedrock mirage in the distance. We found just enough daylight this time to stop and take pictures of our exhausted family standing at the edge of the Bonneville Salt Flats, a virtual wasteland behind us. Those pictures are probably sitting conspicuously alongside the ones of us outside of Cabela's, fuzzy and poorly lit with a disposable camera with no zoom.

There was no stopping on the way back; my parents had to go back to work, and I started school in a few days. The vacation was over, summer was over. I spent a lot of time thinking about alternative destinies—what if we had stayed and I had grown up there? Would I have been like the kids who lived there now? Or would I have found my way to escape as well? This was all before I ever even considered what might happen with my life. I still planned on going to a major university, doing something substantial with my life. It was a time before I ever got stoned, before everyone around me started cocking their hats and tried convincing everyone what they were and why that was important. It was before I realized I wasn't going to play in the major leagues. It was before I thought I was Jim Morrison and before a more-than-disappointing attempt to graduate from high school, running around chasing a buzz. It was before the city blew up and the kids decided they weren't kids anymore. Going through Lincoln, Nebraska, I hadn't figured out yet how I was going to feel about my own city when I got older, was confused as to where I really came from or if it really mattered at all. I hadn't figured out what it was that hurt so much inside yet; the dull ache and the nerves that lived with this body hadn't told me yet what was always there. Even crossing the Iowa border back into Minnesota I hadn't thought about my own potential. I did think about my parents' road trips, and the strange places they found themselves, and how somehow they found themselves back home—the magnetic forces of the universe that made me a kid growing up in South Minneapolis instead of a kid going to school in an obscure town high in the sky. It was a time before anything mattered yet; all the destiny-defining choices had been made by someone other than me.

Our friends in the mountains never made the trip to Minneapolis. We went back to San Francisco several times, but we never drove again. The point came in my life where I started making all the destiny-defining decisions in my world. The ache and the nerves started to create an identity of their own as the world rotated and got more complicated. Mom and Dad did their best to make sense of a very nonsensical generational transition. The Buick Century blew its head gaskets and got traded in for a Ford Tempo. The Trinity Alps and the rest of the mountains in the world quietly and as slow as geologic time continued to move and formulate, tilt and push farther into the sky as plates collide without anyone even noticing it, seemingly staying still as lives begin and end.

Five

MONSTERS AND
FLORAL PRINT SKIRTS

M Y PROSECUTOR called me a monster. I wondered how seriously he believed this. I wasn't any more of a monster
than he was. When I got to prison, I realized that prosecutors
call just about everyone they are on the verge of convicting
monsters. It's a fine piece of theater: the wielding of language
as performance, where they play the good guys and new actors
get to be the bad guys every day.

But being a monster wasn't even a thought in my head
when I was twelve years old. I played so many roles during the
years I went to Hans Christian Andersen Open School. Early
on I was the angel, the mischievous child, the sensitive kid, and
the boisterous one. I grew into the smart-ass, the class clown,
the show-off, and, eventually, the rebel. I was never a monster,
though. At least I didn't think I was. It wasn't something most
sixth graders identified themselves as.

In sixth grade, I didn't even know we had a school counselor until Joy showed up. Our counselor was a heavier woman
with a red face that seemed flush with broken blood vessels
who smiled these big, energy-laden smiles meant for children—
probably not as effective for the newly serious, much more

sophisticated personalities of our sixth-to-eighth-grade class. We were an independent age group where the adult figures of our world were only let in when there were consequences, or if the baby-half of our adolescence was somehow overwhelmed by the sprouting adult-in-waiting. Joy wore these outfits that had the mismatched flamboyance of an uptown thrift store. She sometimes showed up in polka-dot skirts with red sweater vests or floral print blouses in hot pink or lime green. On several occasions, she wore sweatshirts with Labrador retrievers or kittens emblazoned on the fronts. In our young, material-crazy universe, to even the poorest of the kids at our school, a lady in her thirties in black-and-white striped cardigans and puffy corduroys couldn't hold much influence over kids who were just trying to fuck each other or look tough.

We were a mass of early adolescents in hats and T-shirts with team logos of anything that matched our shoes. We were lucky if our families could afford David Robinson's or Cortez's. We were downright rich if we showed up to school in Jordan's or Reebok pumps. We all wanted some kind of starter parka with one of the previously accepted team names emblazoned on the back. They were a cherished commodity; guys were getting robbed all the time at the sight of them in the neighborhood. Really, guys were getting robbed for anything they had that the other person did not, whether it was their shoes, coat, or baseball cap. It was the beginning of the baggy sag. It was around that time that the first real complaints from an older generation surfaced regarding kids wearing pants ten sizes too big and sagging them low on their asses.

It was also the era where kids were dressing like Theo from the *Cosby Show*; in turtlenecks with vests, with African medallions and flip-up sunglasses. Some kids had cheap gold chains they bought at the old International Gifts store on Hennepin. Some would have little handgun medallions or their names or an adjective that was supposed to describe their personalities in gold-plated cursive. The girls hairsprayed waterfall bangs, and the boys got their names or designs shaved into their fade.

Joy made every effort to make her presence known to

the kids, even though her office was in the darkest part of the school, with no windows. It was a silo-shaped space like most of the school's offices, born from the bizarre experimental architecture of the 1970s. The design probably came from the same oddly hallucinogenic place where this woman, Joy, had fostered her style in clothing. She offered her services to everybody, but I don't think very many of us knew you went to the counselor to talk about problems, so she seemed like just another of the strange figures walking around this strangely configured maze of a school.

She would have gone completely unnoticed had she not yanked our Centers class—a rotation of gym, art, wood shop, and whatever other classes they could come up with. The problem was that they were one Centers class short of an entire rotation, and so for a segment of the year we sat in a vacated teacher's classroom without any supervision, watching videos on The Box on a television in the corner. It was a free hour for the lucky group of us to socialize and leverage our positions in our small society. They tried to call it a study hall period, but that was really as an afterthought, in case someone asked why we were unsupervised in a corner of the school.

We had a classroom of girls braiding each other's hair or making friendship bracelets. Kids played football with little folded paper triangles that they slid across the table and flicked like they were kicking field goals. Kids talked shit in stonewashed denim overalls, played king of the hill, banging their chests to gain attention from the girls. And groups of kids would get up in dance teams and create roughly choreographed routines whenever MC Hammer came on the TV, a reaction rivaled only when 2 Live Crew videos appeared. And they did appear, over and over again, sometimes in sequence. Some of the girls would laugh and pretend they didn't mind the raunchy imagery as well. Mostly they were trying not to rock any boats or lose favor with some guy they liked, or one of his friends.

And every day we came in, the TV came on and so did that 2 Live Crew video, the TV version of "Pop That Pu**y" with a house full of women popping it in the pool, in the bathtub with Uncle Luke, or in the kitchen with the Asian guy in the Miami Hurricane jacket and a gold rope. Those not interested in the colorful explosion of sound and imagery mostly kept to themselves and stayed immersed in their own activities. There was a set of twin girls from California who somehow ended up in this part of the city, at this school, and right smack dab in the middle of this classroom. They would read lines back and forth from a play they said they were writing. Mostly, though, it was noise, noise that they did their best to carry over the TV and the sound of ten different conversations. Conversations about shoes or hairstyles were really about their teenage hormones. One of the particularly popular boys would get on a table and hump the surface, in a display that sometimes lasted several minutes. Kids in our class laughed, never even suggesting it was kind of weird.

One morning we came into the classroom and started our usual routines when Joy showed up in pleated jeans and a "Where's the Beef" T-shirt. A kid was hitting the buttons, trying to get to Channel 52 and 2 Live Crew. "Whoa, whoa, whoa, turn that TV off!" The kid's heart sunk, and his eyes went to the floor instantly.

"No, I mean it—turn the TV off. We're not watching TV today. We are in a school, and this is not an appropriate activity at school. And put those cards away. I've got something different for you guys today—I'm going to bring you guys downstairs."

I looked around as most kids did, for the pack's alphas to indicate how to react.

"Just for today?" a boy in a UNLV Runnin' Rebels sweatshirt asked. When he wasn't responded to, he asked the same thing again.

"Just for today, though, right?" Again, no response.

Most of the kids looked at her like, "Who the hell is this?" That's what I did.

"Who are you?"

"I'm Joy, and I'm your junior high counselor."

"What the fuck is a counselor?" One voice propelled from the back of the group, which was now being herded into the

hallway and down the stairs like Moses's people to an unoccupied room in another part of the school. It was the same room
we went to so we could skip out on DARE class. Instead of
listening to a cop tell us to rat on our friends and parents, we
played paper football with the worksheets he gave us.

"Who is that back there cussing? We're not going to be
cussing in this class; we all have better things to say."

Joy had seated us in chairs in a three-quarter circle with
herself at the head—able to move about freely while we were
seated religiously on hard plastic chairs that lived in stacks everywhere throughout the school.

"Why are we down here?" asked a kid in a Denver Broncos
sweatshirt, breaking out from snickers and defiant body pos-
tures. I just played along with the community and threw a remark in whenever I could. Sometimes I got a laugh, sometimes
not. For the most part we all laughed, even when the timing
was poor, or the joke had been told a thousand times. Most of it
was discomfort. We didn't know what this lady was going to do.

"We are here because I was told you guys have been unattended for several weeks watching pornographic videos on TV."

"Pornography? We just watching The Box. You ain't seen
The Box before, lady?"

"I don't know what The Box is. What I know is you guys
were sitting around with idle hands, and you all know what
they say about idle hands. So what we're going to . . ."

"No, we don't know what they say about idle hands."

"Oh, sure you do. Anyways, what we're going to do is talk
about child psychology."

"What the fuck?" one kid blurted out.

"No more swearing! Wash your mouth out with soap."

"But just for today, right?"

"Well, no. We're going to meet down here in the mornings
and talk about stuff as a group."

Heads went down into hands. Some looked for the lead-
ers of the pack to strike out in defiance but just saw sour faces,
cringing at the idea we were losing our free hour with The Box
and Uncle Luke.

A small group created a consensus that this was a life-changing disappointment. It was disappointment coated with teenage animosity toward this odd woman who took it away.

"Well, what are we gonna do? I don't know what child psychology is."

"We're going to think about stuff. I'll pose questions and we'll walk our way through them, like a creative problem-solving course. Have any of you taken a problem-solving class before?"

To this she gets a chorus of creative no's—"Hell naw!" "Nerp." Only one girl reluctantly put a hand in the air, peeking around for possible rejection from the rest of the class, but nobody was paying attention. Everybody was too consumed with their own reactions. Joy, though, was encouraged, and a smile developed.

Very early I created this persona strong in aloofness who could, because I was so cool, speak out no matter how silly it sounded. I had been in the same learning environment since I was in kindergarten; any façade of authority they ever tried to push on us really meant very little to me. I was always looking for a chance to make people laugh—I guess to be liked or loved and have all the girls think I was rebellious and dark.

But also I was only in sixth grade, part of a small minority of maybe a half-dozen kids amidst all the seventh and eighth graders of the entire junior high. I was a pretty boy—but I was young and little—trying to finance the same charm I had always used to navigate through the maze. It was always important to compensate for my youth.

A lot of the boys already had man bodies. Me, I was short and skinny, and where most of the other popular kids lived off of the adolescent animal magnetism of the whole boy-girl dynamic, I had to be cunning to hold my social position. It was all about others' inadequacies in the funniest light. And a thirtysomething woman who still wore barrettes that matched fluorescent-colored Mickey and Minnie Mouse clothing and oversized T-shirts made for an easy target. Typically, adults either looked upon my humor as clever or just irritating and obstructive. However, in this class I was cloaked by a slew of the school's most pronounced jackasses. So my precociousness wasn't that exclusive. I was just another voice of resistance among so many.

As a pack, though, we could smell corny. There might have been some wolves in our class who just didn't want to be mean, but all of that was overruled by the enjoyment of being silly and dictating our own actions. In her eccentricity, Joy had made a bold power grab, but she wasn't much of a disciplinarian. Her control was limited, her threats hollow. The parameters teachers have are marked in nature—and we could smell how far we were able to take one. And Joy's threshold was virtually nonexistent.

To any observer outside of their middle school years it would have seemed that rather than teaching child psychology to this class, she was really compiling some sort of case study, putting together information from our reactions to her suggestions without any real curriculum. She would come with a subject that was met with exasperation due to the freakish reality that we were still there, and a return to what we once were was completely extinguished.

Many years have wiped away all the exact details. I wish I could remember or had a video recording of those class periods. Then I could replay her individual lessons and the preadolescent packets she handed out with little cartoon panda bears and bunny rabbits. What is lasting, though, was her centrality around *morals, values,* and *ethics*—terms only abstractly incorporated into our youthful lexicon through some kids' family participation at church, or by parents as rationale behind their discipline or structure at home. But those were terms either unknown or mostly ignored during these particular years of development.

Joy's most lasting impression was left from the glowing example she used for an exercise about personal property.

"Is it wrong to steal grapes at the supermarket?"

We always sampled the grapes when we went to the grocery store, both green and purple. That wasn't stealing: that was sampling.

"That's not stealing," I shouted out. I mean, really, if my parents and a mob of others sampling around us did it, it must be okay.

"Why isn't that stealing?"

She cross-referenced grapes to everything, especially clothing. It was ironic only because a small number of the kids in the class had built substantial parts of their wardrobes swapping out clothes in the dressing rooms at Dayton's. I was too scared of the emotional confrontation I would get from my mom if I ever got caught.

Joy's ethics speech turned from clothing to items in people's yards and their homes, until she had cast a blanket over everything. It felt like it was becoming a preappraisal of what she believed most of us might become—even though most of these kids would probably still eat grapes at the grocery store but never burglarize someone's home. Most would likely graduate one day and end up in college, and hopefully lead interesting lives. Our participation in her presentation was mostly for the enjoyment and inclusion in the daily unraveling of the adult figure in front of us.

And unravel she would, starting classes with these wide disingenuous smiles and hand gestures seemingly prescripted, but when her script ran short and she was left to improvise and carry her curriculum, she would fall apart like a sick gazelle falling away from its pack. We played her at different pitches, high and low, wavering the tempo, starting slow, and, as we saw weakness, hitting the fever-pitched crescendo until it was like monkey town jumping on the walls—kids doing the Running Man in the circle. It was a symphony and I was its maestro— using every opportunity to ignite fires in open spaces where other kids could get their sick off. And Joy in her daily defeat would succumb to the fatigue, and the flush in her face would redden at the end of broken blood vessels. She would put her face in her hands and let the last minutes of the class period dissolve away.

But every day she came back renewed, seemingly oblivious to the day before and its incessant chattering, smart-ass remarks, and lesson plans from students who had chosen to rap instead of recite. But as time progressed, she became more recognizable in the school. Though she was still an oddball, absolutely recognized by her peculiar outfits, she was also a figure whose name and face were known. She was at every chaperoned event, mostly out of the way, but always available. So I think she felt she was helping, that in small strides she had made a little progress with these kids, was making a mark in the school.

What I'm sure she didn't realize was that we loved her class—not for the reasons she would have liked but, rather, because it really was a free-for-all, without The Box, a place where the entire class would buckle at the waist in laughter every day at the unfortunate expense of this woman. As time went by, we understood fully that the extent to which we could explode and how far were a much greater freedom than any of us could enjoy at any other place in our lives—and we had a real-live talking bear as a central focus.

It really was cruel—and it opened doors to a very cruel part of my own soul. I realized I could be someone so self-involved and in need of temporary validation that I would pick on the weaknesses of a very well-intentioned lady who came to help kids she believed to be at risk, even if most of us weren't really at risk of much of anything. But this was an adult—an adult who should be able to handle children. It was her job; she took out long-term loans and went to school to be this person. And maybe, just maybe, she had underestimated the voracity of the jungle, and the ferocity of nature. Maybe we weren't as simple as she wanted us to be; there wasn't an easy educational fix, and that was her fault, that was her failure. She wasn't the only one failing, though.

So when the final week of school came and it was time to end class, we were all very much intent on replaying the symphony we had all written one more time. Joy had a plan to go out with some kind of multicolored gusto. When we showed up, we didn't know the vice principal would be observing and evaluating one of her final classes.

I don't know now whether I felt any more or less vicious that day, or if the presence of the vice principal had anything to do with what transpired. Joy had planned to use this class and sum up the entire semester to create a comprehensive display for her boss. Her problem, though, was trying to use our input to support her plan. Maybe she thought we understood the stakes as well, and maybe some of us did—but I was the conductor of this orchestra, I was the maestro.

I didn't hold back. She got going on the grapes again, and I was on her. My relentlessness soon spread to the most obnoxious of my accomplices, who had until now been mild because of the vice principal's presence. These were the same people whom I had merely been accomplice to when the class started but who were now following my lead. The rest of the jungle laughed and ridiculed as they had so faithfully all semester long. The vice principal didn't intercede—she just let the hunt continue—and Joy saw it, too: that they would devour her, and the vice principal would let them.

The optimism and whimsical intentions for the day's class were slipping away, and the composure she had no doubt put on that morning with her makeup and probably had pumped herself up for the night before began peeling away. She tried at different points to bring us all back and start over, but our disobedience had become an almost immoral tornado, so far from right that there was no coming back. We had gone from a point of trying to be funny to an outright maliciousness coming from a predatory anger that I didn't understand, that I didn't even know I felt. At one point I stood up—eyes rolling in the back of my head—fire shooting from my mouth, and I think I said, "Why don't you tell the vice principal how stupid this class was—and how none of us learned anything, that none of us ever listened to you?"

At which point my head probably started spinning and whatever possessed me returned back to hell. It seemed bad enough, and then most of the class took this cue to individually raise their hands and contribute their own annihilating remarks.

An unbelievable sadness took over her face as one girl—the one who had raised her hand at the beginning when Joy asked about problem solving—raised her hand once again and asked if it was "morally acceptable to spend our parents' tax money on classes like this that are a complete waste of time and that don't teach kids anything." It even made *me* cringe.

Joy was silent, making a few attempts but had at last lost her breath, and class was finally over. I didn't think about it at all after walking out the door. In fact, I went to my third-hour geography class and took a test on Africa that I had thoroughly prepared for. It was a quiet class, no mayhem, ruled calmly by our social studies teacher. I finished my test and sat back, quietly thinking about summer and baseball, oblivious to the other kids still testing, or to the phone ringing in the back of the room. The phone rang but it meant nothing until my social studies teacher, under control and mild mannered, told me I had to go the office around the corner.

I was sent down the hall where lights disappeared, to a round office that looked like a geometric piece of the building's infrastructure. I knocked on a strange little door that entered into an office with a not-so-unpleasant atmosphere: potted plants, leather-upholstered chairs, framed prints, and a heavy-duty desk with framed photographs of little children I didn't know and with smiles pointing at nothing. There were oak bookshelves with teaching and psychology manuals. And behind the solid, authoritative desk sat Joy in a modest, less-than-Joyesque business suit, what could've been called a power suit—her "make a strong impression and save her job" suit. And drooping in her tweed she was enveloped in a whirl of tears, face bruised with moisture, trying to pat them out with tissues that softened and became soggy.

She looked up, trying to compose something that had obviously fallen to a thousand pieces before I entered. She looked at me in a painfully malevolent way and told me to sit down in one of the nicely upholstered leather chairs. It was a suggestion I almost rejected. I almost just walked out to go hide somewhere. But instead I sat down, a little scared, a little confused.

"I just want to tell you: you are the most evil child I have ever met. Do you know this?"

"Huh?" I immediately retreated, knowing I would only give the most concise answers to whatever her barrage was going to be. She was obviously hurt, and this would be her vengeance. I was alone with her and her vengeance in a forgotten corner. I merely answered, "No, I didn't know this."

Then, as if to break through an emotional wall that divided personal devastation from fury, she stood up with a finger pointed and shot at me with all the rage she could rally.

"Well, you are!" And went into a diatribe about the day's events.

"Do you realize this is my career? And now you have jeopardized this. I have kids to feed, a mortgage, and a car payment. But you wouldn't understand those things—you're too busy being coddled, told you're so clever, and brilliant, and funny! But I know that's all a sham, that's the game, that's the manipulation. I have never met a twelve-year-old boy who was such a tyrant and as inconsiderate as you are. Most children are sweet and vulnerable, but you are rotten. If I could, I would hurt you the way you have hurt me and my life. Do you understand? Do you understand how manipulative you are? Of course you do!"

Now she was pacing, at every lap turning to shun me again with more gunfire.

"I bet your family believes you're just so special. I would call them, but I know that you probably just play games and manipulate them just like everyone else. You can use all that mushy sentimental crap to lure your victims, and then you unleash your venom. You are a dangerous little person. Lord have mercy on those who cross your path in life."

Her wrath seemed to be calming. I think she was getting tired, like a worn-down athlete from a body's natural attrition. Her breaths were longer now, her paces were shorter. She finally settled at the edge of her stern desk and in a less forceful tone, still affected by tears but not completely finished, she went in for more.

"It was a simple class—no homework, no nothing, just a

little class participation. I liked all of you, *even* you. I put up with all the abuse, and the one day when my boss is there—you knew she was the vice principal; you saw her back there writing things down; you knew that she was there to judge my performance, that she has the power to take food out of my mouth, money out of my pocket. Like a true predator, a true monster, you pounced. You couldn't wait for another time, couldn't show any mercy. No, like the impulsive little demon you are, you couldn't let up even a little when my job was on the line. Is it that you hate me so much—huh? What did I do to you for you to hate me that much?"

She sat hunched enough so the tears that fell from her face would fall right onto the carpet, like dew on wet leaves. I was leaning back, my arms crossed in a retreating position, trying to process information and mannerisms as they were hurled at me. It was just like when my mom would sit me down and grill me for hours after a bad report card, or later, after my parents bailed me out of jail. I sat that way as this woman whom I didn't hate, really had no opinion of outside of class, dished out now what she could not over the many weeks of her class, maybe for most of her life even. I had become, as a twelve-year-old kid, her last straw.

"I just want you to know that I have been let go. I won't be back again next year—and I blame you. That's all."

And then she paused and an uneasy quiet hung in the air between us.

"Do you have anything to say?"

I was in protective mode. Anything I would've said would only have been to maintain my turtle shell. I told her I was sorry and that "I didn't intend for you to get fired." She wouldn't believe it, though; nothing I could've said would've been enough for her. To her it was more mushy, sentimental shit, just another manipulation on my part. Maybe it was. All I wanted was to get out of that damn office. What I should've said was, "I'm sorry but is it my fault you let a twelve-year-old dominate *your* class and walk on top of *your* delicate self-esteem?" But I shouldn't have said that either, and thankfully I didn't. Instead

I was taken aback by the tears of a grown woman who some-times wore a full-length vertically striped skirt and a Hello Kitty sweatshirt. On the way out her cracking voice told me, "You're a monster, I truly believe that. Good luck with your life. And don't expect that at any time I'm ever going to give you any space."

When I finally got out of there, I felt heavy, that treacher-ous confused feeling after a deluge of confrontation. I didn't know if it was about her, or about being called on all of my faults, or being told I was a monster. For the rest of the day I saw her a couple of times. We didn't say anything to each other and made no eye contact. I had two more days of school. I could play baseball and sneak over to girls' houses while their parents were at work. I could empty all the poison from my system and leave this woman and the guilt and the emotive role reversal.

The next day we went on a field trip to Lake Rebecca. Every year we'd bring water balloons and roam around in minisquads taking turns tagging each other. Unfortunately, the day we went was cold and windy. It was gray for most of the day except when the sun would peep through for short moments. Some kids swam despite the weather, despite the wicked wind. And it wasn't such a grand day for water balloons, but it didn't mat-ter. Roving bands of young rogues moved across the expanse, terrorizing any vulnerable being. At one probably inevitable point, the group I was in was leaving one of many attacks. After our most recent barrage we were filling up another round of balloons and Joy comes around a bend of trees with another teacher. The roving band of rogues, little adolescent monsters, with which I was aligned, decided from the command of one of the Lord of the Flies kids to attack. I had intentionally done my best to avoid her the whole day, but she was too close. She was going to get this; she was going to be absorbed by this mob. But I wasn't going to be the one, on this cold day right after the previous cold and vicious day, to give her a shower. So I veered to the back of the group just as the slinging began. I intention-ally sloughed off the balloons I had. When I looked up, all I could see was Joy turning a hip as a dozen or so balloons flew at her, many exploding in unison as they hit her white-hooded windbreaker. When the onslaught ceased, a kid ran up a few feet from her and slung a kickball into her upper thigh. And although I was in the back, when she looked at the retreating mob, her eyes fell directly on me. And anything I told her would inevitably be trumped by what she believed.

Later on in life I was able to be all the things she said I was—in a narrative about being young and overwhelmed with desperation and ego. This trip to the office would be a public one, and everyone I knew would get the chance to call me those things—a lot did, some did not. In my heart I knew I wasn't evil, knew they had hyperbolized my image—made me what they could to avoid their own monstrous actions—to get somewhere they were trying to go and impress someone they were trying to impress. I didn't know it right then in that office—and really the visit had made me unsure—but I figured out I wasn't exactly what she said I was. Part of me might have been—I was a kid who wasn't evil but *was* wrong, was malicious, and was headed for some dark things attached to some dark shit that doesn't come out in the wash of time. And who knows where this woman is now, what she's wearing now, as life does to her what it does to sort out all of us in nature.

Six

MARCHING ON
THE THIRD PRECINCT

We are the children
who used to be the future
—*from "These Songs Remind Me"*

NINETEEN NINETY-TWO started as an empty extension of the previous year. It would gradually fill itself with more boredom, and loneliness, and a bitter first taste of depression that helped me see through the superficiality of so much of what I used to think was important. The way I dressed, the way people looked at me, and the cultural agreement over what we were supposed to care about all showed their limitations to me. Our seemingly interesting shiny outer layers could be eaten by the poisons of shame and fear inside us. I still had so much rebellion built up in me that may have really just been anxiousness. I really didn't know how to get *it* or any of those poisons out of me.

We were in the final months of eighth grade, sitting in a school where I had mastered every corner and every semilit corridor in the building. By then, even the teachers were tired of looking at me. I had truly exhausted my run. A group of us had done anything we could to break up the monotony. We had "rioted" at the Science Museum, gone camping where some of us broke off and drank MGDs on a beach. I got high for the first time on some really green weed from California I would never see an equal to for the rest of my life. I tripped on three hits of acid and walked around the house all night melting into the woodwork. I caught the girl I liked getting the business by some young roughneck at a party. And it was the same year I got stomped out and beat with a broomstick walking home from school on Thirty-fifth Street and Fourteenth Avenue.

Yet it was hardly the most exciting year of my life. It felt empty and sad and just like an entrance to more confusion. I would wake up and wonder what the fuck I was even going through the motions for. We really just had to create things to stay awake. I remember our eighth grade catchphrase, which was probably the catchphrase for eighth grade classes from the beginning of time: "All the cool people left last year." I wanted to tell them, "You're not cool just by referencing these people, and I know all of those people, and they weren't that cool either."

It was spring; the final weeks were like trudging through mud. I felt like a zombie. I think we all felt like the run was over months before. Parallel to our misadventures, TV was running wild with the videotape of the super-dusted Rodney King getting shellacked over and over again by Los Angeles police officers. It coincided with several accidental shootings and incidents of abuse by Minneapolis police, and it seemed like the local news simply accepted the law enforcement point of view, even though it all seemed so obvious to me. I became so outspoken my parents wouldn't let me watch the news with them anymore. The idea of justice was fast becoming a joke to me.

And then the news of acquittal came. I wasn't outraged. I didn't have enough experience with the justice system to understand any kind of pattern yet. I was angry because it seemed so obvious. I was angry because it was becoming more obvious that there *was* a pattern. I just couldn't figure out what it meant to me yet. The rest of the country was trying to digest it in terms of right or wrong. With it came quarreling psychologies with a morality culture; the self- and communal righteousness of law enforcement against the withering personal identity of someone who was kind of dirty, and how blurry the lines were between the two.

Like a lot of kids I was always eager to react, but I was probably much more reactionary than most kids at school, even if I didn't always know what I wanted to say. At school on the morning after the verdict, I was surprised by the absence of any mention or acknowledgment of what happened. I shouldn't have been surprised—it was almost the end of the year and teachers were in a scramble to close things out. Sometimes kids needed to be convinced about what to be upset by. And my reaction was probably to a certain extent an attempt at trying to avoid another monotonous day in a classroom.

I had a friend who was an automatic participant in anything I came up with. He hadn't decided yet if he wanted to be a gangbanger or a Black Panther, a drummer in a rock 'n' roll band or a rapper. He wasn't especially good at any of these things; on his best days he thought he was Ice-T. He was mostly just a stoner and two-bit thief. He was a kid with many personalities, none of which was particularly complex. But when I proposed a walkout in protest of the Rodney King verdict, part from anger and injustice, another part from dangerous boredom, and probably to see what else I could get these other similarly bored kids to do, my friend was in.

We started by getting together the grimiest of the student population and convinced them this was as good of a reason to walk out as any. Even then, the good-old-fashioned walkout was the most liberal-sympathetic way to break out of class. In high school there was one at least a few times a year, and staff would look at all the kids as being emotional, politically minded young people showing that they cared about the world around them, and usually excused them. I took those opportunities to get stoned somewhere. Even in deepest meditation I couldn't now tell anyone what any of those other demonstrations were for. This one, though, I could, and I was probably the only one who was even thinking about it. I mean, wasn't this just as viable as anything else we had demonstrated for in our time here?

It didn't take long to get kids organized; kids wanted to be involved—they never want to be left out—so others could later say they weren't even there. We had huge chunks from every class; noticeable empty seats all around with kids spreading the word. It was mostly "This is what we're doing"—instead of "This is why we're doing this."

We moved in exodus without escort from any adults. Usually these things are broadcasted so that an authority figure or figures are alerted to ensure that there is somebody to listen to and validate them. It was the old "I have to do this. Don't you understand we have to?" I was telling kids not to even say anything: "They'll just try to stop you from doing what you know is right."

As we were walking out the doors, one teacher asked what was going on—"Ignore him, he'll only try to trick you." I got a funny look from the guy after the remark, but we kept going, marching to open space in the adjacent Stewart Park for our baby demonstration. No signs, just junior high rants. Then a handful of teachers came, trying to quell the protest and talk us out of our civil disobedience. A few curious students came along with them to watch. "Okay, it's a nice thought, guys. We know you're angry—but let's go inside." When some of the kids realized they wouldn't get the same validation as in some other demonstrations, they turned to go with the teachers. One of the teachers thought he could swing his weight and get the same result as had worked in the past. He knew what kind of kid I was but wasn't prepared for one of the last great thrusts of the Little King that I was: "Hell no! We're not going anywhere!" This was my show—we started early so we'd have plenty of time. They weren't going to decide the guidelines for our unrest.

He suggested we bring it to the great multipurpose room, to assemble the kids so they could talk about their feelings. But I had been there for those things, like the sit-in in the commons in protest of the Persian Gulf War that was also redirected to the beloved multipurpose room. It ended up becoming a scene where kids held up peace signs while kids who never lived during a time of war took turns talking about their fears that it would be like Vietnam and cried that they didn't want to be drafted and go to war. And this same guy who was at the forefront of suppressing our latest movement was there with a videocamera. Others, too, photographed the event like it was what liberal arts education was all about. I heard one of the teachers say he called all the local news stations. "They should be on their way." Only they didn't show up. When I went home I saw there had been at least twenty different metro schools that held protests, making ours not so special. Driving the news van to Phillips rather than less volatile neighborhoods wasn't probably their best option.

They had manipulated that one well, taken the power from the students and isolated it. They had recovered nicely with the whole Science Museum thing, too; but they couldn't have this one. And it started to become evident to the small group of educators standing there, pleading, that this was going to be harder to navigate to our sensitivities and make it theirs. "What is it you guys are trying to say? We can help you." Of course some of the kids who were hoping for parental validation from the adults were all for the submissive option. They were looking for their way out, and rightfully so—we didn't have anything coherent to say. Just frustration and wanting out of a classroom for a while. I really didn't want to have to explain my angle, or my anger, or the invisible something that told me to do things, or that I needed any kind of escape that was viable.

In an act of improvisation I declared, "We're gonna march to the Third Precinct!" While it took the other kids by surprise, some were all for it. Others just wanted the plea bargain the teachers offered so we could have a more watered-down rally inside. But a few of us, my friend in his best version of Ice-T, of course, being one of them, just weren't going to accept the compromise. Finally, the teacher who had expended the most energy trying to redirect our delinquency, tried the classic poker bluff: "All right, I'm going back in. Whoever doesn't want to get suspended can come with me." And he left with only a slightly larger group than he came with.

We were at our crossroads. One girl asked, "Okay, guys,

what *are* we going to do?" During these crucial moments we lost a few more stragglers back to the machine. "We're going to the Third Precinct!" It was a declaration some supported; others really didn't want to go all the way to the precinct and instead shuffled off back to school. We were down to about twenty students walking, with no particular route in mind to get to the station. We had no agenda but to arrive, chanting, "No justice, no peace!" in our fragmented group. We made it a few eastward blocks, but our sense of purpose had mostly evaporated—and like most field trips, chaperoned or not, small factions formed and new conversations were created. Space was gradually initiated between varying small groups until the entire amalgamated party was really just loosely scattered groups spread out as far as a block or two down Twenty-sixth Street through Phillips. On a pleasant spring day at nine in the morning it was pretty quiet, except the occasional barking dog. Most kids were at school, and most anyone else out lingering or on their front steps were oblivious to the unattended procession of middle school kids lazily moving through the neighborhood like adults who had their shit figured out.

And really, by then there wasn't any conversation about Rodney King shermed out, getting beaten by police batons. None of us really knew what it meant when the people on TV said he was high on PCP. Plenty of the kids in our group would know later in their lives when they dipped cigarettes in embalming fluid and got stuck somewhere in some place strange and unidentifiable. Most of us probably didn't realize that when we got home and turned our TVs on that L.A. would be on fire. Or that there would be men and women running in and out of chaos with armfuls of whatever they could snatch in the new anarchy. Or that some guy would get snatched out of a truck at the intersection of Florence and Normandy and get stomped and smashed with a brick. We didn't realize that cameras from helicopters would show us miles and miles of flames and black smoke.

Where we were, there weren't flames or black smoke, just an odd group of mildly delinquent kids who thought they stood for something. We thought that if we played serious enough it would seem sincere. We had members who would at future points find all sorts of treacherous terrain in the geologies of their lives. A few, like myself, would take similar pilgrimages like this to police stations and county courthouses. Some would get babies before they could be what they told everyone they were going to be. Some would say yes to the shit on all the posters at school we were all told to say no to. Some would be Rodney King or Reginald Denny without a camcorder or a helicopter hovering over their heads. Some would just end up in the mediocrity of never wanting anything at all—in a project building, or serving drinks, or giving lap dances at seedy underground bars. And one or two would end up as the young faces on funeral notices because the environment, history, and their choices were just too volatile a mix of chemicals.

We were still kind of clean, still kind of lucid with the iridescence of our naïveté. But none of that could happen to us. Those were just the problems of earlier generations that had lost what it meant to be cool. So while we crossed over into Seward and turned south on Minnehaha, the day was sunny and peaceful, the birds flying overhead, unhunted and whistling freely without any clue of what it meant to fly in a world where something bigger could swoop in and steal that innocence. All the while, in someone else's world, identity and community were on fire. The forces of good and evil and all the dim light in between were at work across the country.

As we got closer we started to consider what we were doing. What the hell were we going to say or do when we got there? We had no signs, no real organization, just bodies—small underdeveloped and growing bodies—with a developing sense of hatred for the symbolic figures in blue. It was hatred that mostly came out of something cultural less than out of anything personal. Some of these feelings came from things that seemed to predetermine battles that were inevitable later on in our lives.

We finally came upon the Third Precinct building on the southwest corner of Lake and Minnehaha, recognized by all of us who lived in that part of the city. As part of the busy intersection tied to Target, the Cub and Rainbow stores, a liquor store, and one of the last sauna houses in the city, the precinct building stood out. A fortress built from stacks of stone with blue lettering and a shield to tell everyone just who they were, with an American flag waving in the sky. We had no approach. Our game plan was just to get there; what happened after that was completely up to improvisation. Without any coordination, the action turned out to be a bunch of kids standing out front on the steps of the building yelling whatever we felt like, maybe every so often joining in chants of some agreed-upon mantra. Usually the mantra rhymed or had a catchy alliterative pattern. "What do we want? Justice! When do we want it? Now!" We stood out front, our fists pumping, our faces scrunched in defiance, yelling things that no one in the building could even hear. It only took a few minutes before somebody in a blue uniform noticed us and came out to address the strange collection of kids in cocked hats, pagers, and dirty Nikes.

"Why are you kids standing out here?"

"We're protesting the acquittal of the cops who beat up Rodney King!" came from the mouth of a young Asian Gi-Gi girl in a pair of Filas, whose clothes might've been a little provocative for a fourteen-year-old girl. All I can remember of her outfit was a pink pager clipped to the front pocket of her extra-tight white jean shorts.

"Why are you *here* then?"

Then another voice from our crowd—a small squeak manipulated into sharp edges, empowered by the Asian girl's directness struck out. "We're sick of the cops beating on us and getting away with it."

"Well, this isn't the place for that. Why aren't you kids in school right now?"

"We walked out and marched here in protest." It was already starting to feel ridiculous. Unless someone specific stepped forward as the spokesperson, we would end up looking pretty dumb—but I wasn't going to be this person. I enjoyed the revolt; I wasn't ready to govern after a revolution.

"What school are you from?"

"Andersen."

"Where are the teachers? Do they know you're here?"

"Maybe," we told them. But whether they believed we'd ever make it instead of just skipping and running off into the neighborhood was still unclear. I don't think any of the kids in our party really cared about what was happening back in school. My nerves were vibrating. I'm sure I wasn't the only one. I don't know if we ever thought we'd get an actual verbal encounter. None of us—not even my dumb ass—had any real platform for our campaign. We didn't have arguments or talking points; we had random swatches of reaction without continuity or rhythm that came from the news, or personal experiences of people we might have known or heard about. We had a decade of assorted beatings and accidental murders we hadn't actually been involved with.

And then we had the video, raw and actual, that displayed for our young minds all we needed to know about imbalance and disproportion. We saw the flailing sticks, and I could feel defeat, being bullied by a force none of us could beat, couldn't strike back at even if we thought we could. And if you did strike back, there would be the news, with society and generations of police shows and movies, and hundreds of years of public opinion right there to make one of us the bad guy. But we didn't have the words to explain all of that, or even much of anything to say at all. What we did have were a couple dozen kids with a few pieces of ephemeral memories and a little hurt in their hearts all yelling at once, or not yelling at all, hoping someone other than the cop would put to words what they felt. They were hoping that somehow the force of their presence would mean something.

What we had was only a stimulus for an adventure. The officer, probably some kind of receptionist who used a pen rather than a gun or a billy club, asked us to come in from the street so we could discuss what we needed to in the lobby rather than having twenty shorties standing outside all day. Initially we refused, thinking it was a trick, or that we might be softening under the flex of the police. Realizing we were at a particular dead end, we finally accepted and were escorted to the media room, with a roomful of chairs and another American flag in the corner. On the way in, we were walked past numerous uniformed officers standing around with their guns and the whole police persona, laughing at us, holding dumb-ass smirks, as if to ask why the hell we were there. One stood there in black leather gloves with several sets of handcuffs draped on display over both arms.

"We want to know why it was all right for those cops to beat on that man over and over," my guy told them, in his freshest Ice-T stance.

Then we got the very predictable, very vanilla press-friendly explanation law enforcement officials had been distributing throughout the entire run of the story about all the dangers of the job, and the extents to which they sometimes have to go to maintain the safety of themselves and the community. They didn't say anything about racial profiling, or the abuse of the War on Drugs concentrated in poor, urban neighborhoods like the ones we lived in. It was just more drag like we were starting to get used to hearing.

"We don't believe the officers reacted unjustly. They were trying to restrain a dangerous man under the influence of a very powerful drug that makes people paranoid and hallucinate. All the while this man aggressively fought back, endangering the officers. In these instances our officers are trained to use the means at their disposal to restrain such an individual."

Five or six juvenile voices that soon became ten or twelve or fifteen or sixteen all started at once, yelling boldly, guns or no guns, billy clubs or no billy clubs, videotape or not. It was just a cacophonous blob of words and noises, no new arguments. There was nothing particularly moving or insightful going to come out of the way we were arguing our points. The sheer brashness and the volume level were our strongest and most wonderful testament in the debate. The cops had to stop us several times just so they could focus on a single voice. They told us to keep it to one speaker at a time, so we did our best to set up an order so anyone who wanted could get their one great chance to yell at the cops, to say whatever the fuck they wanted.

And most of these kids did say what they wanted to, in bold, living color—graphic, personal, sometimes obscene and unintentionally abstract with references to Malcolm X or to the JFK conspiracy. The stuff became the best kind of entertainment for the officers—to which they all laughed and looked at each other in collective amusement. A kid who was probably thirteen but looked like he was ten or eleven, whose voice any of us may have only ever heard a few times all year, got up to speak. Using only a handful of syllables each time, he got up and told the police in the least linear, least connected manner about his cousin, and his cousin's friend, a toy gun, and a shooting involving the toy gun. The point was discernible, but the actuality of exact details and the five Ws of what really happened were unclear, to say the least. Even still, as he got further into his story, his eyes started filling up with water and little tears rolled like mercury down his cheeks.

The cops told us all of our stories were fine, but that we didn't have a point. Then the guy who invited us in, who acted as their spokesman, told us one more time that we were wrong. He told us we exaggerated our stories, told us our cause was a fraud. He told us Rodney King was a *monster,* told us he was what happens when you skip out of school behind dumb ideas that weren't rooted in reality. I cringed a little at the use of that word. As his voice rose, and the still very vocal parts of our group started to recognize the condescension, it spurred a realization in us. We were being diminished, played like children, talked to like dumb ghetto kids who just didn't understand the complexity of what law enforcement was or the streets we lived in. But *should* we have understood?

We wouldn't understand these things as much as any of us could readily understand the perplexity of our own futures. The saddest part was that even most of these adults, who likely didn't live anywhere near any of our neighborhoods, or in the city at all, were the ones with badges and guns. They were the ones who pulled people over and put battering rams to people's doors early in the a.m. or made enhanced statements to help a district attorney send people's fathers and brothers to cages. It was members of this same group who had helped fragment family structures for generations. *Those* people didn't understand the perplexities they were telling us *we* didn't understand. And they were grown, given responsibilities that were beyond their own comprehension. But we were the ignorant ones? We were just little kids who felt the bullshit and reacted without the raw, aching consequences. And we were supposed to be wrong for recognizing what was blatant and real: that billy clubs hurt, that four beats one, that rich eats poor. And that people do ugly, treacherous things to other human beings. And they shrug *us* off with self-righteousness and build walls to divide our ideas.

From this I knew a couple of things: that I still felt the same way about these cops from when we left the school in the morning, but that I felt even less respected, less important. And while we weren't that well organized or perfectly well intended—and we weren't all that articulate or well thought-out—we weren't wrong. Our methods may have stunk, our intentions not wholly collective, definitely not completely right, but we *were* kids on the preemption of being the next targets, who didn't know it yet but felt it acutely. Instinct told us that we were the next wave to get what was happening to our older brothers and sisters right now. We were the next group whose opinions and whose space and choices wouldn't matter when the Man decided you were insignificant. We were the next group whose voice would be muffled because he or she was high on PCP, or whose credibility had been pissed on because of a felony that came from a choice made trying to creep out from behind poverty, or even just from the obscurity of being young. We were the next generation to get shushed out of a police station—or yeah-yeah'd from the front of a camera. The next wave of imperfect young people to get older and become an excuse to get stomped by a mob of strangers while a celebration of family stands around watching and supporting our attackers. Whether we knew it already, felt it, or had any idea at all, we were the next cycle to die, or rot in a cage, or simply fall apart from the cocktail of everything combined.

To add insult, a small crew came from the back and joined the already present officers. Somebody told us it had gone on too long—and it probably had. So the on-hand mini riot squad herded us out. No matter the level of our defiance, angry or not, we were forced out the door back out onto the street. Some of the kids felt a mild empowerment: "At least we *did* something." Others were just disappointed. The rest of the bunch were mulling over the idea of whether or not to go back to school for the last couple of hours of the day.

This was it—if the Science Museum had been our Woodstock, then this was probably our failure at Altamont. It was obvious to everyone that there wouldn't be a gathering to express our feelings, no community of boys and girls crying in support of each other. There could be no groups organized to protest injustice, no adults to validate the claims. We were just a random assortment of kids who looked like they were just looking for a way out of school. We were rejecting the same ultra-liberal learning environment that had for so long nurtured our rebellious ideas. It *was* the end of the run—there was nothing else they could do for us. I didn't need the validation. I didn't so much care what they thought, and it seemed like everybody else was left with a realization that we were on our own. In the summer we would all break apart and run around in the sun waiting for high school. In the fall we would find a new flock, and some of us would play football or put on a cheerleader uniform. Some of us would get closer to drugs or to the streets. By winter or the next spring this entire experience at the Third Precinct would be expelled or packed to the back of the dark places in our brains.

We were left standing on Lake Street to decide which direction we would take. I went with a small group to play pickup basketball on the rim at my garage. And the ugly part of reality existed at that moment where one thing was happening while at the very exact moment something else completely unconnected happens as well: Los Angeles burned, I played pickup basketball. I was already unconsciously getting ready for the end of the world, the blurring edge of perspective where seeing anywhere beyond where I was standing was nearly impossible. Less than five years later I saw the deeper insides of the Third Precinct—this time in handcuffs, with a lot less exuberance, a little more understanding, but with a whole lot less purpose and expectation for the future.

II. Life: What I Would Be

But that was before
City Center was Mecca
and kids made Hajj
stealing Girbauds from Dayton's
and looked at all the people they knew
on the wall in the holding tank
in the basement.

That was before I became time,
stories accumulated in the walls.

I was still standing on the rooftop
watching tricks circle the block.
I was still on the bus
behind a janitor's uniform
and the smell of fryer grease.
I was already on fire.

—from "Before I Was Anything"

Seven

PRAYER AND RESURRECTION

"**W**OULD YOU LIKE TO JOIN HANDS and say a prayer for your friend?" said the man in cheap gray polyester, who had made a living—albeit probably a meager one—of joining hands with the disparaged on late nights for just these very instances.

"In the elevator?" one of us asked.

"Or whatever. It is times like these where it is important to surrender our needs to the Lord's will. Was Justin a Christian?"

"Does it matter? He's not dead yet—what does it have to do with you wanting to pray with us?" It was the snap-back reaction from the Argentinean girl who only hours before had been at work with Justin, and a bunch of other people who worked with them at the neighborhood organization that created public works of art from inner city youth in the Phillips neighborhood. It was supposed to be a safe haven; it was supposed to be the sort of work that would save him. It was 1993, and it was only one and a half years after our protest outside of the Third Precinct. Now I was with my friends taking a break from the trauma to smoke outside of the emergency room entrance.

It was that phone call, the phone call everyone will get at some point in a lifetime. The surprise—picking it up, expecting one thing, and hearing something instead we are never prepared for. It was one of the guys, who had just heard from Sid, who had just walked up on something horrible. Something ghastly and surreal while on his way to meet with Justin and the other guys at the empty house Justin's mom had left a month earlier to live somewhere else. It had become a flea-infested structure beaten up over the years from the growing pains of family living. Jus and Cheesesteak, his best friend, stayed there, mostly abandoned, with mattresses on the floor and the TV on all the time. I think there was a couch, but most of the rooms were empty with busted-out chunks of sheetrock from the walls. The itch from the bounding fleas made it unbearable sometimes.

The plan was that we would all meet there when Justin and Cheesesteak and Rich and Cuzzo got off of work at the Art Spot. Sid would come from work at the New Market on Lake and Blaisdell, next to the K-Mart. Me and Jackson were supposed to come through later. We bought some acid, and most of us were going to take it and kick back. I was at home. It was just me and Mom. Dad was on his yearly fishing trip to Leech Lake. Besides being a school night, there wasn't anything else going on. Jackson was still at home, just waiting for everyone to get back from work. I hadn't decided if I was going back to Justin's or not.

Then the phone call.

This is the part of the story Sid should be writing—the part where he got off the 21 bus on Eighteenth Avenue and strolled. He only had a block and a half to where he was going, and the block was quiet, the first subtle waves of evening, nothing odd, fall breeze, warmer than most nights at the end of September. Until he saw something on the boulevard—something familiar but too surreal to be what it probably was. A mass, dressed in human clothes, Dickies and a flannel, laid twisted and jagged on the grass in front of him—Justin, at least a tattered and discarded version of his body covered in blood, left alone on the street. A disgustingly surreal moment with just him and his friend, nothing else. Looking around he had to wonder what this was, how rooted this moment was in reality.

Then a squad car pulled up, its bright lights so strong it was tough to see the passengers in the backseat. One of them looked like Rich to him, but it was hard for him to tell if there was anyone else in the back of the car. The headlights were too bright, the lines of sight too complicated to understand. Standing over the body, one of the officers shooed him away. "This one's dead." That line reverberated, would be repeated in the retellings. It had to be a sinking feeling, a pulverizing piece of information given to him before being sent from the scene by police order. An ambulance came, and more squad cars, until the night was lit up with red and blue. Steadily a neighborhood oozed out of their homes, crept up to the edge of yellow tape, and watched what he could not. Without any resolute explanation for what had happened, he left and got back on the 21 as fast as he could. When he got home, he called Jackson, so by the time I got the relay call, Justin was dead, Rich was in custody, and Cuzzo and Cheesesteak were missing.

In a blur I hung up, got some shoes on, shot my mom a garbled version of what I had heard—that my friend had been killed. Despite protests and motherly concern, my momentum was much too great. I got on one of the bikes from the tangle of stolen bikes left in a pile on the porch. I rode it through Powderhorn and across Thirty-first Street to the red and blue flashing lights.

By then, the entire neighborhood—parents and kids and pets—were all crowded along sidewalks watching the circus. I just stood there, propped up by my busted old ten-speed listening to all the bystander remarks; I didn't know any of those people. Then I saw Cheesesteak, handcuffed, brought out in front of several others, no doubt being asked to identify someone, but he shook his head negative. He looked over and saw me, made eye contact, shook his head again, and they ducked his head back into the squad and rode off. I stood there for a while, hypnotized by the flashing lights and the drama. Drunken onlookers tried to analyze something I was having a hard time doing myself. I rode my bike back home to relay the message to the guys: Cheesesteak was alive and now Cuzzo was the only one unaccounted for. Mom was frantic, flagging calls from Sid and Jackson, plenty of others, trying to put all the pieces together.

By calling all the local hospitals we figured out a single black male had been admitted at the Hennepin County Medical Center. We didn't know if it was one of *our* guys. We were hoping it might offer us some needed information to make the situation clearer. We all thought it might be Cuzzo, but it turned out to be Jus. We all assumed he was already dead, but he wasn't. Mom brought me and Jackson and Sid to HCMC. We were the first ones there, the first ones to find out it wasn't Cuzzo, that it was Jus in emergency surgery. As it was happening, it was so hard to process what was real and what we were supposed to feel. Something obviously treacherous and life-altering had happened.

It wasn't very long until the community started to arrive in clusters of interrelated people. It never takes long for these kinds of things to get out. The friends and family in the network learned what happened and found each other in the lobby of the emergency room. Eventually the hospital moved us upstairs where we had the entire floor, gossiping, passing what little we knew around, recycling it until everyone there grew tired and frustrated with the same old information.

Then the noise of sorrow, weeping, overwrought emotion coming through in a tornado moving through the hallway toward us—his mom being held in the arms of friends or family, overwhelmed, not knowing whether to sit or stand, lie down or be held in place by those around her. She was proof to me that there was no cliché to describe the way mothers grieve for their children.

||||||||||||||||||||||||||||||

HE WAS SUPPOSED TO BE tougher than the rest of us—most of us, at least. Jus was definitely tougher than I was. That's one of the reasons why it was so fucked up. The skinny, long-bodied kid in a Georgetown starter jacket he wore in the summer to baseball practice without a shirt underneath. Back then he wore a necklace with a laminated picture of his sixth grade girlfriend.

Cheesesteak told him he was a simp. He didn't care, though; he just smiled that smile, someone glad to be alive. It was the smile that made people like him, made them follow and trust him, with lots of teeth, a brow, and eyes that squinted uncontrollably when he grinned. He had those long arms that helped him throw punches from his six-foot six-inch frame. He was lanky but fluid and natural, very much comfortable in his skin.

He played baseball for one of the teams my dad coached at the diamonds on the north end of Powderhorn. But by high school we all just skipped school and smoked weed between the garages in the alleys along Thirty-second Street. That previous summer we all hung tough in Phillips because a lot of our people worked for an art project on Eleventh and Franklin in what used to be the old Franklin Avenue adult movie theater. They called it the We Claim Our Lives project—a mural in four sections on the side of the People of Phillips building across the street from the theater. Everything that went on the wall was art constructed by the kids, a diverse mix of styles and points of view. It was run by a woman who had spent her life putting up murals in Minneapolis. She wanted to believe that art could save the kids. It felt a little exploitive at the time, but I was making judgments from the outside.

We spent most of the summer buying sacks from the Blue House on Fifteenth Avenue. We probably kept the spot in business with all the trips we made. By that time Jus had already taken a bullet, maybe two. He and Cheesesteak had already started to sell dope, although neither seemed to make that much money. He was already a man, at least it seemed like he was. I was hardly even grown yet; I was just trying to avoid it being too noticeable to everyone around me. We were supposed to be claiming our lives, but I had absolutely no intuition of any such thing.

We were all over the place in those days, tagging our crew name all over mailboxes and bus seats, or anywhere generally we ended up squatting. Mostly it was Rich, though: he had this intention we would be some kind of tagging crew. Guys started stealing markers and spray paint from the Walgreen's on

Franklin. The rest of us didn't care. We just did it as recreation until we ended up into it with another crew a lot older than us, nineteen- and twenty-year-olds still trying to get their diplomas. I still only weighed a hundred pounds and I had grown men in bulletproofs riding down on me at Burger King.

We spent the summer linked as this strong little unit. From it, personalities changed, language and inflections in our voices changed; they became morphologically faster. A friend of ours who typically spent his summers with his dad in Virginia said he came back and didn't understand anything we were saying. Our boundaries had expanded, too: there weren't any more places in the city that were too obscure or forbidding for us to be. We went anywhere. It was the start of the freedom years, without many attachments or commitments.

Then school came back, and the obviousness of everyone's situation and the lives we were declaring became apparent. I don't think Jus or Cheesesteak were even enrolled at school. If they were, their names were just truant slots on a piece of paper. They did go to South every day for lunch and afterschool smoke-outs. Me, Jackson, and Cuzzo were the only ones trying to hang on at school. Sid was on the verge of scrapping the high school experience and getting his GED, and Rich was kicked out of all Minneapolis public schools for beating up a kid with a vacuum cleaner pipe, so he had a tutor homeschooling him.

I was coming back to South after an abysmal freshman year, ending it with back-to-back underwhelming semesters. There were plenty of lectures from my parents and start-overs, but my brain was somewhere else—listening to the *Menace II Society* sound track and *The Chronic* on loop or *Cypress Hill* at Washburn parties until I threw up in a backyard.

I came back to school with every intention I could stay focused and do better. But I didn't figure on my usual fall crash. I hadn't figured out yet that my fall crash was a part of a depression that would stay with me for my entire life, or how much a part of my being these crashes would become, no matter the perspective I entered them with. I would get lost somewhere and it would morph into something else, most of the time derailing my earlier intentions. It was supposed to be a *new start*—it was unbelievable how many times that term would be used in my life. Usually by others, though.

Cuzzo came back to South that fall without any sort of transformative expectations. Cuzzo was probably my oldest friend. Through years of social reconfiguring where the crew changed names and faces, even during times when we weren't necessarily so close, we could look up and the other one was still there. He had always found little ways to skate through tumult, though without an exactly flawless execution. It was always the right shot through the woods: his compass found the right gaps to get out into the clearing while others did not. If most of us were smart, we would have just followed him out wherever we could. We usually didn't, though. But this night, I couldn't help but think he must have picked the wrong direction this time, because nobody knew where he was or whether he was dead somewhere.

||||||||||||||||||||||||||||

IT WAS LIKE WE LOOKED UP at some point and the operating room lobby was filled with people we knew and just as many we didn't. There were clusters of family and friends just there waiting on something. Children were running around like it was normal but probably knew it was not. Some were playing tag late at night in a hospital waiting room with sobs and wrinkled expressions all around. Every so often a new announcement would come about his status, and it would get passed in whispers from group to group.

"He's probably going to die."

"They don't think he's going to make it."

"It went right through his spine, too close to his spinal cord."

"He's lost too much blood."

"If he does live, he'll be brain-dead."

"If he does make it, he'll be in a wheelchair for the rest of his life."

We were up and down the whole time. We would be

hopeful, then news would come and we would fall right back into despair. His mom, wrecked with tears and sorrowful expression, kept reentering prayer circles, adding and releasing members as the night marched and new faces appeared. Nobody even mentioned Cuzzo.

I stayed pretty well clustered with all of my friends. I had met his mom several times, but on this night I was unrecognizable to her, just like so many of the people there. We all waited, we all wanted a certain reassurance. After a while even the new news wasn't really new—we were all there to get the singular bit of information of whether or not he would live through the night. As part of our youth, most of us still lived in a world where decisions were made in single instants, with results expected in the corresponding moment. Waiting on babies to be born or parents to get old was sometimes unfathomable. I think we felt like if he got through that night that he would be okay, that the fight wouldn't be as severe. Sitting there, it was hard to imagine weeks of fighting with death, attached to machines—or months of recovery, and maybe years of not being what he was. We wanted to know: did he win or did he lose?

The woman who ran the Art Spot project on Franklin came in a gust of wind with her own swarm of paparazzi. The whole energy of the place changed, pointing out who people were, framing the story in her own way. She gave Jus's mom an exaggerated embrace; they were old friends. It helped for the narrative that was going to be told from then on.

This woman with a haze on her face from the burnout of the sixties and seventies, took over the area—composed, a woman who understood her moment, understood opportunity, and where and how grant money was obtained. It seemed disingenuous to me.

"These are all Art Spot kids—we're like a family." Many of us were not and had no intention of being included in her PR push. Most of the kids from the project were *not* there. I said something to clarify that we were not all kids from her project.

She hardly expected the outburst, the bursting of the bubble, the noncompliance with her use of horrifyingly raw experience as a means to make a personal statement about community and her program. A program "that can always use some more funding." Something about the woman stunk, but I had always said that. I wondered if anyone else was seeing what I was seeing. Something felt gross and self-serving. It was the evidence for the assumptions I held from before that night, and it was now blaring in hot-red flame in front of everybody. But nobody except Sid and Jackson seemed to understand it.

Soon after the room started to suffocate with bodies and assumptions and random chatter, we got up to smoke cigarettes or breathe the cool fall air. That was when the alert came—the Code Blue went off on the radio of a hospital employee standing by my mom, the alert none of us knew was happening or what it meant.

We were in an elevator, five or six of us trying to escape the dead air of that room. And the chaplain—I'm sure usually embraced and especially sought after in times like this—was on us, mouth chattering, trying to get us to say prayers for Justin's soul. It was true: the chaplain had spent most of this night with a head bowed, delivering words from brain-muscle memory, deliberate and automatic parables in language that for years was meant to carry ease, I guess—I really don't know what word this is supposed to be—or hope or guilt or destruction. I wonder how many people, on nights like these, have turned and submitted to forces greater than they could understand.

None of us wanted to say the prayer with the stranger. And while probably genuine in his intent, he seemed like most of the other strangers who come around in dark times—social service workers and police investigators who show up with a card and looks on their faces that say, "You have to let us help you, you need us." To me, it seemed like a prayer for our friend's soul from our mostly unreligious group would mean we were ceding that he was going to die. And while most of us knew how strong the possibility of his death was, we also knew that the spewing of words and the gathering of our hands wouldn't generate enough spiritual force to stop it.

Then his heart stopped beating. Detached from the world,

we were standing in the emergency room waiting area. Justin's light flickered on and off for a series of moments. It was the critical gathering of energies, the tug of war between the physical world and the other side. It was the space between. It was that pivotal time in the lives of parents they never forget, fearful of losing a child—the moment between yes and no. And still the light flickered: on, off; light, dark; now, or later. People die every day, at decibel levels that shatter the worlds built around them. But he probably wouldn't even be the first one to die in the city that day. It was a fact of life, people die and new life grows from out of the ashes. We were all trying to gather what the lessons were. Was it about violence or the community? Was it about making bad choices, walking into bad situations? Or was it that he was sent to teach us all about pain and loss, about the abruptness of life so that his experience could maybe save us?

His heart started beating again, not strong, but enough to fight a flat line for a little while longer.

All of that happened before we got back upstairs to the packed reception area. And although no one knew exactly what was happening in that operating room, whispers still circulated. My mom told me about the Code Blue, but the word hadn't come, no one had been told whether he would live or die. Then coming down the corridor, three figures, like ghosts: Rich and Cheesesteak and Cuzzo appeared before us. They would be able to tell the story, put some of the pieces together for us. I don't know if Cuzzo realized how we had believed him to be dead all of this time. They were sullen and exhausted looking, beaten up from a long night that was supposed to be a party, that ended up being hours spent downtown.

From them we got what happened: the coincidental encounter, the confusion, and the flash that lightning strikes in the dark; how in the chaos they had all gone different directions, somehow come out alive, without bullet wounds. Cuzzo saw the flashes, all the power of the charge that lit up the night, saw the energy transfer from the trigger into Jus's body before he could run away. Justin's mom hugged them all and engaged them in prayer. She even embraced Cheesesteak, whom she had so boldly held responsible before he even got there.

"I know you know why this happened—I know you're responsible for this—I know you know something—I know you had something to do with it!"

He tried to tell her, but she wouldn't let him tell her anything: her mind was made up.

As a group we all talked until everyone was too tired to say anything else. The waiting room thinned out. A lot of the people who stayed had found places to sleep or were barely holding their eyes open. There weren't any new updates; he had survived thus far, barely, but nobody knew what his body had left to fight with. At close to four in the morning he was still alive. We all went home except his mother and some other family members. There wasn't anything else we could do for him, or his mom, and we hoped we weren't leaving him when he needed us most. There was school the next day, but we weren't going. I slept in until the early afternoon and awoke to news that he was still fighting.

There was a candlelight vigil the next night at a vacant lot in Phillips on Fourteenth Avenue. People came from the neighborhood, some none of us knew, and sang songs alongside the Art Spot woman, who earlier that day was broadcast on all the local news channels talking about Justin's shooting and his impact as a community activist. It was a very Art Spot–centric piece rich with shots of the project and the mural. We only stayed for a short time. Jus's mom didn't want Cheesesteak there anyways.

The next day we went downtown and were able to see him for a few minutes. He was lying on a gurney, naked except for a hospital gown and thick bandages and a brace around the wound on his neck, hooked up to wires from all sorts of machines. He couldn't speak but his eyes were open. We were able to tell him we loved him, and that we knew he was going to make it. All he could do was look at us; we couldn't tell if he could hear us or with all the anesthesia know what was happening. I wanted to tell him how we thought he was dead, that our world had changed because of this, but I couldn't come up with the words. He looked back at us, eyes bugged, restrained, and wounded, a silence that told us the confusion we were experiencing would continue. It was hard to see this person, so strong and confident, broken down, made human with wires and IVs hooked to him, without the words to say what he needed us to do.

Less than a year earlier I sat in a different hospital room and watched a friend of mine writhe in pain when he got shot in the face. He was a little further along in his recovery, so he could speak and express what he needed to say, but his jaw was enormous from the swelling and he mostly just cried. Strong and invincible, made a child again from a bullet.

I was a lot closer to Justin, though, and looking at him it didn't feel like him, as though he had left that body and instead there was just the flesh and moving eyes left. And it looked like what it was: destruction. When we came, a young pretty girl we didn't know was waiting, crying a whole face full of tears, with a belly large and full of a child ready to come out. She acknowledged us but went back to her crying. Nobody had anything to say to each other on the trip home.

That weekend me and Cheesesteak took the acid we were supposed to take the night of the shooting. We sat in my room for a while listening to old Ice Cube, *AmeriKKKa's Most Wanted,* and let the world spin. We went out with friends and the night got weird, voices reverberated off the shrinking dimensions of the car, and voices and words piggybacked off of each other until Cheesesteak flipped out. We got dropped off at his house across the street from the Little Earth projects on Cedar, and at some point in the night Cheesesteak, chalky and ghostly, scared to death, told me, "Zeke, I died. I'm dead, Zeke." I told him he wasn't. After that, I was through playing around with acid. There were some dark things in us I wasn't prepared to face yet.

After that, everyone started to reconfigure what they were doing with themselves. Certain things were different now. The Art Spot ended for the season, and we all had commitments to school, where most of us had fallen behind again. But we stayed a unit, unified by the trauma. Jus was in and out of surgeries, and we couldn't see him for whatever reasons his mom thought were necessary. He was the centerpiece of our thoughts, but we didn't see him at all.

We all went to South's homecoming, except Rich, whose mom put him on Don't Leave the House Status forever. I only remember two things about that night: sitting in a garage by the school drinking Old English out of 64 oz. bottles; and splitting my lip by accident shadowboxing in the commons at school, leaving a lifelong scar on my lower lip.

We saw people we knew in the street, and they asked about him. One time a guy I hardly knew caught me coming out of the gas station on Thirty-fourth and Cedar and asked me, "You guys gonna kill them guys?"

"We're gonna try." What? I was out of my body, offhandedly making an allusion to killing something. I didn't own a gun, I didn't even have a car, and I didn't have any real idea as to who I would be looking for, or really any sense of who I was. It was a reaction statement: I could have just said what the truth was—that I was hoping he made it so everyone could move on with their lives. What kind of idiot just puts that kind of mojo out there with somebody as vague and random as that particular guy? I didn't know what I was becoming.

IN NOVEMBER, as the first frost hit and any lingering reminder of the summer was pulverized into wet, leafy mulch, we found out Jus had been transferred to Abbott Northwestern for his rehab. He was going to live. I went with Rich early one afternoon with the one rule that we couldn't tell Cheesesteak he was there. Jus's mom still swore he was the one who let it all happen, even though he had just been a victim that night like the others.

We navigated our way through the hospital chaos and found the corner of the institution where he was supposed to be living—but we couldn't find him.

Then a mechanized sound came from one of the rooms and a wheelchair emerged with a headful of uncut curls much higher than the back of the chair, turning a corner. His posture rigid and straight, his neck held straight by foam and a steel brace as though the chair made him part robot, with a hand that maneuvered anywhere he could go. When he saw us he smiled with a childish exuberance, as though awakened. But his glow wasn't there; it was simply gone. He was so skinny despite being flanked in oversized flannels and corduroys. I was so glad to see him, but his presence wasn't the same, his strength was gone. He still had the smile, but it wasn't the same—there was fray at the edges. He was trapped in a chair, even when he wasn't; he was trapped in a body that couldn't get out of bed by itself. There was a month and a half missing from his life, and he had to ask Rich what happened that night because he couldn't remember. It was hard because the story had become too separated from what and where he was the previous five weeks to absorb what actually happened. It couldn't make clear the accelerating moments after he took that bullet, and the rest of the experiences that followed while being in a hospital.

"Where's Cheesesteak?" he asked almost immediately.

"Your mom didn't want him to know you're here."

"Fuck that. Bring him up here next time. And bring some weed, too."

"You sure you can smoke like this?"

"Yes, and bring Cheesesteak." Again.

We were a bit conflicted whether or not to bring what he told us. I told Rich, though, "You know we're going to anyway." He smiled, "Yeah, I know."

And so we did. We grabbed sacks at the Blue House and showed up in force at the hospital with Cuzzo, Jackson, and Cheesesteak. The reunion was surreal; maybe now he could tell us what it meant, maybe we could all be resurrected now that he was.

He was instantly redrawn to Cheesesteak. It took time for him to tell Cheesesteak about the dream he had of him while he was under. He called it a vision. Cheesesteak stood there with his mouth open, telling Jus about the acid trip, and about thinking he was dead. They looked at each other dumbfounded, maybe thinking the other was full of shit, but didn't care, just grateful for the revival.

We took Jus outside and wheeled him around, pulling on joints we rolled on the counter next to the sink in the bathroom of his room. His hospital room became like one of our bedrooms, jackets hanging over chairs, seeds and stems in the toilet. There was comfort, some relief believing that some things were arcing back in a saner direction. I had to leave. It was night and my parents still expected I would go to school. The world could only be on hold for so long. Before we left, Jus's mom walked in on all of us standing around him. She didn't care about the rest of us; it was Cheesesteak standing there that was her focus. There was no explosive outburst, nothing outwardly confrontational—just recognition of his presence and an internal combustion mostly held to herself. They'd known each other for so long and any blame would have to be repressed for the moment. She made us all come together in prayer before we left.

And so our ritual of going and smoking with him every day began. Sometimes we just took over the heated smoking box designated for smokers. We took him on walks around the block. He even fell out of his chair once. He got too dusted and got to moving his heavy head too much, and his center of gravity shifted and he fell out.

Another time he came back and got into bed and got a head rush, something he had forgotten existed in his time out, and flipped out a little. The male nurse attending to him told him, "You gotta take it easy. And get some cologne or something." But he didn't. For a while we were like poorly trained orderlies, lifting him from his bed to bathroom to chair and back into bed. None of us knew what we were supposed to do.

Soon the pretty girl from the waiting room was just about to have his first child. He had another pretty girl, who would later have his second and third children coming through, sometimes locked in the bathroom with him when we showed up.

He got so comfortable in his chair that in the middle of November he was pushing it by himself the six blocks to the Blue House on Fifteenth. A woman would come from the upstairs apartment to sell a guy in a wheelchair and blue flannel shirt a ten or twenty dollar sack. And then for Thanksgiving he was able to go home for the day to eat with his family.

By Christmas, Justin was at home with his mom and his siblings in a rundown duplex apartment on Twenty-fifth Street, right across the street from the Children's Hospital, a block or two away from the dice spot on Columbus. He was being chauffeured around making appearances at everyone's house. When he got to my house, he had shed his chair, taking stairs with some help. He was a lot taller than I remembered, but skinny—skin on bones. When he walked, his right leg dragged, his right arm dragged, too. He had to do everything with his left now. Sometimes he actually had to lift up the right arm with his left for balance. Everything was a coordination of mechanisms trying awkwardly to get to know each other again. His long neck showed the severe scars where the bullet ripped through, missing his spinal cord by millimeters. His chin and parts of his face bore the collateral nicks of being so close to the explosion. He held his head up shyly, moving his entire body to see anything happening on his periphery. He was alive, yes, but wore every scripture of what happened to his body. It was the first that most of my family had seen of the wheelchair-clad mechanical man trying to learn how to walk again.

Everyone believed now that he wouldn't have to be in a wheelchair for the rest of his life. And besides all the weed he still smoked, it was apparent he wasn't brain-dead either, like they feared. He would have a partial paralysis for the rest of his life, a slowed use of the right side of his body. But despite it, it seemed like he was going to beat the tragedy trifecta of death, brain-death, or complete paralysis that often comes from those kinds of gunshot wounds. It seemed we wouldn't have to figure out for ourselves what the lesson in all this was—he would be able to tell us himself.

Slowly he got better, the wheelchair went away, and by

spring he went back to work when the art project started again.
I sold out and got a job at the art project, too, mostly because
it was summer and it was where our family was gathered. And
they needed someone to set up scaffolding and wash brushes.
Certainly he didn't move like he used to. He couldn't run or ride
a bike, but he figured out almost immediately who he could rely
on for free-ride service—service he had no problem abusing a
little bit: "What? I just almost died."

Sometime before the completion of the mural project, the
kids from the art project went camping somewhere around
Siren, Wisconsin. It was extracurricular stuff meant to show
perspective in contrast to the everyday brick and concrete
constructions of the inner city. Me and Jus snuck off to smoke
something in the woods and saw a black bear and her two cubs
late-afternoon foraging about fifty yards away.

"Look, Jus, a bear. How cool is that?"

When I didn't hear his response, I looked behind me and
all I heard was rustling brush from the scooting of his mechanical legs in their fastest hop-trot out of the woods.

"Where are you going?"

"Shit, you can get away. I ain't as fast as you—I ain't fucking
with no bear," he told me, standing, out of breath on the road
just outside the woods.

He seemed to be doing all right, though. He had his newborn son, who was aptly named after him, and he was vigorously
working on another one, probably several. He could be, for the
most part, the same man he was before—indiscriminate and
unapologetic for his experiences— hopefully better.

He was becoming, as expected, the poster boy for the art
project. And while I wanted it to be blatant exploitation, it
wasn't always. He really loved the attention. In fact, he courted
and charmed it. When we went to apply for grants, the great
resurrection of one of our own never went unmentioned. But
that was how the game was played. He would smile and automatically assert eye contact with one of the more or less attractive women in the room. He was addressed, as a lot of the
individuals in the program were, as a community artist or an

activist against violence and poverty and the destruction of the cultural ethos of so many different groups in the city.

To us, though, we early on recognized this superhero suit as laundry threaded from mostly pure hustle. Because he, just like most of us, took his paychecks inconsistently distributed and usually late, depending on the financial timing of the manager of the project's own bill and grocery needs. We spent our money on cheap beer and sacks of weed. They were for Jus, just like some of us, vices he hadn't shucked despite his rise from the dead. And in addition, he held on to an insatiability for gambling on just about anything. It was the continuation of some of the patterns that would operate for the rest of his life. Sometimes the only time any of us would see him over the course of a day would be a glimpse of his hunched back balancing himself with a fist clenched around paper Presidents, and the other hand either blocking or rolling dice. Like the rest of us, he was around all the same people as before everything had happened. We may have felt different, but we were in all the same places and participated in all the same activities as before. But the rest of us didn't have the reminder of months of surgery and rehab walking around with us in every step.

He was a spokesman whether he knew it or not. He was selling something, a part of himself in exchange for all of those things he may need later—a ride, a shot of pussy, or a small loan. "But it's me, Justin." Of course it was, and he was great at it. It worked on all of those who were unsuspecting, without the sharp point to poke through the smiling surface. It became a joke to a lot of us as to how full of shit he could be sometimes. None of us knew what would come from the mechanical re-creation he went through on that hospital bed. There could have been a lot of different variances; but when the sweat was wiped from the mirror, it was just Justin. Without the scrap or the fluidity of body, but with the same fluid jazz, same sinewy charisma—part angel, part crook.

It was unpracticed charisma, which didn't have all the "speak" or language hammered into a ready-made, press-conference-like format. He would be asked to make announcements on the radio, or say a few words at events to bolster the mural project, which he did with all the temerity of a pro athlete with just enough smoothe-over to get through an uncomfortable interview. But he didn't have to be Nelson Mandela—his wounds alone were supposed to be the figurative representation of the message. I'm not sure if he fully understood that himself; what he did understand were the short-term favors his willingness provided.

From the inside I was able to see the workings of community organization, with all the strange hierarchies of purpose, individual interests, and the disagreements and competition over grant money. It was the hustle and grind of the arts most don't realize, the smiling mask of goodwill that comes from constant fund-raising. The city was on fire, so it was easy to validate the need for anything to help the kids. It felt necessary when the local news was keeping a nightly body-count tally: "We're at forty-eight, and it's only June."

There was naturally the small bit of Kool-Aid we were all expected to drink—the caustic beverage from which some drank more than others, those who believed some sort of community revolution or revival would come out of it. And if you drank enough of the fruity elixir, you might not notice some of the more blatantly unorganized parts of these kinds of community programs.

It may have in fact saved some of the kids in the project. And if it didn't save them, it created the right benefit they needed to propel them into their chosen lives. A couple of girls maximized the opportunity and learned some things about how the art world worked. They learned how to write grants. Our friend, the girl from Argentina, became the youngest person to earn a grant to meet local artists on a tour through Central and South America. It helped me to later be a lot more forgiving to what the project was and what it was able to do, and to see that I was probably looking at everything then through an obscured lens.

ııııııııııııııııııııııııı

AFTER THE PROJECT WAS FINISHED, the kids involved shot out like fireworks in the different directions of their lives, and not necessarily great directions. At least six of us ended up in prison at some point, and there was an assortment of shootings or other hoodlum outcomes. There are, though, pictures all over the place. I'm absent from most of them because I was probably the one asked to take them. I wasn't exactly the face of the project. The face was of course Jus, in corduroys and a Dickies T-shirt with his hair in plaits in the middle of the photo, with blank stares into the camera or off into the distance somewhere.

There was the eventual unveiling of the mural, for which the community came out to celebrate its completion. It was generally very well received in the neighborhood and created a pleasant sense of accomplishment, even for me, the kid who was most apprehensive to give anything of myself. Many involved spoke on behalf of the project, including Justin. There were mostly nominal meanderings hard to hear because of the shrieking reverb of the microphone that came off more symbolic than inspirational. There was, though, a genuine acceptance that it was the end of something that for better or worse had been a significant force in our lives.

Justin, being the one who "took the bullet" for the project and for whom most were concerned with keeping afloat, was given a job with the Phillips community organization. He had a desk in the very building the mural was painted on. He was given an apartment in a Social Security building on Twenty-first and Minnehaha, soon after his second son was born.

Sometimes we would listen to him doing promotional work for the People of Phillips on KFAI, the local radio station on the West Bank. He wasn't much more polished than he'd ever been. We would listen and laugh out loud, knowing his employers had probably given him a bullet list of things to remember to say, but he probably lost track of them after the first couple of points, and he freestyled the rest of the way. We laughed at knowing about the likely smell of smoke on his clothes as he walked into the station.

Then a bunch of computers were stolen from the People of Phillips building. A whispered pandemonium ensued, a shock and subsequent injury to the community organization that at least in the criminal sense trusted its individual parts. The suspicions turned to assumptions and conspiratorial conclusions that most often pointed at Justin. Even if it was technically impossible for him to carry out all of those computers through the back door with his handicap, theories stretched and fingers were pointed. The idea had become that it was Cheesesteak, the fallback villain who coaxed or was in cooperation with Justin, the partly handicapped josher, with his good foot still in the streets. To many, the Golden Child—the poster boy, the inspiration and star of the Art Spot story—was also a crook.

It probably felt to them like he had taken on the kindness and generosity of people who were only trying to help those in the community like him. He used it for a small-time come-up with his grimy-ass partner—whom nobody there ever trusted, whom nobody wanted around, but who sort of came with the package of Justin. Some of them had always kind of blamed Cheesesteak for his influence on Jus. They had always kind of put a whole lot of unfair blame for the fire-tempered fragment of steel propulsion that bore a cavity through Jus's spine and existence. There was a lot that could be said for Cheesesteak, but they couldn't say that. But they wanted to.

And in their betrayal, their kindness disregarded, when victims are trying to cleanse themselves of the abuses they've endured, they needed a face, something with a name to expel in order to move on. And with a confusion of opinions, conflicting angles of emotion and point of view, they fired him. The interrogation was simple: "Do you know who took the computers?"

"No." And that was it, a decision had to be made, and it was.

But the truth, however abstract and obscure as it always is, was somewhere outside of the small box they were looking into.

"What happened to the job?" I asked him one day after it all happened.

He told me about the computers.

"Wow, that's some grimy shit. Did you?"

"Fuck no! That's a hype move."

"It *is* a crackhead move. You sure you didn't do it, though?"

"On my right hand to God, I didn't have nothing to do with that shit, and Cheesesteak didn't have anything to do with it." I knew he wasn't selling any bullshit—we were all criminal enough to not try to pretend we weren't in times it was seemingly so obvious. There were others it could have been. Employees with not-so-secret crack habits and obscure vendettas and all kinds of snaky possibilities. It was a strange coincidence, though strange coincidences don't always make for truth.

He was left on his own for the first time since that fateful night in the fall. He was fine with it, though. It gave him extra space and freedom to consume as much beer and smoke as much weed as it took to put him to sleep or lose enough of his SSI money shooting dice. He found a niche working for Cheesesteak's sister selling Web sites and long-distance service for a telemarketing place. To him it was the same as anything: the same grind, the same hustle as he had always done, with a new disguise. When the Feds showed up with warrants because there was something bogus about what they were selling, Jus was back the next day with a new script selling long-distance service to people sitting around all day at home.

But he had ravage—ravage that came from the recklessness of drinking too much and filling your lungs with bad trees and menthol cigarettes. It came from throwing money that was meant for the kids into the furnace every time he flung a set of dice onto the carpet at the spot on Twenty-fifth and Columbus. It was this ravage that left a worn fray along the edge of everything in his life. It made it difficult to be the parental figure he intended to be. When he was in the hospital he always believed the kids would be his salvation. He thought like a lot of people who come out of all different kinds of tragedy that if he built his flock they could be the foundation for all of the things he wanted out of life.

The great purpose that was built out of the revival of his breath would be that he would get another shot, unencumbered by the dual traps of the poor, the two-headed monster of death and prison. Now his life revolved around his nightly trip to the liquor store for cold MGDs and daily dice games at the gambling spot. It ended, though, with a life full of continual underachievement. He would be the first to ask who decided what the expectations were supposed to be. He might have been lucky that there were certain desperations he just could not go back to—his handicaps just didn't allow them.

It was the part of the ravage that might have otherwise put him on a corner or a thumper in his hand to go rob or hurt something. It was that part of the ravage that put Cheesesteak in jail. First a couple of months, then a few more, then a few years; it set up the pattern that stuck with him for the rest of his life. The build back up and the break back down: nothing new, maybe in hindsight a fitting denouement, though.

Jus just drank more beer and competed with me and Sneak for sales to people in his building. He would gas and dash at all the nearby gas stations until a manager at the Holiday on Franklin came stomping out one time with a mouth full of threats and a whole face full of bluster. Jus handed me an empty 22-oz. beer bottle: "If he tries something, hit him with this." We'd show up at the apartment sometimes in the middle of some of the dumbest arguments ever between him and the second baby's mom. A little while later there was another son on the way, no doubt with a *J* name.

I went out with him for my birthday that year. I remember trying to ask him about what he was going to do with his life. It was a dumb question simply because it came from an eighteen-year-old kid who had no idea his damn self. "What the fuck are you talking about?"

I was talking about the boy who died and was resurrected but never became Jesus as was promised. The young man whose symbolism must have gotten inflated with the same sense of disproportion that everything from that time did: the local news and the pleas from the police for more officers, the crises of every little small organization, and the competing sales pitch to win the coveted grants and donation money.

The young man who saw the actual light on the other side but was yanked from it at the last second for more work on Earth. The boy who never told us what all of it meant. The man who was a walking representation that pain isn't calculated in singular moments but in the long, slow pressure of living—the long, slow drag and the fraying of experience. The person I had every intention of killing for. I guess I was also talking about myself and the less-than-shiny world I was coming up in, no more motivated than Jus to be anything either. A person who was just thirsty but didn't know what for. And wanting freedom, even with all the empty spaces it leaves behind.

"What the fuck are you talking about?"

I don't know.

Eight

THE BLOCK CLUB
|||||||||||||||||||||||||||||||||||||||||||||||||||||||||||||||||||||||||||||||||||||||||||||

N EIGHBORS GATHERED TOGETHER, like they were doing
on blocks throughout the city. Even my own parents were
now in collusion with families and oddball eccentrics they
hardly knew lived in the neighborhood, all to expel the un-
seemly aspects of our part of the neighborhood. They brought
untouched casseroles and two-liter bottles of pop to compare
outrage with the varying things they believed were making the
city unlivable. Everyone, depending what part of the block they
lived on, had their favorite villains to point to for the problems
they didn't understand. Most of the focus was centered on the
tenants of the red brick apartment buildings, who many believed were the roots of everything sinister in their worlds. My
dad's own nemesis was a guy in a white Cutty with customized
license plates who harassed my mom in the backyard while she
worked in the garden. On at least one occasion Dad chased him
off the block with his shotgun. In 1995, I was not quite eighteen
yet; I was one of the "good ones," they thought. There was no
way I was touching any of those casseroles, though.

That year the whole city was hot with youngsters shooting
out of the backseats of moving cars and dope fiends lined up
around city blocks for crackhouses run by people from other
cities who had figured out how sweet Minneapolis could be. In

the middle of it nobody was calling it Murderapolis; nobody realized it was just a short stretch of time in the history of the city
where the murder rate skyrocketed and people's views of what
the city was would change. Most in attendance believed it was
just part of the inevitable spiral downward of their community.
A motley crew of neighbors, mostly unfamiliar with each other,
came together in that kitchen; the adults drank coffee and
smoked cigarettes and compared their own personal stories of
disbelief, accentuated with enough exaggeration and populist
rage to make the meeting seem meaningful. There were gunshots every night, but twenty minutes at that block club concentrated solely on the old woman at the end of the block who
didn't secure her recycling well enough, and bottles and news-
paper would blow up and down the alley on windy days.

The cop sent to speak at the city-sanctioned block club
gathering told everybody at the meeting to call them every
time they heard gunshots. The cops got so many calls between
'94 and '96 they probably couldn't respond to most of them. On
the mornings after, out watering flowers or trimming bushes,
neighbors assembled in half-sun to compare statistics. A couple of summers previously, they all still believed green lawns
and crab apple trees made a neighborhood safe. Now, they got
together with their nightly tallies to compare and contrast.

"We heard them four times last night."

"Oh yeah? We only heard them three times right after the
news, then during Leno's monologue, and again sometime after
we went to sleep Michael heard some more."

"Yeah, four times. Two shots, then a three, then a whole
six or seven, and another two when Margaret got up to use the
bathroom at 2:37."

As long as I could remember there were two worlds to my
block on Thirty-fifth Street and Twelfth Avenue. On a summer
day a person could walk around the entire block and not see
anyone. But after five, a stroll through the alley was like pushing aside the flora to another world. It was a well of activity,
between basketball games on garages and the smell of charcoal and barbeque, contrasted with the spoil of overflowing

garbage. There was a house on the block that had been getting raided since the eighties, yet most of the focus still fell on the two apartment buildings with a more transient population that wasn't as familiar to the longtime residents. It was suggested not to let anybody from the nearby apartment buildings into the block club's top- secret meetings for fear that covert information would get passed along to drug dealers.

When new gossip was exhausted, the gatherings were overshadowed by mention of a neighborhood peeping Tom— a wiry little man with round glasses and bug eyes who was spotted by several women on the block, peering into bottom-story windows late at night. He was pretty easily recognized as a guy who lived in the middle of the block with his wife and two kids. The family, himself included, were present at many of these meetings, even as stories of the peeping Tom were being shared. He would sit silent on a chair in the corner and listen to the group talk about their disgust with his actions.

During one of many insignificant hot summer nights I was at home, drinking beer upstairs in my room and playing Nintendo for five dollars a game with Cheesesteak. Cheesesteak was still as shifty as ever. Even with everything the guys had gone through, he still stole cassettes or reset *Madden* when it looked like he was going to lose.

He had the sleight of hand of a street hustler who will nickel-and-dime someone out of their last piece of change, because he *was* a street hustler who nickel-and-dimed people, even his friends. It made him easy to blame for things. If the world blew up, it was easy to point a finger in his direction. He had a rough kind of charm, though, with funny quips and sound effects, enough bells and whistles for any of us to assume that someone was coming up with empty pockets.

Cheesesteak came through before my parents went to bed. We spent several hours betting the same five dollars back and forth before we just got tired of playing. Of course it was after he got ahead. When he left, he let the screen door rattle and shut with a startling and irritating clang. I pondered my buzz for a few minutes, a little irritated with Cheesesteak, a little snaky and bored, and stuck for the night. Hidden in a sock and wrapped in a sweatshirt in my closet, it sat there without any sort of calculated purpose—.38 Special, heavy in my hand, its black steel and classic wood grip had a history I didn't know. Revolver with a snub nose like a bulldog. I had no idea what its power was yet, how it could take so much from someone, how it promised safety and protection but didn't give it necessarily. Most of the time it just sat there, its purpose hidden in the stack of clothes I didn't wear anymore. I held it flat in my palm and ran my thumb over the cylinder and the hammer, opened it and saw the same six bullets that were in it when I got it. It occurred to me that we were strangers to each other, a secret relationship with something nobody knew I had. Despite planning to, I hadn't shot it yet. I closed it and started to wrap it back up, but I had a thought. It wasn't a complicated plan; there were still several hours of night left, and there was an empty park across the street. I looked out the window and Thirty-fifth Street was dead. I could slide into the park and fire some shots off, and slide right back in and go to sleep.

I ran across the street into the urban forest of Powderhorn with the pistol hanging loose in the pocket of my shorts. Cautious, I took off into the void, finding a spot just low and camouflaged enough by trees and slope to stay unnoticed. I pulled the .38 out and held it out in front of me, facing the island in the middle of the lake, and fired off the entire six shots. I did it with very little rush or flux in my nerves, just a buzz and a nostril full of gunpowder. I wasn't thinking about jail or that stupid block club, or the city and the murder rate. I just jogged back up to the house, watching both ways on Thirty-fifth Street for traffic, with the gun still in my hand.

I went back inside and lay down for the night. After sleeping through the morning, I found a spot to sit on our front steps. I was eating orange slices, a little hungover, spitting the seeds onto the grass. Mom was in the backyard gardening. Dad was in the garage. My niece and the neighbor kids were running around the yard full speed, zigging and zagging, knocking things over, and zagging out of the picture again.

Mom came around the house, pulled me up close to tell me: "You know after Cheesesteak left last night? He went across the street and started shooting at something."

"Huh?" I asked, only then remembering what I did.

"Yeah, Margaret and Ronald said they heard gunshots right after he left, like exactly. They saw him running across the street afterwards. Did you know that's where he went when he left?"

"No," I answered, slightly amused the neighbors couldn't tell the difference between me, a tall, skinny white kid, and Cheesesteak, who was short, stocky, and black. There was obviously some collusion going on between Mom and the neighbors.

"Tell him he can't bring guns over here or he's not welcome. I would have thought after Justin he would understand that."

"No—I don't think so, Mom. How do they know it was him? How do they even know who Cheesesteak is? It sounds like a coincidence and they're overreacting," implying that I knew she had let our neighbors drive the car to a conclusion, and she was riding right along with them.

"Oh yeah? It was right after he left, Zeke. Like a few minutes, only," trying to pretend she hadn't been steered by anyone to come up with her assertion.

"How do *they* know when he left? I'm pretty sure it wasn't him. I never saw any gun. I think that if he had the money, I don't think he'd buy a gun with it."

"Are you sure?"

"Yeah." Likely he would have bought weed and a case of Bumpy Face gin.

"Well, okay," knowing it would take too much time and energy to find the truth.

She looked at me like I was being sneaky, or naïve, being taken in by the shifty Cheesesteak. She let it go with the satisfaction that she had figured something out, even if I hadn't yet. After she left me alone, I meditated on a way to clean it up, create a reasonable explanation for the synchronicity of events. Or every time Cheesesteak came through, it would be an unspoken but heavily sensed issue. Soon after, I caught a glimpse of Ronald and his wife, Margaret, both looking over at me, then back at each other, repeating the highly exaggerated gestures a couple times until Ronald came over to me. I wanted to not know why, but how could I not? I was still swooshing an orange seed in my mouth when, without a hello or anything else of any cordiality, his mouth opened.

"Zeke, does your friend Cheesesteak carry a gun?"

"What?" How did they even know Cheesesteak's name? Mom, of course. But why, even with what my parents may have suspected, would either of them let our neighbors in on their hunch? Were they serious—really? The bluntness of how he presented it came off as a bit corny to me. I decided anything they asked me I would give them the most basic and to the point answer I had.

"No." My eyes scrunched up as I told him, still swooshing the seed.

"Are you sure?" What did he mean, am I sure? And if I was keeping it to myself, why would the "Are you sure?" addendum to the question push me into revealing something?

"Yeah, I'm pretty sure." And I spit the orange seed onto the ground a few feet from him, catching his attention.

He looked at me like this was his moment—his police moment—the months of writing times and frequency down, calling and reporting them. It was his take-back-the-streets moment. And it was so easy for him to confront; it was right next door. He was going to clean up the block one shot at a time, one stone or one stem at a time. I looked back at him: this was my So what? moment.

"No, I know plenty of people with guns, but he's not one of them." I could've easily added that he was plenty shady without one, if that was what he wanted me to confirm. I wanted to say there are dozens of shots every night—what did six more matter in the middle of one particular night? I guessed people in powerless situations tend to puff out their chests most in those fights they think they can win, or bluff out. I've done it many times myself. Ronald just kept looking at me as though he were looking for a tell, or some kind of breakdown. I just turned from his attention and walked back inside.

I knew there was more he wanted to say, but he wasn't going to get that chance this morning. He could bring it up with Mom and Dad or take it to the block club. For the most part they used the encounter as a reason to not talk to me, which was cool. It was only a matter of time before they would move out, to a neighborhood just as volatile as ours. Soon, they stopped telling people to call every time they heard shots. Once they got all the federal funding for new officers and departments, there was no need to record everything.

There had to be a lot of phone calls logged somewhere with times and personal descriptions. Yet the shots didn't stop, their volume didn't diminish, and people kept dying. I wonder if there is a ledger somewhere with every call, every testimonial from those years. It was fifteen years before my mom found out where those shots really came from.

Nine

FATHERS AND SONS,
MEN AND BOYS

||||||||||||||||||||||||||||||||||||||||||||||||||||||||||||||||||||||||||||||||||||||||||

W E PULLED UP TO THE FUNERAL HOME on Thirty-first and Minnehaha, a building I had seen hundreds of times, seen the illuminated logo on its lawn coming to and from the grocery store for most of my young life, not realizing that it was a place where people get dressed up for one last party of love and grief. Looking for a place to park, I saw a guy I used to play hockey with when we were younger. He was walking around the triangular block by himself. I never liked him, and the years had helped me forget him and how I felt. In a plain moment we caught eyes and a simple expression of grief expelled itself from his face, leaving only a small trace of the old arrogance I hated about him. And yet, here we were in the same place again, and none of that really mattered now.

My parents had come to get me from school that Tuesday, picking me up in the family car, a '91 Ford Tempo. It was fairly new then. My dad had his tweed blazer on and a pair of khakis, and my mom was in the navy-blue suit she'd worn to work. I remember my dad's tweed coat because it only came out of the closet for weddings or funerals. I had on what I had worn to school that day: dark gray Dickies and a blue-and-gray flannel.

It was hardly funeral attire and was a style that had had its day, but even though I knew I was coming, I wasn't prepared.

Getting in meant walking through a confusing cordon of security, a mixture of friends and family in airbrushed RIP T-shirts and plainclothes police officers with exposed side-arms, wanding everyone as they came in. Small units moved frenetically with walkie-talkies, engaged in some kind of activity. The lobby was full, with family members I remembered from years past from barbeques at his house. I saw his mom in sobs in the arms of someone I didn't recognize. She didn't recognize us, but that made sense: it was not a reunion—it was too harsh for that, the pain too new—and in sorrow we'll walk past history, even if we were in it. I saw several people I knew once, all in their own stages of loss, not saying anything to me, just moving in unison with their grief. All the people there astounded me, the few I knew, and the so many I didn't, all coming and going from the lobby to the main hall and back to the lobby, from small group to larger group, security watching perimeters and coordinating movement, consolidating space amidst the large crowd. When my great-grandmother died, there were a quarter as many people, and she was ninety-two, so the pain wasn't as rich, tragic, and spontaneous as this was. This was new. A generation coming to know death so young, and he was *so* young, so charismatic.

||||||||||||||||||||||||||

WHEN WE WERE KIDS, Junior was one of my favorite people, lived on the same block, played baseball and football at Powderhorn with me. His parents got him a facemask like Walter Payton, because he wanted to play running back. We would collect baseball cards and hold them out proudly when we lucked up on something the book said had value. In the summer we played baseball. Our dads coached the team together: he pitched and played the outfield, and I played shortstop. During the long summer days we ran around the neighborhood playing pickup games in alleyways and church parking lots. This is the point where I could oversimplify times, make them seem carefree and innocent. I could conjure images of kids running in full stride with giant smiles and water flowing from fire hydrants. But no matter how young we were, and no matter how prototypical the childhood motifs may have been, even then things were complicated. There were always strains of our struggling family structures and all the social dynamics of being young. And we all felt these things acutely. We all knew Junior's parents' generosity and concern for their children before everything else, even after it became obvious they were a family deep with hustlers. Every once in a while, a dumpster in their backyard would be filled with stuff ruined during the raids. It was something I noticed long before my parents ever did. It was impossible, though, not to see how great his mom and dad were to him and his sisters. And it was hard not to love his dad, Coach, always present, always with a smile for the kids on the team.

He and my father had a natural relationship, a relationship between men raising kids in a city that was different from how it had once been. It was becoming what growing cities with changing populations start to become when all of its varying elements are left to interact with each other. Parents tend to blame themselves when things go wrong. They'll blame themselves for being too lenient or too strict—letting kids watch violence on TV or movies. Kids have so many things they want to blame too for how things end up, or get messed up—divorces, abuse, parents going to jail all affecting how they saw the world. My mother swore she should have never moved us back into South Minneapolis to the exact neighborhood where Dad grew up. She thought we should have stayed in a small town in the mountains or moved to the suburbs somewhere, and that it ultimately would have saved us from much of the hurt that touched our lives. But that's not reality. Because by accepting this idea would have meant traveling back in time and condemning all the people and experiences the three of us ever had during those twenty-one years. It would mean that all the things any of us learned—the jobs and the creation of our personal identities—had no value. It's like a person blaming himself for not understanding the future, or for not being someone else.

Baseball was a big part of how my dad and I knew each other. He started throwing balls to me before I could even sit up. So when I was growing up, I played catch with my dad every day. He always worked blue-collar jobs: fixing roads for the city of Minneapolis; he worked in the lumberyard when we lived in California; he worked a super-shitty welding job for some dick at Flying Cloud Airport, where he came home every day bitter and dog-tired or injured. He caught metal fragments in his eye once and slipped a disc in his lower back another time. For months he laid on his stomach in front of the TV in the living room. But when he was able, he came home, grabbed the gloves, and threw the baseball with me at the park across the street for hours. He threw me ground ball after ground ball and tossed it high into the air so I would run after it and try to make dramatic catches. On at least one day a week he suited up to play softball with the team he'd played with most of his life, and I got to see him make those diving catches himself and throw people out from left field. Afterwards I drank pop at Mortimer's while he and his team drank beer. When I was about fifteen, some of those guys would buy me a beer, too, until a waitress would come steal it from me and bring me a Coke instead. Then they'd just get me some rum or cognac and pour it into the Coke.

For years our relationship was centered on baseball. We went to games at the Metrodome and watched mediocre Twins teams play on green carpet. And he would tell me about all the players, and about seeing games at the old Met Stadium. We would get a stack of punch-out All Star ballots and vote for who we wanted to see. We brought my friend Junior one of those times. We brought our gloves hoping to catch foul balls. We went early so we could lobby players from the opposing Red Sox to sign the baseball cards we brought with us. When we were going to take our seats, Roger Clemens was tossing pop flies to Ellis Burks and accidentally overthrew him, and the ball came whirring into the stands and bounced on the concrete steps in front of us. My dad tried to catch it for us, but its trajectory was just too great coming off that concrete.

Eventually, as we got older, those times faded into childhood ether. Social circles left the parks and the neighborhoods and migrated to schools. He had his friends and I found my own. Sports didn't matter much anymore. I never got much bigger, and I just couldn't hit the pitching of the bigger kids and it stopped being fun. I realized I wasn't going to be Cal Ripken.

I would see Junior at parties with his people, and we'd hang out for a while and kick it about our dads, or look at the ass on some girl there. But that was it, a pound or a handshake and we went different directions. We were still in the same city, the same neighborhoods, but we were in different schools, had different cliques. I always heard about him, though. Never anything bogus or underhanded, just that he was kind of raw now, doing his thing. But I never saw him anymore after that. I even bought weed at one of his spots, a dilapidated apartment complex on the south side of Lake Street, but he had just left. We sent one of our guys into the building past a few guys with guns in their waistlines. They patted him down and broke down some dimes from a table with a monster pile sitting on top of it until he got the sack and left.

At some point after that I heard that Senior, his dad, got locked up. He got a bundle of years; I can't even remember how many. It seemed like so long back then, so irredeemable and permanent; I just didn't know what any of it meant. Later we would have our own guys go away, lean back into the shadows and disappear. We would hope we weren't the ones to disappear. I don't remember if I told my parents about it then; it probably didn't matter, though.

It was in the early fall of 1994, the night of South High School's homecoming, a Friday, of what would have been my junior year had I not been so many credits behind from the previous two years. I went with Cuzzo to pick up my first government paycheck, from the part-time job at a discount retail store downtown. Me and Cuzzo cashed our checks and bought *Ready to Die,* as though we were.

That night we drank cheap beer and Seagram's gin with generic orange juice at a friend's house down the street from the school. Some of the guys wanted to go to the homecoming dance. I didn't, though. I thought they were lame. Just two years earlier, as a freshman, my science teacher ratted on me to my parents about how hammered I had been at the winter Snow-Daze Dance. Initially, he told me he wasn't going to say anything, but then he called the house anyway. I think he thought he could save me. Wrong. We ended up throwing bottles at his house after getting drunk in the middle of one particular night.

Out front of this house, where we sat on the porch listening to dope-fiend stories from the tragically drug-addicted older brother of the friend who lived there, there was a navy-blue car. It was probably a Cutlass from the early eighties; it could've been a Regal or a Monte Carlo. Somebody else telling this story might've known for sure, but to me it could've been any car. It just sat there, not belonging to the block or anyone from the neighborhood. It sat there ownerless, by itself, exactly in front of this house. Apparently it had been there for several days already, its doors unlocked, unclaimed. The fellas had already been through it, under the seats and in the trunk. The older brother told us it was a waste of time to be messing around in it. He said if it was there any longer, he would scrap it and sell its parts.

Except the glove box was locked. And while in all of his dope-fiend meticulousness, the older brother and the rest of the bandits in our party before us had chipped out the trunk, torn apart the seats, and ripped through every other aspect of the car, they neglected the most obvious idea to bust open the locked glove compartment. So me and Cuzzo sat in the front two seats, each with a hand gripping at a small crack at the edge of the glove box. I told him, "Whatever is in there, half of it is mine," not anticipating much, just wanting a claim on whatever it could be. We made a rough count of three and yanked at the door, breaking out the plastic around the weak locking device, and the plastic flap fell open and several bagged blocks of mineral-like hunks of wax or soap fell literally into our laps.

They fell in chunks—larger than either of us had ever seen in real life—of already rocked-up cocaine, several ounces of it.

In our confused drunken states, me and Cuzzo looked at each other, confounded by what this meant, what we would do now, how we could make it relevant. In order not to draw attention to all those who had missed what we had stumbled upon, we cuffed the blocks of dope and pocketed it so nobody else could stake any claim to it, downplaying the amount. We didn't talk about it much after that. Instead we just drank more and eventually tried to get into the dance, but the building was full. I was lucky I didn't go to jail, because I had my stash in my underwear and I got carried away calling the officer at the door a bitch.

The next morning we went to work, hungover, ready to bag up and make money. When I got off work, my mom picked us up and on the drive home told me the sad news. She told me Junior had been shot to death the night before, just a few blocks from homecoming, and where I had been most of that entire day and night. I didn't have an outward reaction when she told me. I ingested it, but I didn't understand it. I didn't understand how I should react, or how I was supposed to feel. My heart was hardening. Something inside me understood that this was unnatural, but not uncommon. I didn't know whether to be overwhelmed with grief—or if I wasn't, if that meant I didn't feel anything at all. I didn't know if I should be afraid—if maybe there was a bullet out there for me. I didn't know if I should be out there asking who did it—if it was my business, or if it was just more stuff being flung in my direction to process. I didn't know how I was obligated to feel, or what to do if I ever encountered the person who killed him. Or if I might already know the person—that would just complicate the mix even more. So I stayed quiet and absorbed the blow. I didn't know what it was going to mean in my life, now or later on. I had no idea what the dope I had in my pocket would do either. Mostly, though, I wondered about Junior's dad leaning back in the shadows of a prison cell somewhere.

||||||||||||||||||||||||||||

PEOPLE FROM THE FUNERAL HOME were making last announcements to view the body before the funeral. My mother kept encouraging me to go see him. They had both seen him already the day before at the wake, in a hat and football jersey, in his colors. But I was too ashamed, felt too disconnected then. I didn't know why I was ashamed then. I still don't. It could've been the immensity of the event. All the people I didn't know, the lifetime since we were kids where so many other people had appeared and he wasn't just one of my best friends anymore. I had become another bystander behind the yellow tape of another person's life. Even if I had loved that person once. I was only one of many who had a chance to love a part of this person. All the cats in his crew were lined up in clusters of red and black, cliqued up, knowing him as he was right up to the moment of his death. They might have understood the context of his death, and maybe something more. But I didn't, and I didn't know any of them yet to ask, so I chose not to look.

I sat next to my parents many rows back in the funeral hall, itching to capacity, people standing to hold the last remaining inches of room space. I followed along with the prepared program printed out on baby blue paper folded in fours. People stood up and spoke about the things they speak about at funerals, grief and loss, a chance to reconnect with God, and all those personal anecdotes that will become this person's folklore in the future. And they spoke in tones that reverberated over and over in inner cities or anywhere young people died, about a young life lost too soon; the endless possibilities over the proverbial frontier; if only he or she could've dodged the cosmic inevitability of a bullet or a blade, a dirty dose or a runaway automobile slingshot at their destinies.

One of his uncles took the podium and read something written by his father. Something about losing his closest child, the only boy, the original promise of something better, and the first mustard seed tossed into the wild winds. I wasn't sure then but was told several years into my bid that Senior had been present the day before at the wake in an orange jumpsuit, manacled in cuffs and shackles, escorted by guards from whatever institution he was housed in at the time. I tried to think about what that trip was like for that man, my coach, taking a break, only to have to see what a bullet had done to his son. And to not be able to see all of these people who had loved his son, gathered to say how much they did.

I was sitting next to my own father—stolid, serious without any appearance of outward emotion. He was the steady presence amidst the hysterics of my mother and me. I'm not sure if it was conditioned in him as a child or as a young man in the military. But it was this reserve that made him the man of the family. I certainly wasn't. I had to smoke weed every day just to get through my day. When I didn't smoke, I felt awkward and insecure, unclothed—I hadn't smoked yet that day so I felt out of place, even next to my dad. Even at the funeral of his own father, who was his best friend on earth, not a single public tear came out of his eyes. That's at least how it has been told to me; I was too young to notice. I had to leave early with a family member because I had climbed into the casket next to my dead grandfather and tried to wake him up. But this stoicism in the wake of my father's grief became a part of personal family history, brought to the surface by my mother anytime death was brought up. The part of history that doesn't get mentioned was the two weeks my dad disappeared after my grandfather's funeral.

On this day, though, as words came indirectly from a man he knew and respected, absent and unable to be that presence to his own family, expressing the jagged sorrow over the senseless loss of a kid who had eaten dinner at our house and taken batting practice from him countless summer afternoons, I looked over to him on my left and saw the running moisture of teardrops on his face, unmoving, fixed forward. The moment confused me and water came to my own eyes for a second, but my nerves seized them, my awkwardness took over and took me back to the water and saline flowing downward into the beard of my old man. In a stretch of seconds in which he wouldn't look over at me, the film over his sight froze him in his own personal moment, in private thoughts to himself. In that moment he was a man to me, and a father who had been to war and skated past death, narrowly escaped the heroin epidemic when he was in Vietnam, and hurt his body working like a monkey at those shitty jobs for those shitty people just so that there could be security for his son. In the city that he too had been a kid in, had grown up in, and played baseball at the park, unsure of who he was, who he was going to be, or where he might end up. And he sat there, finding tears that could only have existed previously in another world, in another person, crying, nearly weeping for the loss of a child of the man who could've been him. A man who had spent his life trying to save his own son, in the city that had become a wilderness, and where the over-active violence of nature lived on its streets. It became a place where the angelic intentions of being a parent are often overwhelmed by the inherent adolescent need of kids to navigate their own way through the woods, and the ways the path can change them are infinite.

But I didn't know what any of this meant. It wasn't a revelation or anything. I didn't see myself in that coffin—or in an orange jumpsuit shackled at a loved one's funeral. No, I didn't, because we were different people, at different points in our lives. I didn't even carry a gun around back then. I didn't feel like I had to. But I was trying to figure out how I was going to sell all this crack—how I could get some of what I was trying to get. I could say it made me realize those years, baseball in the park, riding bikes, and running around in the neighborhood, were over, they were gone. But I knew that already. I knew the city was different, that it had changed people: I was different, my dad was different, my friend and his dad were changed from it as well, and what we would become was in that ether somewhere. I could say that we were just kids, but we weren't just kids. We were kids of an era that ate children, met them on street corners and in dark alleys and drowned them, children of parents with a past—pasts that bled into what presents the future. And children of a city just like all the other thousands of cities out there, that will remember a small few and forget so many, be broken down and built back up again—re-created time after time.

I didn't make nearly as much money as I thought I would. I never flipped the dope over like I probably should have. But I went back to it on several occasions—bought or consigned packs to get on my feet. I sat in other people's crack houses and watched them, sometimes without gloves or masks, cook soft into nonuniform shapes of hard that would break down from fissures in their structures into innumerable little pieces. And I would ride my bike to corners on Chicago or Nicollet and Franklin and participate in the grind of desperation. Or I would sit up all night at a crack house the first few days of the month stuffing twenties into the toes of my shoes—until naturally, I went to jail. Scared to death, 119 pounds, with grown men, who already understood this kind of upheaval. And it hurt. For some it was a trade, like a plumber or an electrician, but there wasn't a union, and the allegiances there were too fragile to rely on. For others, it was religion—life or death and all the things that mattered in between. For me, it was just another way to convince myself the sky would never fall down on me.

In the years that followed, my friend became a kind of cult figure. I would see his name RIP'd on slabs of concrete on city sidewalks or tattooed on some girl's ankle. When I went to prison, I met guys he used to bang with, some who would get to go home, and others with a million years. I was even in a unit for a while with the cat who killed him; nobody wanted to let him forget about it, either—year after year after year. I mean, motherfuckers loved Junior. There's something magical about people who die young, still strong and vibrant. They don't get the chances to do all the despicable stuff that makes us ugly—or boring—or invisible. The stuff that puts us in prison—or in a living room somewhere with a woman we don't love watching *American Idol*.

In the summer before I went away, I saw Senior at the

Hi-Lake Liquor Store. It was the first time I had seen him since I was a kid. So much had happened already, and I didn't know what to say. I wasn't sure if he would know who I was in this context. I guess he had been out now for a while. But what do I say now, after all the things that might've connected us had gone away years before? So many people enter the traffic of a single lifetime; it's hard to remember someone crossing the street so long ago. He was getting out of the car alongside of the passenger-side seat where I was sitting. On the verge of leaving, I rolled down the window and caught eye contact for a moment and said, "What's up, Coach, how have you been?" And he smiled, and we pulled out of the parking lot.

Ten

CLASS OF 1996

NINETEEN NINETY-SIX was the year I ran around like an idiot with a mouth full of stones wrapped in cellophane, in some of the grimiest spaces I'd ever seen. It was the year I thought I could get totally free if I just grinded hard enough. It didn't really matter to me how many other motherfuckers were out on those same corners competing for the same little nothing. I was starting to understand how those varying conductive elements got together and made electricity, turning it loose as new energy. I wasn't afraid of the future and was more prone to letting new things come into my environment without worry of consequence; at least I believed I wasn't afraid. It was part of what was my freedom summer, the scarce piece of time in between the expectations of school and the later legal entanglements of jail or probation. I wanted to hustle and be free, but the two things weren't necessarily intertwined.

It was the year I was supposed to graduate, and it would have been had thirty credits not dropped from my pockets somewhere along the way wandering around the blocks near South High, looking for a piece of freedom. This was it—this was the time I was supposed to get that freedom. It was the same year I walked out on the discount retail job where I was secretly working instead of going to school. It was the year that

I got my GED to forever sever any tenuous bonds I may have still had with the Minneapolis Public School system, or with my childhood.

The GED I earned was the same piece of paper, watermark notwithstanding, that my mom refused to accept as completion of twelve years' investment and active involvement in school functions and organizations, and punctual participation in parent-teacher conferences. It was all that existed to say she had gone over and above what parents were supposed to do for their children—the unhappy ending that in her mind was merely a dead end. There was no way she was going to accept that this measly slip of paper held even comparable weight to the diploma she swore I would get if it was over her dead, decaying body. She still had it planned out: I would continue to go to the alternative school on the third floor at MCTC and earn credits at an accelerated pace, maybe even enough to walk with my class in June. Then there could be the forever life-affirming moment: the hug and a photograph of me in a cap and gown that spoke about perseverance, the tough road that was conquered by good parenting. Then I could go to college, something that was becoming more and more abstract as the world was revealing itself to me.

I originally intended on making the whole thing work. I thought maybe getting away from the familiarity of high school would take away some of the distractions. I didn't anticipate running into another kid as far behind in his credits as I was, and even more immersed in the streets. We drove around in circles in the parking lot smoking blunts and then sat on a couch at the end of one of the school's long hallways. He would set a cocked 9-mm on the coffee table in front of us so it wouldn't go off in his pocket. Of course I never got those credits.

Dennis and I got our GEDs at a place on Franklin across from the daily labor spot on Chicago. They were giving away a hundred dollars to anybody who completed the tests. When I finally told my mom I had passed and that I was officially through with school, she flipped the fuck out and actually refused to honor it at all. "You *will* go back to school, and you will get those credits—and you will graduate next year." No, I wouldn't.

When the invitation came for the GED ceremony at Parade Stadium, both mine and Dennis's diplomas came to our houses, but I didn't even pretend to entertain any ideas my family would attend. To my mom, it was like celebrating failure. It was Dennis who showed my mom the invitation; as it got close enough for her to see what it was, she snatched it and flung the envelope across the room. I didn't want to go anyway; I was just glad I was done. I would never be under the anxiety of underperforming in one of those window-scarce buildings again.

||||||||||||||||||||||||||||

SUMMER WAS COMING and finding work was the last thing I was trying to do. The energy I got from my parents was far less reassuring. For the first time in my life I started getting threats to move out of the house if I didn't find work soon. Every time I was sitting on the couch when either of my parents came home from work, or I accidentally set the alarm off coming in the house after 2:00 a.m., there was a potential explosion. Dennis was sleeping on a mattress in the basement at our house. Because neither of us had a job, or much intention of finding one, it was usually best just not being there when my parents were home. The threats from them to move out just got sharper. We were for the most part displaced for a while, trying to find angles to put a few dollars in our pockets. We spent a stretch running petty hustles and sleeping wherever we could.

I bought a pack with the $100 I got for getting my GED and went to Justin's to ask after some spots to get my stones off. Through the not-so-coincidental workings in the universe, I ran into Sneak, an imbalanced, sinister kind of figure who had been around for years on the grimier fringes of my social world. Or perhaps I had been on the squarer fringes of his social world. He was fresh from the Youth Authority in Colorado with long braids and nicks and scars all over his face and hands from his collisions with the universe. I had heard stories about him for years, but I didn't know him that well. He had a pocket full of stones, too, trying to catch up after his time away. For some reason he took to me—the unlikely, light-as-a-feather white kid who showed up looking for crack spots to pump at. He brought me with him to all the different street corners, alternating sales on the move. I'm not sure why he was so quick to take me out there with him; we met each other at a point where I was trying so hard to figure out what this kind of life felt like, and he was just low enough to accept where he was. I was transitioning into the streets; he was in between jail and being back in the streets. Neither of us really knew if we would ever get to where we thought we should be. It wasn't anything we talked about— we just woke up and stumbled back out to the block.

llllllllllllllllllllllllllll

DENNIS AND I went to a graduation party for one of our friends who actually *did* finish high school. He was one of the kids who grew up in the Bermuda Triangle of Riverside Park with Dennis. Their moms had been close friends, so he and Dennis's destinies were supposed to be linked that way. Dennis's mom had taken a job in Maryland the year before. She even brought Dennis with her to finish high school there, but after a summer and his eighteenth birthday passed without a high school diploma, he was back in Minneapolis. Our friend Ritchie had moved with his family during those important years, and he actually hung on through his own struggles and graduated from Washburn. Now he had family and friends stopping in and out on their Sunday tour of all the different graduation parties going on, dropping off envelopes with crispy notes inside of them. His mom, a diminutive Japanese woman strong in spirit and tough in dedication to her son in a similar way as my own mom, was sitting with us in the kitchen, wistful and proud. She spoke to Dennis about all the glorious dimensions of the day and how things happened over the years: "I remember me and your mom used to talk. We used to talk about this day— we were supposed to have this party together. But you know, things happen, life happens. I wish she were here, though, so we could have shared this."

And for an instant we were doused with anxiety that we might have missed out on something important. I did, at least—the moment that was waiting for me that I wouldn't get to be part of, the rites of passage of graduation, or any of the other things that came to define that period of time. I never went to a prom either. I was a little melancholic because I knew I could never get them back, but it was so much more important to feel free then. I intentionally forced myself to ignore most of those feelings of sentimentality when they came, but I couldn't help but recognize what regret might feel like. When we were getting ready to leave, Dennis had a seizure in the driveway. He had them once in a while when he didn't take his medication. When we were all just eleven years old, the same three of us were in my room one day when he had one; we thought he was playing so we started punching him until we realized he was not. Now, on the day that could have been his own party, he lay there, with his head in a tire groove in the driveway, the grouping of us standing over him, still confused as to what we were expected to do. Do we just let it happen, keep him awake, make sure something inconceivable doesn't happen? None of us really knew what to do—with him, with ourselves, or anything at all.

⁣‌‌‌‌‌‌‌‌‌‌‌‌‌‌‌‌‌‌‌‌‌‌‌‌‌‌‌‌‌‌⁣

I DIDN'T KNOW what to do with myself, so I looked for freedom in the most destructive ways. I stayed out on corners during a lot of late-winter and early-spring nights that extended right up until daylight. Me and Sneak did everything on the run: bought a beer, drank it on the move to the next spot, bought a bag, broke it down, split the blunt, and twisted it while in motion, discarding the remainders in the gutters. We smoked it while we spit stones out of our mouths at customers. When it got nicer out we rode bikes from spot to spot, stopping in to see friends at the The Spot on Twenty-fifth and Columbus, or at Sid's on Twenty-third and Franklin. We'd have a beer and scoot out, or we'd sit on someone's stoop or the benches outside Taco Bell on Cedar and Franklin and flag down customers.

There wasn't as much money as I expected. I thought I'd get rich. But for the first time I was an active player in my life. I was out there around people and things I didn't understand before. They weren't specifically pretty, but I was controlling the movements of my life, or so I thought. There wasn't any specific place I had to be, ever—so I was everywhere.

I was also spending a lot of my time with Robin, a girl I had known since I was eleven at Andersen Open, and running around with friends by Minnehaha Creek. We hooked up the previous winter. She kept saying we weren't together, but she kept coming around. She was a year older than I was and a lot more mature and independent and worldly than I was. She certainly had much more game than I did, but we had something unresolved from childhood that I think kept her around. Being with her also made me seem more interesting to other girls for some reason. She was also kind of a voice of calm to my parents, who would have much rather I spend my time with her than with some of my other friends or other girls around them.

At the same time, my parents were dealing disparately with the disappointment of being parents to a child who wasn't becoming what they envisioned. I wasn't enriching their lives the way they expected. It was invisibly affecting the ways they interacted with each other. Dad was becoming apocalyptic, Mom was becoming neurotic. We were a fragmented household, each vying to be as far from each other as possible. We had never been that way before. It was mostly unconscious. I thought I wanted to be gone, but not for the reasons that had much to do with the family. My parents continued with their own issues, and I felt like the more they saw my face the more they were reminded they wanted me out of the house. Dad was in a period of his life where he thought he was Clint Eastwood. I came home on many nights to him on the couch with a handgun under a cushion next to him, and a bitterness I didn't recognize in him. I couldn't discern how much of it was related to what it was I was out doing, and how much to all the other uncontrollable forces out there.

This force had already been going on for a few years but seemed to be hitting a crescendo. One summer we had a lowlife in a white Cutlass speeding through the alley every day hollering all sorts of nasty shit at my mom. Dad chased him off the block with a shotgun in his hands. And there was an incident where he also chased some kids I knew from the rim on our garage with a baseball bat. Mom thought he was going crazy; my friends thought he was kind of a gangster. I knew this wasn't what I knew of my father when I was younger, but I thought maybe his protectiveness was a role I wasn't supposed to see before and was just now showing itself. It was certainly out of character for my father to be so reactionary over things that didn't seem that serious all the time. I certainly wasn't going to stick around to witness it up close and personal.

⁞⁞⁞⁞⁞⁞⁞⁞⁞⁞⁞⁞⁞⁞⁞⁞⁞⁞⁞⁞⁞⁞⁞⁞

WE STARTED SPENDING most of our time at the Cedars 94 apartments, at the spot our guy Sid had moved with his sister. It was a single-bedroom that smelled like the cluster of kittens that ran around chasing each other all day and night. It wasn't uncommon for there to be people strewn out on couches and all over the floor in the living room. Soon June had just about evaporated, and Dennis hadn't found a job, so his mom sent for him from Maryland. Apparently, she had a job for him if he agreed to come back. About the same time, Sid took the job as an assistant manager at the Dairy Queen in the Seward neighborhood. With nothing else to do but hustle, I took a part-time job working for him and under a miniature woman with lice. It gave me all the time I wanted to run around and hustle in the neighborhood all day and still be able to tell my parents I had a job.

Dennis left in July, the same day I started slinging Blizzards. That meant the mischievous energy I shared with him shifted to Sneak and, without exact consent, to Sid. We all got up early to buy Nas's second album on its release date at Electric Fetus. It was an experience trying to dodge one of the clerks there, a local rapper who always tried to peddle his tapes on us. I dogged the guy every time he opened his mouth.

Dairy Queen turned out to be a party. I figured out early about the button on the register that meant extra money for me and took advantage of it as much as I could. Once everyone we knew figured out we worked there, people came all day to get free stuff. And because it was free, we hardly ate anything else. Sid started throwing up some sort of green matter every night after his shifts, gagging until the unnatural substance heaved itself from within. His subconscious was probably trying to expel whatever poison was gathering inside the both of us. The poison made him sick; it *empowered* me.

While the rest of the young world moved from old obligation to new obligation, I was riding around the neighborhoods on a suped-up bike with chrome pegs I stole from a kid over North on Twenty-sixth and Aldrich. On days when I wasn't working at Dairy Queen I strolled around Seward and Riverside. Sometimes I tried to sell stones in the vacant lot on Cedar in front of Twin City Cycle. I usually got my toes stepped on by the twelve-year-old kids out hustling packs for someone else. Robin, who had by then decided I *was* her boyfriend, had no problem telling me, "Be careful: one of those little kids is going to shoot you in the face one day."

︎iiiiiiiiiiiiiiiiiiiiiiiiiii

THEN THERE WAS EVA, the chubby, oddly shaped, sub–five-foot daughter of the store manager. Dairy Queen was her only job; she was the "Dairy Queen." She worked the summer months and then went on vacation somewhere for the winter. She was a strange little woman. She rarely washed her hands, and her stubby little fingers always had dirt or some kind of grub under the fingernails. Her clothes were dirty and reeked of smoke and BO. All of her work shirts were saturated with fryer grease and had splattered lines of ice cream across the front. Actually, every employee had the same splatter on our shirts because Eva broke the splatter guard on the Blizzard machine and never had it replaced. We all took orders looking like her, with a line of Blizzard at chest height on all of our shirts.

She spent most of her workday sitting on the concrete benches outside the building, smoking cigarettes with a regular

crowd of the zombies from any one of the Social Security buildings that lined the streets on that part of Franklin. A culture
formed on those benches around the tiny building, an amalga-
mation of friends and acquaintances of the people who worked
there, gathering for little stretches of afternoon or evening. On
days when Eva didn't work, our friends waited outside smoking cigarettes and shooing away yellow jackets from splotches
of the sticky film left on the store benches.

Right before the end of one of her shifts, she was smiling
and telling stories. Offhandedly she made a comment about
wearing her hair a certain way: "I can finally wear my hair the
way I want after I got rid of those things. They itched so bad I
started breaking the skin. See, see the scabs?" She parted two
clumps of hair to expose small wounds that had been scratched
to blisters. I didn't understand right away what she was talking
about until the sixteen-year-old girl who was working with us
said something out loud about some kind of shampoo for lice.

"Lice? You had lice? How long ago?" I didn't know people
still got lice. The word brought associations to being in grade
school and getting letters sent home warning parents about
outbreaks. I remembered teachers having to tell kids not to rub
their heads on the carpet.

"Oh yeah, I just got rid of them maybe a week ago. It was
pretty bad. You guys probably want to get checked for them,
too."

I was flipping out inside. I had an entire week to get them
and pass them on to everyone I knew. I had a visual of her thin-
ning, dusty blonde hair being attacked while the lice rested on
pillows and stuffed animals that hadn't been washed in years.
I imagined the piles of unwashed clothes and stacked dishes in
the immediate vicinity of this woman lying on the bed flipping
channels and dropping crumbs on the sheets.

It seemed like Sid was the only one as horrified as I was. In
between customers we ran into the bathroom to examine every
inch of our heads for bugs.

We went to the old caves by the Wabasha Bridge with two
girls from Southwest High School. I was most afraid I was going

to give the girl lice. And through the course of the night, the fear I felt at every itch didn't end until the girls left. I went to a drugstore and acted indifferent to the giggling store attendant who led me to the shampoo in a small box that was supposed to kill the little something I was not so sure I even had.

IIIIIIIIIIIIIIIIIIIIIIIIIIIII

WHAT I DID GET FROM THAT TIME were the many personal stories out there on the streets and inside of those spots. Wheelchair Will, an old man paralyzed in Vietnam, who had openly given up on everything in his life, except getting high, spent his monthly Social Security check to create the temporary oblivion he was searching for. It didn't make him happy, though: rather, his bitterness was like his wheelchair, with him no matter what happened. Sometimes we caught him out on the block in the middle of the night trying to keep his high going. Sneak and I ran into him wheeling around the block by himself one time. Sneak hopped out of the car to ask him about some money he owed him. While belligerently trying to tell Sneak why he didn't have it, he fell out of his wheelchair and started screaming at us to help him up. I went over to help him; Sneak squinted his eyes and told us to leave him. "Help him up when he gives me my money." Me and another guy got him into his chair anyway. It was harsh, but a couple of weeks later Sneak helped him move new furniture into his apartment. Their relationship was conditional upon what day of the month it was. On the first, Will was like his uncle; on the Twenty-fifth, when he owed Sneak money, he was just another lowlife. I didn't want to be like that, but I also didn't know if that was the kind of thinking that could get in the way of getting what it was I was out there looking for.

The residents at the dope spot where I was working came home after five. It was an apartment in an old brownstone across from Justin's building on Twenty-first Avenue. It was rented by a married couple in their forties from Chicago, by way of Mississippi. They lived there with the wife's mother, and all three of them smoked crack. The grandmother was a sweet woman who loved me for some reason. I tried to do right by the three of them—or as well as someone selling dope to them could. She fried fish and chicken for me like I was a family member, or something other than I was. They made me think about the world we were living in, and what it could become sometimes. I liked these people, but it was hard for me to decide if what I was doing was right or wrong, or if it was just an arrangement of needs. The man looked at it like he had a pretty good life, a steady job without some of the urban failures he left in Chicago messing with his buzz. He told me that as long as he had a job and could stay in his apartment, it was nobody's business. I couldn't tell if it was the truth or not—it wasn't *my* business.

I sometimes got careless keeping the lines between what I did in the streets drawn sharp with what I didn't in the little time I was at my own home. My parents were cleaning the house one day and found a stone in the cushions of the living room chair. I played naïve, of course, said it was a friend's. Mostly I had to convince them I wasn't smoking it. I told them I would make sure no one else ever brought any dope into the house. It wasn't a satisfactory explanation, but it was all I was willing to give. The façade was cracking and could only be a couple of mistakes away from exposing what it was I was out there doing. My dad spotted me on the corner of the block getting into a truck at 4:30 one morning. I didn't have much explanation for him.

But it was my freedom summer and not much could obstruct that. Me and Sneak drifted through neighborhoods, a conspicuous duo of a rail-thin white kid dressed in red, in a Cincinnati Reds hat and a beeper, with a super-grimy dude, with an ugly stare and a sinister aura around him that scared people who didn't know him, and he did nothing in his approach to change people's minds. There were so many mixed reactions to the two of us hustling in the middle of the Zone, trying to eat from the same plate as the rest of the grinders. Some neighborhoods just didn't want us snatching sales from them. There were always more collisions—close calls and fights over corners. But Sneak had a knack for getting away, being teleported from the midst of any chaos we found ourselves in. There were always times when he was able to skate through when we thought there were no possible ways to avoid a bullet or a trip to jail. Being around him made me believe I could be as lowdown as he was and be protected by the same force that pulled him out of these situations time after time. But I didn't have that same protective force. I just thought I did.

And there were things I had to forfeit to keep a barely grasping hand on the identity I was trying to maintain. The night the Fugees came to First Ave with Goodie Mob and the Roots, I was at a crack house. While I was out hustling for pennies, trying to figure out who I was, the culture crackled, figuring out what *it* was. B-Boys and B-Girls had been waiting for this—the coming out of its darkness into the light. I was still in the dark hoodlum shadows, even though I was supposed to be an adult. I showed up to the after-party at New's on Twenty-sixth and Twelfth, sardine-packed with backpacks and Kangols and Adidas tracksuits. There were break-dancers and ciphers of teenagers rapping mediocre freestyles and holding each other's nuts. There were plastic cups covering the place like red confetti, and a collective of people I knew hanging out in the cut. I came to catch up with Robin and some of my other friends, but I couldn't find them. I'm on an old videotape somewhere for a few minutes, long enough to ask New where my people were. "I think they all just left," he told me, and that was it, I left too. My spot held, firmly entrenched on the fringe that would follow me for years.

For as much freedom my new career seemed to offer me, I knew this wasn't who I was. I knew it was stupid—at least part of me did. Another part of me didn't know anything, played dumb, deaf, and blind, didn't care what happened: a bullet in the head or a nasty, unfurnished apartment with snotty-nosed kids running around unguarded while their parents beamed up in a room across the hall. I sort of understood the emotional sorrows, but I wasn't built for the kind of physical sorrows that existed, or the lack of heart or respect for the game. It was fast and unrestricted outside in the wind, but inside of those houses and apartments it was a dreadful life with a dreadful view of human nature. Motherfuckers were really thirsty, kids were really hungry. People would kill other people for what seemed like nothing. I spent a couple of days at a spot with a smoker who was dying of AIDS, sitting in the spot all day, letting himself die behind a lighter and a stem made from a car antenna and brillo. In the course of a couple of months I watched the man diminish to bones in the streets. I had miscalculated this life for being exciting and vitalizing. I thought it was my schooling for something greater and eye-opening. I hadn't done it long enough to see it was a dead end—enough to hold me still in life until the roles reversed and I would become one of the losers in an unfurnished apartment, with kids I couldn't take care of. I thought the few dollars I could scavenge from doing something thirsty could create enough thrust to blow me up like some of the other kids from my generation. For as carefree as I felt, something deep inside of me knew I wasn't precise enough, and knew I wasn't grimy enough. The child I used to be who wanted to help people like this lost faith that anything could be done for them. That same something knew the summer was almost over.

Despite Sid's ritual urlings and the less-than-hygienic working conditions, the party continued for a while at DQ. It was obvious, though, that Sid was overstressed by all of the energy around the place. I was too self-involved with my own issues to give his worries over the changing dimensions at the store and the accounting for missing money much thought. He was a manager, but I was just a random part-time employee. The risks were different. During the first week in August, I went with my family to a cabin in northern Wisconsin. I was thinking I would come from the cabin and get right back at it. But Sid quit. He'd had enough of Cedars 94 and the congestion of personalities hanging around every day, all waiting on their chance to blow the world up. So Sid moved to a place in St. Paul and took another job. He knew people's attitudes were changing and that all of us coming up were willing to take bigger risks and disregard some of the personal consequences hiding in the shadows. Eva hoped I would stick around for the last month of the ice cream season, but without Sid, I quit, too.

It was really just another decision that could make me some money or might put me in jail. It was another point where I should have asked myself again about the things I really wanted. It was probably more about how Sid so easily up and escaped any potential turmoil in the simplest ways, but how I had convinced myself that I was so connected to it, as though it were an actual part of who I was. It was about how he could be an adult, but I just wasn't ready yet. Soon it would be September and starting to get cold. I quit the job at Dairy Queen, but I was still riding around on that ridiculous bike hollering that I had "Work" for sale. I rode through Seward sometimes and saw Eva sitting on one of those benches outside the Dairy Queen, with a cigarette, waiting for the end of the season to come.

I knew for the most part it was over. I just didn't know if it would fade out or if something abrupt would bring it to a halt. At the end of August I went with Sneak to a party and watched as a bunch of the kids I grew up with staggered ignorant and inebriated to their cars and toward the rest of their lives. I ended up bouncing with Sneak to the house on Twenty-fifth and Columbus and shot dice for a while. The guys over there already had most of the rest of their lives planned; I didn't know why, but I was willing to be like that, too. I went and got greasy again. I bought double-ups and chased after the few dollars the smokers still owed me. The guy with AIDS made a habit of running full speed from me every time he saw me. He only owed me fifty dollars.

If I hadn't figured it out already, it became more obvious how little money I was making. The kids I was used to seeing were going off to college or had other things happening. Robin was getting ready to go to school in Miami. My parents stressed to me again that it was time to move out. "Get a job and get a place—unless you decide to go to college." I could hardly even process their demands before that weird dread started to come back to me like I was going back to school. It was dread over shorter, darker days, and anxiety over whether I had enough nuts stored for winter. Unless I figured out how to make some more money, I would have to get another job, and to me that would mean more enslavement. I always felt like *something* was coming and I had no idea how to prepare for it. The fear on the other side of *this* fall was so much greater because all of the things that were constant before were the most uncertain things now—where I would live, where I would hustle— the other side was open-ended. I was out riding around neighborhoods that knew winter was coming; I couldn't smell the charcoal from barbeque grills or see people gathered outside watching the neighborhoods bristle. The only people out there then were the grimiest, most thirsty kind of human beings. The summer party was over.

I was coming home from Justin's one of those nights, tired and hungry, cold from the chilly wind whipping at me, when I ran into somebody I had never seen before on Twenty-seventh and Bloomington. It was near the end of the month, and I was having a hard time getting my stones off. I only had a few left and I was trying to get rid of them quick so I could re-up. I ran into the guy in front of an old abandoned storefront across Bloomington from the fire station. An older, short cat with gold fronts flagged me down and I sold him a half. Naturally his name was Goldy. I don't know why I did it, but I gave him my pager number. I guess I was hoping I had found a good trap, but there's really no such thing as a good trap in that part of the neighborhood. It was way too far from any of my spots, and it was too cutthroat of a neighborhood for me to be grinding in.

I woke the next day to an aggressive vibration coming from my pager. As certain as death it was Goldy, trying to buy as big a chunk as he could from the gullible white kid he just met the day before. I only had the small bit left, but it was all I had and I needed just about all of it to re-cop. Half-asleep, I agreed to meet him where I had seen him the day before. I was scared he was going to try to beat me for it. I thought he might bring someone with him to try to take what I had. So in a split second, devoid of sense or reason, I made the decision to take a gun with me—something I knew could only make a tricky situation more complicated. I had been told never to do this; instead, take the loss and get it back later. But I wasn't thinking like that. I figured if they tried to rob me I could pull out and change their minds.

I showed up and saw the lowlife standing on the corner by himself. I was hoping that meant everything was good. In classic crackhead style he decided he didn't want the whole chunk, so I broke him off a piece of the whole and held the rest of it clenched between my teeth. I don't know why I didn't think about the police. I was so preoccupied by the idea that he would try to beat me I completely disregarded the possibility. It might have been I was still so naïve about how dishonorable people could be in certain positions. I think I overvalued the general loyalty to the game. I don't think I understood yet some of the disparate levels of the human experience.

After I got the money and turned to go, a squad car turned the corner with its lights blaring, moving to catch me, eighteen years old and free. Before I even got to the end of the block they ran the car right into me. They got the gun, the crack, and the marked fifty-dollar bill they had given the rat-smoker to buy the dope. Goldy just slithered off with the dope somewhere to beam up. While I stood there on the hood, with the cops all up in my shit, a class of school kids walked by with their teachers. One of the little girls pointed at me and yelled, "Ooh, he's going to jail." The other kids giggled, free and unconcerned yet, walking past a sign posted on the street declaring this a Drug-Free Zone.

I sat in the back of the squad car listening to the cops in the front seat make snide, boastful remarks about the hurt I had coming. "Who were *you* going to shoot with this big-ass gun?" He was holding the gun up in the front seat. He had unholstered his own weapon and held the 9-mm next to the .45 they had just taken from me, comparing the two: there was an obvious disproportion. There was no humor in it to me; all I could think about was the end—the end of running around without obligation, the end of my summer of young love. It was the final dismantling of my freedom summer. There was a transforming of self, a mincing of identity for the confused kid running in the wilderness like it was an amusement park, as though there weren't wolves and other predators out there lurking. I only ever wanted to be free, and now I was absolutely not that, suffocating in the backseat.

Eleven

THE FIRST STRIKE
|||||||||||||||||||||||||||||||||||||||||||||||||||||||||||||||||||||||||||||||||||||||||||||||||||||||||||||||||||

T HE CLAUSTROPHOBIA starts in the backseat. The harsh shrinking of free space with hands in cuffs, clicked to the bone of my wrists. I just kept thinking there had to be a way out—but I knew I wasn't going to kick out a window and crawl out. I was there in the backseat stuck on the way to County. Less than a year before I had been dropped off at Juvenile after a beating from the police. Everything there was carpeted, and they sat me down on a couch while they called my parents. It was just a speculation, but I had to believe this would be different. I was eighteen and going downtown with grown men and grown problems.

They pulled the car into a dark garage, the light of the day closing when the garage door shut. I wished they had just taken me to the river and whooped me like they used to do when I was a kid. I ended up at the electric door against a Plexiglas window getting a pat-down, with someone from the sheriff's department talking crazy into my ear. That was the end of anything personal; everything from then on would be completely impersonal. I came in, got weighed in at close to 120 pounds, six feet tall, in clothes I threw on in a hurry. I had a hundred-twenty-something dollars on me and a wholly defeated look on my baby face.

There were eyes looking at me from inside all of the holding tanks. I got put in a room and stripped down naked, opening my mouth and lifting my balls. I was standing there naked with some guy asking me to spread my ass cheeks, probably a demand he had to make over and over to every new man who came through the door for his entire eight-hour shift. My first assumption is that he likes this—that it fed something ugly in him. It didn't matter who it was; I was just like the last guy or any of the ones who came after me. It was a common embarrassment—part of the original breaking down of the individual. They gave me a set of county blues, the smallest size, and they were still kind of baggy.

I ended up in a holding tank with a guy who smelled like old onions and Wild Irish Rose. He didn't seem like he had the kind of energy needed to hold a conversation; he just lay down and rested his head on a roll of toilet paper. It was a good thing, because I had nothing to talk about except the future, a blurry, kaleidoscope-view future. They moved us to the main holding tank where they took my first mug shot—an expressionless blank face of someone who was never going to be the same after this. They took my fingerprints. I was in the system now; there was definitive proof that I was a crook. Somewhere on a card, filed into the universe of the criminal justice system, there was my name and a set of prints that said, "We knew you weren't worth a damn, now here's your number."

We waited for hours in a room that just kept filling up with bodies. I was learning that anyone who had ever been through the county jail system already knew about how slow everything took; even the guards talked slow to us. People slept under the benches people were sitting on. There were a couple of men who would pace the unoccupied parts of the floor back and forth until someone got annoyed and told them to sit down. They didn't have anywhere to sit, though, so they stood and walked in small circles instead. The only break from waiting was to see a nurse and to get my one phone call.

I called my grandma because I knew she would be home. I told her I was in jail and that she needed to tell my parents.

I told her I might not see her for a while. I'm sure it caught her by surprise. I'm sure there was the ceremonial shattering of those glass expectations we leave our childhood with, but I was trying to block most of the outward emotional projections. I couldn't get caught up trying to gather together all the things that might go wrong. I went and saw a nurse who was very nice, kind of motherly. She looked at my paperwork and winced a bit.

"Why on earth would you be in a place like this? Why on earth would someone so young be out there selling drugs?"

"I guess because I just always wanted to be free," I told her, high off a cocktail of fatalism and desperation. I could've just as easily told her, "Because I'm not real smart, or ambitious, or really value my life very much." The deputy over her shoulder jumped in to insert his own opinion.

"Well, you ain't free now, are ya?" I just shrugged and went back to the holding tank. It seemed like the tank had even more people since I left, and everyone was so old. I felt like I was the only one my age; most everyone else looked like they were at least in their midthirties. And they all seemed like they were drunks brought in for being too wily, too early, at the bars.

There were a few guys who had been picked up on parole or probation violations. There was an older black guy who they snatched up at work; he still had his janitor's uniform on. He was mostly worried about losing the job and when they were going to feed him. And there are always guys in the tank who don't shut the fuck up. "What are you here for, what are you here for?" over and over again to every man who walked in. Then there is always the guy who's beating on the Plexiglas because the process isn't moving fast enough. He was the guy who when not yelling through the window was trying to get everybody else complicit in his anger. When they brought a line of women through from the women's jail, some of the men in our tank hurried to the glass to holler things at the women, who mostly looked like streetwalkers or dope fiends. I was really not anyone to talk: I had just woken up and was dressed kind of like a crackhead my own self.

Everyone in there acted so angry, probably to deflect the

fear of what might or might not happen. The ones who had been here before were obvious because they played so acutely on the sensibilities of all of us who hadn't. I've always had this claustrophobia that came when I was in spaces where I couldn't leave, and it took a whole lot to keep it in check, to keep myself from gagging. They showed up at one point with a bunch of bologna sandwiches that mostly went uneaten. The veterans collected all of the extras from those of us who were just too sick to eat. I was hungry, but I couldn't imagine eating one of those things. One of the guys ended up in an argument back and forth with one of the deputies over the process, and he got yanked out of the cell by an enormous football player–looking guard and was brought to another tank with a group of other deputies, where he got maced and put through some kind of gauntlet. Once he was gone, there was another guy who took his place as the tank's most irascible.

I was stuck thinking about all of the things that were set to change. I kept hearing "three to five years," and things like "mandatory minimum" and "zero tolerance." I went through the list of everyone in my life and imagined what might happen between me and all of them. It was so hard to look too far into the next week; trying to envision three years in a place like this was a nightmare. I just kept imagining hearing the same voices and personalities that were in that tank repeating themselves on a loop for the next few years. I was scared; I didn't think I should be, but I was. I felt stupid, really stupid, and most of all I felt little—even the smallest men in there were bigger than I was. This was my first taste of this; most of these other people were somewhere further along on their journey of disappointment. I was scared because I was trapped: getting used to being trapped takes a long time, unless you are one of those people who feel like they've always been in a state of entrapment. Then this becomes only formality. I wasn't one of those people yet.

After what felt like most of a day, they walked a whole group of us in handcuffs to a crowded elevator and brought us to a room to pick up the standard issue: blanket, sheets, pillow, plastic cup with a toothbrush, toothpaste, and a miniature bar of soap inside of it. They moved me to one of the thirty-six-hour probable-cause pods where they put guys before charging them. It was a dorm, lined with bunk beds and plastic cots designed like boats, with a TV locked inside of a cage. It was substantially larger than the holding tank, but the claustrophobia was still there, still fighting against my breath. There was also a scratched-up window, reinforced by a screen that looked out over what would several years later be the new county jail. Guys were watching *Jerry Springer,* arguing during commercials with guys who wanted to watch the news.

It was already night by the time I got my bunk. There were guys all talking loud about anything they could think of. It sounded like every other person in there was there for some kind of drug case, except the guy who went to South who was in there for opening fire at a concert downtown. Most of the guys sat at steel tables and played spades for hours, listening to the guy from South spout off about what happened or didn't happen at the concert. I just pulled my blanket up over me and read the only available book in the entire pod. I can't remember what it was about, something about a snow or ice storm. My mind was cluttered with thoughts running so fast through my consciousness; some would race right through my mind, others would leave and come back as paranoia or panic. My instinct was to look for ways out, but there was just jail and big, immovable steel doors. And there I was, my world shrunk down to just the variables of that small space with people I didn't know. That whole night I did my best to empty my mind so I could fall asleep and escape for a while; but that was unrealistic and images bombarded my head of my family and friends and the questions they would ask me. The thoughts just pushed more unease through my blood. It was one of the in-between moments I would get so used to in my life—between the familiar and unfamiliar. I even started to pray. I'd never prayed in my life. It was the classic pity-me prayer—for mercy and, mostly, for a way out.

The next morning I woke up and saw the sunrise in crazy orange and purples through the marked-up glass. They fed us an orange, milk, and some kind of frosted sweet roll. After breakfast, I paced the perimeter of the room for a while, trying to move and get some of the morning energy out of me. It was also the first whole day I had gone without smoking weed for years. It was a natural coping mechanism for me, and I didn't have it then, so I had to move around, start running the scenarios through my head that were larger than the world I was currently living in. There was a morning count where the deputies came through talking supercrazy to people who were at the crossroads of their confusion. Afterward, I got back to my bunk and tried to sleep the time away. It was now a Friday, and if I didn't get charged today, I would probably be stuck in that same room for the weekend, at least that was what people told me. I had no idea what the next pod, or dorm, or cell would look like.

Around me there was a slow cycling in and out of people. Some bailed out; others got to see a judge or went to see investigators; and others, like the guy with the shooting at the concert, went upstairs to a more long-term living arrangement. In less than twenty-four hours, the culture in the pod changed, the voices were different, with new stories being told, about the same things but through the lens of new eyes. I just waited. I didn't call home when I had the chance because I was too embarrassed. I couldn't even theorize the sort of hysteria that was going through the house at that time; or maybe it was agreed this was a good place for me, a lesson I couldn't get any other way. I sat and waited on the next phases, still with three to five years as my baseline. Trying to look that far into the future only exhausted me more.

I got into a few simple conversations with guys in the pod, mostly just to compare circumstances. Mine were not the worst, but they certainly weren't the best. Lots of petty thefts and fifth-degree possessions. The pistol made mine a tougher outcome to forecast. I didn't have a clue; I just picked it up from the chatter around me. One of the guys had smuggled in a small piece of crack in his hair. He somehow got a spark from somewhere and beamed up in the bathroom. It was a source of amusement to most of us. I compulsively played games of solitaire as something to do—part of the autopilot program I was on, that I felt I would be on as long as I was in there. The night before and the course of that day were so long and uncertain. Everyone else was too preoccupied with their own futures to really care much. People came back from court in the morning with either a smile and a thumbs-up, or with violent looks of disdain on their mugs.

I tried to suppress my regrets by making bargains with myself over what I would do with my life if I could get out. I didn't know where I was going to work, or if I would have a place to sleep, but I knew I was done selling crack. I realized how much I had been lying to myself, trying to convince myself I was doing anything or making any kind of real money. I didn't have any money to even bail myself out; I didn't drive, and I didn't own anything at all besides a watch and a gold chain I got for collateral from a smoker. Yet I thought I was independent and grown-up, riding around on a bike trying to look shifty and dangerous so girls would like me. I had only been inside a little more than twenty-four hours and I was already feeling reformed, until a young dude from over North pulled me back to reality. "This ain't shit. It's all part of the game—if this is too much for you, you got a hard life coming." And he was right: I had always felt somewhat exempt from this kind of experience, but it was happening then whether I wanted it to or not. I could do all the rationalizing I wanted about the momentum that had begun. It was part of the hardening of my armor, hardening of feeling and dismissal of fear. But I did feel it, and I was afraid. The kid was right—so I braced myself for what was coming, as hard as it might get.

When I didn't get charges that Friday, I figured it would be at least Monday before I saw charge papers or a judge. Everybody I had sort of gotten to know had already been charged, released, or bailed out. Most had moved to pods upstairs to start the next chapters of their fight with the judicial system. Any short-term bonds I established had expired. After going a day and a half without food, I was able to eat—my body wouldn't allow me to pass on the hot dogs they gave us. I stopped wanting to read that stupid book, and I paced instead; a whole bunch of guys did. We would walk from wall to wall at staggered paces, lost in the bargaining process. If I wasn't pacing, I was on my bunk trying to go back to sleep, though I was really just covering my eyes with the navy-blue county blanket. I hoped I could sleep through the nightmare, or at least hide from it under the covers.

The guards came through again for another count. They brought in a whole new crew and came around and made us say our names out loud to the one holding a clipboard. Every time I said my name I got some asshole comment from one of them: "What kind of a name is that?" I got every possible pronunciation they could come up with, turning back to the others and laughing as they looked through the spaces around the bunk to make sure none of us had stashed any food. Then they were off to harass the next person in line.

There was always this talk of being bailed out. Most everybody had this acute awareness of every minute and every hour. They knew you had to be charged to get bail. They knew they couldn't get charged after a certain point in the day on Friday, so every moment that went by without news, the tension grew in everybody's hearts that bail would never come. I didn't even think about bail—I didn't want to even ask after it. There were so many who came through who just hoped for a conditional release on good faith, because there was either nobody or no money out in the world to make it happen for them. Some guys ran around angry, proudly irritated about their people not getting them out at the exact time they wished. They were not-so-subtly rubbing it in the faces of the guys who knew they would have to fight their cases from inside the county jail.

I was on a second day, and I didn't know what to do with my new cocktail of boredom and panic. I tried to imagine years of this, walking around in rubber shower shoes and county blues—but I couldn't. It was just too far removed from what I knew of living. I never foresaw jail or prison. I saw death, maybe a gunshot wound, but why hadn't I thought about jail? The people I knew didn't go to jail—except that they did; Sneak just came back from jail, and Cheesesteak just got three years. There were guys who were always in and out for this or that. It wasn't implausible, yet I had blocked it out; I had told myself I wasn't as far gone as those guys. Now I was the one wearing clothes that didn't fit me, standing out like the unmistakable sore thumb amongst a room full of greasy fingers used to holding on to steel bars. I thought about the guys out hanging out drinking and smoking, talking about how I wasn't going to be coming around for a long time, and I thought about how after a few seconds they would just pass the blunt around and disregard it all in an instant. But I couldn't let that matter to me. "If this is too much for you—you got a hard life coming."

At some point in the evening, after it got dark and after any hopes of getting charged before the weekend had dissolved into mist, I looked out through the scraped-up window and watched the lights of downtown Minneapolis reflect off the glass in windows or the plastic of parking meters. It looked like it might've been raining, but it was hard to tell with all the names scratched in the plastic. Everything was obscured, forms without lines or meaning.

I heard a voice scratching an announcement on the P.A.—maybe the nurse or mail call. I couldn't tell through the trebled muffler the voice spoke through. It came over again and sounded kind of like my name. Nobody else heard what it said either, so somebody hit the emergency button to ask the cops what they were saying. Irritated, the scratchy voice said: "Caligiuri—to the door!" I went to the door and cuffed up. They brought me to a room with some guy I didn't know sitting behind a glass barrier with a janky smile on his face, holding on to the phone on the other side. At first I didn't realize what I was supposed to do; he gestured toward the phone for me to pick it up. He told me he was a lawyer my family had hired, who had somehow got the judge to file charges for me and set a bail at 10 p.m. on a Friday. He told me it was all on the way, that I'd be out in a couple of hours and that I was supposed to call him when I got home. He nonchalantly turned the other way and was gone. No worries, no restraints.

I walked back rejuvenated, feeling loved and looked after but ashamed. I knew there was still a whole bunch of bullshit in front of me, but I wanted to be out of there so bad. It was hard for me to tell any of the guys in the pod I was getting out because most of them were not, at least not that Friday night. An hour or two later they came for me again. I gave a few handshakes, told a couple of them I'd catch up with them when I ran into them in the world, and I bounced. I dropped my linens off and went through the maze on my way down to property. A woman handed over whatever junk I came down in. Jeans, a sweatshirt, some socks and drawers; no ID but the money I had was in there, and some change. They opened a door that led to a dark and empty corridor, which led to the lobby of the Government Center. The place was abandoned for the weekend. Just like that, the compression I felt—the shrinking walls, the shrinking future—eased, at least for a while.

I was alone in the darkened rotunda area on checkered marble floors of the Hennepin County Government Center. I tried to call home from a pay phone in the lobby, but no one answered. So I called Sneak and told him I needed a ride. Without questions, he said he would come get me.

I went out into the rainy, free air of the downtown night, and just like the cliché I got down and kissed the wet ground. I walked around trying to absorb the exhilaration I felt to be out of jail, at least even for a little while. I knew what it felt like now; I wasn't sure how it was going to change me or change my mind, but there was a certain cleansing—the flushing of a certain experience that was poisoning me.

Sneak showed up in an aquamarine Neon Geo, with a big-head girl we knew. He told me when he first got locked up, his dad told him, "I love you son, but you're gonna have to man-up." That was it before he went away. Seventeen years old: what would happen would have to happen. It seemed harsh, but a couple of hours earlier it felt obvious to me. They dropped me off at my grandma's, where I got a look and an embrace. She told me, "I guess we got some filling in to do, huh?" And she brought me into the house. There wasn't much to say, though, so it went unsaid. I called the lawyer; he told me things would be fine; that was all I needed to hear just then. I knew the real moment would be later when I got home—the "never going to be the same" moment. I called Robin, unsure of how much longer I could call her my girl, or if I'd be able to muster any sympathy at all from the people in my life after this. I could feel a dread coming, knowing that the euphoria I felt from being exhaled from jail would be short-lived and that the cycle would begin. There would probably be more jail, and probation officers, and Reporting Center visits downtown. And this new cycle would merge with all of the old cycles of depression and social uncertainty that had only hidden themselves for a time.

Yes, the momentum had begun. I went and had a few drinks, knowing my freedom summer was gone and I was crossing into an entirely unique new world, before I had ever really had the chance to even enjoy it.

Twelve

SNAPSHOTS OF ME
AND HER IN NEW YORK

W HEN SHE ASKED ME to come out there, I was in a period of relative stability. I was almost a year into a job at
Nordstrom. I was still kind of a scrub, certainly not rich, and I
certainly didn't have the rest of my life planned out. But I had
new shoes for every day of the month, plus some. And besides
occasional probation visits, my dope case was finally behind
me. My parents were still pushing to get me out of the house,
but that was going to really happen, so they weren't sweating
me. I was certainly a lot steadier than when Robin left to go to
school at Parsons to run around Manhattan and be young with
a whole new brand of dude staring at her ass. I knew I couldn't
rely on this steadiness too much longer, though; things didn't
work like that in my life. I would need to make a decision about
what I was going to be and what I was going to do with my life.
The stability offered just that—it didn't offer me a whole life.

She called me just about every night since she moved to
the city. I was still in my bedroom at home; she was in her tiny
apartment at Fifty-sixth and Lexington that used to be a seedy
hotel and now was seedy student housing without even a kitch-
enette. She told me about school and the people she met. She

always met people wherever she was. She drew them to her; just like at home they could smell her sexuality, couldn't understand it but went to it naturally.

One of her friends was out there with her, doing an internship at a record label. They told me how the rappers who people at home had been mythologizing and restructuring their realities through were really just like all the dudes they knew in Minneapolis, and everywhere else either of them had been in the world. She talked about the "brilliant artists" she went to school with—she brought up names over and over again and tried to draw parallels between these people with people we both knew, but I didn't care about any kind of artist. I just let her talk. It would've been easy to not want to share her with them.

I was surprised she still called as often as she did. I didn't want it to be, but I had expected this to be a natural separation after a significant stretch of relationship without exactly clear lines. I knew I was an attachment to home, but she had all kinds of friends she could have used for that purpose. And her friend was there to get into all the secret things they got into together.

I wanted her to call, though; I loved her. We had been in an on-again, off-again limbo since my freedom summer a couple of years before. It was around that time I caught feelings for her like most of the other dudes she'd messed with did. She was around all the time, and I misread what it meant sometimes. I felt stupid because I had seen how those other dudes acted. She would come over with her hair in French braids and a summer dress with sunflowers on it she had designed and sewn herself, from her portfolio that she applied to art school with. The dress helped emphasize her womanly body and made her tan skin glow in the summer sun.

I had known her since the sixth grade when she alphafemaled our junior high, picking and choosing from the roster of boys following her around sniffing at her earth. As other girls were growing into their woman bodies, she had hers already, hips and thighs, and ass. She had a pair of tight-ass navy-blue pants with white polka dots that everyone remembers.

Her energy was what made boys love her. I used to say they could smell it on her. It built guys up and broke their little hearts. There were a lot of guys who wasted a lot of time trying to catch back up with her once she bounced out on them. It was an energy that made stalkers out of guys. I fucked up too one day and told her I loved her during a perplexing phone call where I gave away all my leverage. "What the fuck do you mean? We're not together!"

It crushed me, or maybe more just embarrassed me. Embarrassment was the something that I tried to protect myself from most during my time with her. She was the first girl I ever told I loved her, and she shucked me off like I was a little kid with a flower and a crush. She didn't go away, though; she kept coming to the house, sleeping over, and messing with my head.

There were other girls around then. I liked the idea of other girls wanting to be around me. I wasn't used to getting that sort of attention, and I really didn't know how to manage this new interest in me. Sometime that summer, I don't know how the conversation went: she must have smelled those other girls on me because she decided she wanted us to be together. It was *her* saying she loved *me*. I wasn't used to hearing that, and it weakened me a little and I succumbed.

She bought me a shirt and a pair of shorts at the Gap, and I guess that meant I was hers. I never quite trusted her angle, though. Throughout the time I knew her there had always been these secret relationships that existed, partnerships with dudes with fuzzy details. I had already felt like a trick the time I had declared my love and got kicked right back down. It was hard for me to get rid of that feeling I had when she told me my love wasn't real. I did my best to avoid all the serious bullshit. And besides, I had other girls passing through my life at the time. I was in no position to be sweating her flow.

Me and Robin seemed good. I was kind of dizzy from the affection. I just wasn't used to it. It made me start to understand how people could get so smitten in love with people. I was starting to understand the energy that had wrapped itself around all the other guys who had been in her life. I was still cautious, because she was the girl who once told me nobody owned her: "I fuck who I want to fuck with." Somehow during the close-to-three years we were ever together in any capacity, there aren't any pictures of the two of us together. I guess if there weren't any pictures of it, then it probably just didn't happen. "It doesn't matter because *we* know."

She talked a lot about going away to school that fall, and about dreams and ambitions. I didn't have dreams anymore, except maybe a bag of weed big enough for me to sleep in. She still had these ideas that she would get rich and successful because she was meant for something bigger than where we were. I could hardly see who I was yet—the freedom was just too exhilarating at the time, even though the actual things that were happening weren't all that exhilarating. She was quick to let me know where I was falling short.

<hr />

SO WHEN SHE GOT TO MANHATTAN my expectations were much more subdued. She still called, though—talked sweet, said she missed me. I said the same shit, and I did miss her. We talked nasty—about the raunchy things we wanted to do to each other. And she would use that voice—the really cute, vulnerable voice that anyone outside the parameters of being in love would swear was some trick shit. *She* said she wanted me to come. She said she wanted to show me this great big wide-open world she was looking out over every day, learning from it as she inhaled from it.

Just like when we were young, she was still trying to show me something new, give me a grander perspective outside of my generally ambitiousless life; it was one of those things that endeared me to her. She told me I was smarter than I was. She told me I needed to stop smoking weed; she told me to get rid of my friends, get a license, and get a car. She used a voice that sounded like she didn't care if I did any of it or not. "I'm just saying." Sometimes after sex her voice would be sweeter but was really secret code for "If you don't—I'm leaving." It was what made me believe she really knew me and what I needed for my life. In this regard, she was right about me. I had lost the confidence to think big about my own life outside of some street money and new clothes. It might have been what most endeared me to her. That's what people do for people they care about: they show them other things and hope they find something relevant so they don't have to leave them behind.

But I thought I was doing good—I was still working. I was saving money, and philosophically I felt like I had bounced back from the dope case that I thought was going to explode my life. The same one that made me break down in front of her, and she wiped tears from my face after taking a handful of mushrooms that only illuminated the crisis and loss of control in my life. Here I was now a year later, more safe and centered than I had ever been, but also kind of stuck, insulated from what the streets can do to people.

She said I could come out and stay with her—it could be like it was before for a few days. We could fuck on each other and watch the traffic blur from the window. I was only thirteen when I had been to New York the last time, and only caught a glimpse of its immensity. I was always intrigued by it, though—so I said I would come.

It was October, and I had just turned twenty. I was supposed to be there for four days. I would get there on Thursday and fly back that Sunday morning. But the flight I got would bring me in on Wednesday instead, and this somehow became the worst thing I could do—I didn't realize what a big deal it would be to her. I should have but I didn't. When I told her about the extra day, she made it seem like it messed up the entire equilibrium of her new world. She was so good at taking something and projecting it to be something huge. It was always one of her strongest tactics, her excuse to be angry and off-center. She could maximize leverage as well as anyone I've ever known. I don't know—maybe she had decided she didn't want me to come now, but it was after she had convinced me and time had been taken off, airfare had been paid. So she got stuck with me, and the extra day added just made it worse.

Extra day or not, I came in through JFK and got a cab that

took me to Fifty-sixth and Lexington. I got out amidst the bus-
tling jungle of midtown. People and automobiles filling every
square foot moving in directions to places I had no idea of, most
oblivious to everyone around them. I went to a pay phone to
call her and tell her I was there, to come find me, bring me to
where she was. Within ten minutes she was on the sidewalk on
the other side of Lex with a smile, shape poking out of jeans,
her curves flexing from her clothes. A smile I had seen her use
so often without any exact emotion charged behind it. "Hi,"
she said with the usual small talk about flights and time, and
she took very little time to start her passive-aggressive needle
about that extra day, all intertwined with the usual getting-
situated stuff. When we got upstairs her informality relented a
little, and she gave me a hug and the kiss I remembered. It was
short-lived, though—she got going again when she found out I
hadn't brought some of the things she asked me for.

She still had to go to school that afternoon. But before that
she brought me to some restaurant in the open air in Midtown
on the cusp of the Upper East Side, and her intensity had eased
a little. For a moment the collision between the forces of old
and new smoothed at its caustic edges, and she could be the
girl I knew, only superimposed over a brand-new, enormously
complex background. It was the same pretty face with the two
braids that I always loved, making her face so bright.

Afterwards we walked through Central Park, yellow leaves
everywhere, hanging on gently to switches in the sway of the
air and laying as a blanket over the ground. The park was alive,
just like it always was—just like it was when I had been there
before, and just like it would be during the times I came out
later. There were people in varying states of motion and stillness, the atmosphere holding that dew in the air that makes
up the New York intoxication that takes over when people get
there—the randomness at which all the things in the city coor-
dinate. We walked through one of those famous Central Park
overpasses that find their way into photographs and as back-
grounds for scenes in movies and TV. She pointed out everything as we walked by.

"Don't you think that's cool? I think it's cool." I was still tired from the flight.

We sat down on benches at one of the ponds, watched ducks or geese float around. She talked offhandedly about things and people I didn't know, omitting the parts I would've been most curious about. "You'll meet them sometime—you'll see." I probably already understood then how voluminous this new stimulus entering in and out of her world was. The time and focus to process it all were too limited—and trying to rewind and refill these anecdotes with texture and backstory was impossible. Plus, one of her great talents was her ability to sling information while excluding large significant slabs of detail. I knew she banked mostly on the idea that I was too dusted and out of focus most of the time to discern all of the minutiae. She just slid things past me. She knows now I don't forget any of that stuff. It is the craziest anomaly in my stoner life that I can remember right down to the exact phrasing of certain conversations, even within the con and subtexts. It was because of this that her very little comment about some cat she knew in Miami who had hotel hookups would stick with me forever, despite her professional diversion. She was a hustler—at her best and sometimes most sophisticated—and my time with her had made me super-receptive to all the janky little edges that came with conversation.

We walked through the park, some places more inhabited than others. I smoked some of the weed I brought in a little homemade one-hitter I kept in a plastic case that hung around my neck. She took off for school in the direction of a nearby subway to catch the D-Train to the Lower East Side— the NYU–Washington Square side. She told me she'd be back sometime after six and told me to just walk around, see things. I couldn't be in the building without her, so I really didn't have a choice but to walk around all day. I was exhausted from the early morning flight, but what could I do? She told me which trains I could take, and where I should probably get off so I didn't end up in Marcy or Bed–Stuy.

I walked and I walked—mostly just watching people and

staring up at the skyscrapers. I realized quickly that without company you're just alone, and I really had no idea what to do wandering around by myself with a million people moving around me. In it, though, there was a loneliness I kind of liked— an anonymity in a sea of civilization, millions of souls oblivious to me and the decisions I've made. At home there was no avoiding the community: everyone was in your business. It was refreshing to be invisible while my entire world went on separate from me. Even early on in that day my perspective of where I came from and the miniscule place it held in the universe was changing. I started to realize that the ridiculous things I was doing running around in South Minneapolis created such a baby ripple in the universe. Those things were small and insignificant, despite how dramatic it all seemed to so many of us—but really it was all just stuff that helped support my underdeveloped consciousness.

I walked around the Village. I considered seeing a movie but conceded how ridiculous it was to see a movie that I could see at home while I was on vacation. So I pretty much wandered like that until the time she was supposed to be back. I called but she wasn't there yet. I gradually made my way by foot back toward Lexington, merging with the mass exodus of the afternoon workforce—the afternoon sun slowly starting to fade as I trekked. I tried to call again an hour later but she still wasn't home yet.

The temperature was starting to cool, feeling more like fall than the deceptive sun the afternoon had provided. Before I realized it, it was night, and it was dark and colder than it had been all day. I ducked into a store and bought a slice of pizza and a Heineken. I ended up sitting on a large marble bench in the plaza of the office building across the street from where she lived and started drinking the beer still wrapped in a brown paper bag. Soon people came from the building—not people in suits but in janitor's outfits drinking something out of brown paper bags themselves, talking to each other like they met there every night. It was a rich dialogue, heavy with "Naw mean's" and "On the strength, son's." They didn't talk to me, though, and I didn't say anything to any of them either. I just sat there, getting up to use the pay phone every once in a while, until at 9:05 p.m. she answered and came down to meet me, with a half-hearted apology for getting back later than she said she would, but she didn't pretend to offer explanation. I didn't ask for one. I still just let her do her thing, expecting she'd be straight when stuff did come up—even if she wasn't able to do it a lot of the time.

She asked me about the things I did, the places I saw, and the things I ate. At different points she mixed in all the speak that people who have only been in the city for a little while believe to be gospel about where to eat and all the other bullshit. I was just glad to be inside and warm. Right away she introduced me to the girl who lived in the other half of the two-part apartments that shared bathrooms. She was from Alaska; Robin had mentioned her several times over the phone. She was cute, but not particularly all that attractive. She had small town oozing from her, but it was evident she was already adopting that "big city has changed me in two months" kind of attitude. She thought everything was a setup for a joke, asking questions then automatically laughing at the answer. She asked me what I did. I told her, "I run the stockroom in the men's shoe department at Nordstrom."

"Yeah, so you're a stock boy?" and she starts giggling.

And while there was definitely a stinging truth to what she said, I was too proud to take instant criticism from this wide-eyed stranger who thought she had the world all figured out because she had ventured into the big city with her half-hearted dream to design clothes. I was feeling good about how I was doing at that time. I was working steadily someplace where the people didn't treat me like shit, didn't judge me too heavily when I had to go to jail for a month on the drug charge. I was saving money for the first time. I was even partially rebuilding part of the relationship with my family that had been damaged over the whole "not graduating, not going to college, going to jail instead" thing.

I felt like someone who was climbing back up from a self-induced injury and finally had some steadiness in his life. I was someone actively learning about himself and the world. I was a crook who had chosen to lay low and figure some stuff out, but the song says there's no such thing as halfway crooks. Even at my most ugly, I was always only part of the way. And this girl— no older, no wiser than I was—was taking a shot at my life, like my experiences weren't credible, like the fight with some of those brutal times—nearly escaping bullets or being eaten by stronger, more overpowering forces—was insignificant. In the first five minutes, my life, my friends, my city, the very real tears and torment of my parents were all made to be wack because this girl saw some bright lights, had soaked up some of that game Robin had doled out to her in small squirts. She thought she was in a position now to diminish me, the person who was just trying to take some time out of his life to see the girl who was probably the main lens through which this other girl was now seeing the world.

All this comes out of me twelve or fifteen years later—after all of the self-examination, failure, breakdown, and build-back-up of life in prison. I didn't have those experiences back then, though. I just got indignant trying to defend myself, and it came off overly defensive. I didn't have a snappy comeback to express how I had been in some dark places, seen some dark shit, and I was trying to be a regular person now, who wasn't in jail—that was the biggest part. But to these people a "regular person" was a fate as tragic as a jail cell. In ways, it *was* a jail cell—except when you are actually in one. I tried to say that I *was* a stock boy but that it didn't define me. I shouldn't have to say that; just saying it sounded corny to me. There was no way I could've sounded that would have made me more of a man to her.

"But you *are* a stock boy, though?" she said again with a jazzy little smile. I've never been good taking any kind of needling. A trigger is released and I get consumed with embarrassment, disgust, and rage, or I'm washed away with insecurity. I was teetering on that line, until she brought it up again with that stupid little smile.

"What the fuck are *you*, then?" I told the girl I had only

known for a bundle of minutes. She looked at Robin who looked at me like *I* was out of pocket.

"I'm sorry, damn. Why are you so sensitive?" the girl asked me, still kind of smirking.

"Don't talk to me, then," I said to her, short with irritation and short on rationality, rich with immaturity. I had been walking around all day after getting off a plane I boarded at 6:00 a.m. and was drinking beer with strangers in the dark across the street, and she wanted to tease me. She obviously didn't understand what I *could* be. I didn't either completely, but I knew it was the sort of ugly I *did* know. She looked nervous then, probably wasn't used to a reaction like this from boys. It was most likely her playful attempt to be flirtatious, but it was timed wrong and I took it crazy. If she had received similar reaction from others she'd given this treatment to, she most likely learned quickly she could lean on Robin to offset it.

"She's just trying to talk to you, damn! You work in a stock room—that's all she's saying," Robin jumped in, even though that wasn't all Alaska girl was saying, and Robin knew that, too. Then she turned to her roommate: "That's the way he is. He's like Shannon. You know how Shannon gets when you question something he says? When he swears he's right, talking about where he comes from and stuff? Zeke's like that, too." Robin said this while I was standing right there as though I wasn't there, like the bond she had with this lame-ass roommate for a couple of months was enough to front me off. Who the fuck is Shannon? The roommate just nodded her head as though she was receiving the answer she needed from Robin's psychoanalysis. There was an entire analytical discussion going on completely separate from me. It was enough for the roommate to go back to her room: it probably had a lot to do with getting away from me.

Robin told me then, "I've been telling her how cool you were and then you talk to her like that. This isn't the 'hood. She doesn't know about all that shit." Now it was *her* ignorance we were speaking to. It was a great start.

That night, after months of the tension of not being able to be together, we fucked but it wasn't so great. The hours on the phone didn't make this anything particularly special, and really, it was kind of wack. I remember her sitting for a while in the open window next to the bed smoking a cigarette, a habit she didn't bring with her from Minneapolis. I just ignored it; I tried to ignore the whole day.

The next day I did more of the same wandering. She was back earlier in the evening though. We went to eat dinner and did the whole tourist thing in Times Square. We saw *Seven Years in Tibet* at a theater right in the middle of all the lights and the billboards. When we got back she ordered some weed from a delivery service that apparently one of her classmates in the building knew. So she went downstairs for what ended up being forever. I just sat by myself in her apartment that had nothing in it but that window and a radio tuned to Hot 97, playing the same ten or twelve songs over and over again. I heard enough Mase and Puffy for the rest of my life.

Then some guy, a black dude with a dyed-blond patch of hair on his head and rhinestones embroidered on a red T-shirt and jeans came through the door with the Alaskan girl, but without Robin. He came and sat down next to me in Robin's room and starts kicking it. He was kind of normal, besides the rhinestones, a lot like someone I would have gone to school with at Andersen or South. This, of course, had to be Shannon. He went into a whole vibe asking about if I knew how talented and gifted Robin was. I told him I did and asked where she was. He told me she was downstairs hanging out. For probably half an hour I had this cat, who was, according to Robin, apparently one of the "brilliant artists," in my face, trying to breathe on me. He seemed more like Blood from 30s than anything else. It probably wouldn't have been so bad had he brought a blunt up with him. Mostly, though, it was obvious he was just sizing me up, weighing his own chances at Robin. Then the roommate came in and engaged herself between us, so I had both of them trying to talk at me. Her roommate was sitting there with the same dumb smile from the night before, watching for the dynamic Robin had been talking about.

After most of the evening either alone or talking with those two, Robin came back up with the weed from the delivery service; no doubt it would be her primary reason for the length of her absence. The two visitors finally broke off. The rhinestone guy tried to dap me on his way out—"Yeah, yeah, peace, Kwame." Robin could probably sense my feeling and rather than let me say anything about it, she jumped it and explained:

"I was stuck downstairs waiting on this weed, *for you*. There was a bunch of people down there. You wouldn't have liked it."

I told her I appreciated her thinking for me, "but I got the condensed version while you were away."

We got high—smoked a blunt with the weed she got "for me." After brushing our teeth and doing all the things people do before going to bed, I tried to pull up next to her, trying to get down with her again. She told me she was tired, she had to "do the school thing early." I didn't really mind. I lay down to go to sleep my damn self. But she pulled this move telling me the bed was too small—that she wanted me to sleep on the floor. I thought she was kidding. "What?"

"Yeah, there's not enough room with you poking all up against me."

"Yeah, okay." And I lay right back down.

"I'm serious—it's too small. I'll get you some sheets and shit, but the bed is too small."

"Fuck no!"

"Well, leave then!"

It was a stronger chess move than I had because I didn't have anywhere I could go. The chess move was how intimidating the city could be without a place to go. I learned that the night before. I didn't have a credit card to get a hotel room. I wouldn't even know where to go to find one. My ignorance was her greatest piece. So despite the knot of anxiety in my heart sinking into my stomach, and the unprepared confusion of confrontation and unrecognizable environment running through my head, I lay myself down on the floor under sheets on the rug next to the bed. I lay there, humiliated, regretful I ever came, and feeling like I should have X'd her out of my life long before this, like I shouldn't have ever gotten so attached to her. I felt emasculated. I still get that nervous feeling thinking about what I had resorted to on that floor in Manhattan. In the morning I didn't even want to look at her. She left for school and I went out to go hang out with Dennis, who came for only that day to hang out with another of our friends from River-side Park, who was living with his brother's family on the West Side. I would've gone over there the night before if I thought it was possible.

It was nice to hang out with the two of them, to run around with people other than myself, and I was already trying to push the night before into the back of my consciousness. The three of us walked through the park, smoked blunts, and drank Heinekens on city benches. We watched a homeless guy walking around pissing out the fly of his pants, just a stream arcing through the gap in his zipper, walking around drunk and staggering with a sword of urine swinging around, changing directions as he stumbled in abstract patterns on the curb.

Our guy from Riverside still had the enthusiasm from just getting there, and it helped to start making it feel more like a vacation, eating slices and talking about characters we all knew back home. When it started getting dark, I dreaded the call I had to make, telling her I was coming back.

"You having fun?"

"Yeah, it's all right."

"Can you just not come back?"

"Sorry, unfortunately, nah."

And I went back to another night like the previous one. I was already thinking about going home, about how I had always been too polite, how sentimentality was a ghost to me. I felt like a sucker for loving someone like this, believing love meant anything to me. How the fuck was I going to feel anything for anyone after this? I was through with it, through with passively believing love had anything for me. It was a sham; I felt like I wasn't good enough. The things I had done were just too small to impress her. I started thinking about the things that had me on a corner a couple of years before. It was better not to feel—that corny shit was dead. What should I have expected? "She fucks who she wants to fuck." I couldn't help but think that even if the chances I had to take to be somebody didn't work and I exploded, so what? Because it felt worse to not be good enough.

The day after that was the last full day before I would leave the following morning. She had softened a little—probably just happy I was finally leaving. I was certainly ready. We walked the stretch to go see *Boogie Nights* at some small little theater. Afterwards we ate at a Cuban restaurant—nothing special but pleasant. Our conversation was almost like the speak you would imagine after a fire or a bomb. "What are you gonna do now?" We were just trying to maintain a peace so things could go back to normal, but sentimental things had already been burned. I remember feeling muted, letting her take the conversation where it should go. I already had my mind made up, and I was too exasperated to hold down a point of view.

When we got back, she invited me back into her bed—an invitation much more impersonal than ever before, maybe coming more out of thirst than from genuine emotion. It was only a little bit like it had always been. She still used certain phrases and noises that usually came out when we got down, probably taken from stock and part of her core lexicon of expression she brought out for anyone she wanted to. I always suspected most of it was just game; now I had convinced myself that it was absolutely game—part feeling and a whole lot of drag. We spent the last night there, detached and emotionless. She was probably tired of me, regretting the invitation. I remember not loving her anymore, being certain of it. I remember being violently unsure if I loved anyone at all at that point—even myself. It all brought back the confusion I often felt about what the fuck I was supposed to do with myself, confusion compounded by a smallness I absorbed looking out over the millions of people moving, indifferent to who I was. The world was morphing and reshaping, and I knew that it would take the shape it would and then transform again and again no matter what I did, or who I was, or who I loved, or if I loved anything at all.

I got up the next morning to catch an early flight; she was still asleep, only kind of moving at the bustle of my gathering of things, and I left, no kiss, no hug, no chance to send me off with one of those stock phrases in a stock voice that would have before sent me off dizzy. I was dizzy, but from a new comprehension of the world, still limited but rearranged significantly. I went down to the street, the world moving as it always has—as it had the day I got there, exhaust and honking horns, feet moving in the direction of life. It moved the way it still does now—with some of the same people, and a whole lot more new people chasing after their views of themselves. I caught the first cab I could and took the Long Island Expressway to JFK. In my bag was a disposable camera, unused and still in the box.

When I got back home, it was overcast and cold, the South Side was just sitting there waiting for winter, as if waiting for me to come back, getting ready for me. The colorful leaves of fall blown into wet compost in trapped spaces. I went back to work and carried boxes, aligned boxes of shoes in the stockroom, and dreamed of bigger things, things that in actuality weren't that much bigger. But they made me feel like less of a sucker, less like a stock boy and more like the controller of my own universe. There were other girls, and even when Christmas came and Robin came back to town for the holiday, I messed with her a little bit. I knew I shouldn't have, and it never really mattered. I learned what I was going to learn from her—that the world *was* cold. She was tempering my spirit for what was to come—even if neither of us knew what it was yet. It was one last piece of game she had for me. Toughen up: no one else in my life was bold enough to say that to me.

She came back the next summer when she was done with school. I messed with her a little bit then, too, but after a while I just stopped calling. She was never going to love me any more than she ever had—probably not even close. It didn't matter. Being in Minneapolis only made her more like she was when I went to see her. And it was hardly bearable to think about that trip to New York that glowed in my memory every time I saw her. She just stopped trying to call me, too. By the fall, we didn't even see each other anymore. Sometimes people really do have to leave us behind.

She found somebody else, who was always just somebody from before who I just didn't know about then, whose name I probably knew, had heard of in an intentionally different context in a story about something else. I found the Bridge to Oblivion—a burning bridge to latch on to, unfeeling and without a beginning or an end, just enough chaos to throw forever into the fire.

Thirteen

A HOUSE, A NEIGHBORHOOD

WE CAME BECAUSE it was South Minneapolis, because it was where my dad had grown up, because it was across the street from Powderhorn Park, just a few blocks from Granny. We came because my parents wanted to own a house. It seemed like a natural succession. It was not the mountains of California, but the disappointment in having to leave the mysticism of that place had to yield to this. We came because it was the '80s and a whole lot of things I didn't understand yet about the passing of time and not being able to eat off of myth and idealism. We came because of everything it was; now it was supposed to be home. We came because it was Powderhorn, the park and the neighborhood.

She was virtually bare; the rug and the coffee table in the living room were gone; just a couple of months before there was still a Christmas tree and the semblance of a home and family unit. Now, there were just the old wood floors that welcomed us when we first came to live there. One of my earliest memories was sitting with my mom while she tried to teach me our new phone number in the empty living room, repeating the same seven numbers over and over again. There weren't boxes or furniture yet. There was just a phone, an ashtray, and a single blue-gray ribbon of smoke flowing up into the air from the end of a Merit cigarette. The sun poked through the stained and leaded-glass windows that had spanned the many lifetimes of that house. Back then, our family was our religion, and over time the house became our church.

⁣⁣⁣⁣⁣⁣⁣⁣⁣⁣⁣⁣⁣⁣⁣⁣⁣⁣⁣⁣⁣⁣⁣⁣⁣⁣⁣⁣

IT WAS STRANGE to see the house like this after fifteen years. The early '80s had become the late '90s without any of us noticing. My parents were separating and my mom had already moved out. It had become just my Dad and me living in the house for the past few months. The rugs and furniture gone, the brass-framed black-and-white photographs that had adorned her for so long were taken down and packed in boxes, all the plants transplanted to my mom's new apartment. At times I tried not being sentimental toward this house I grew up in. At others I tried to inhale my last heavy breaths inside the vessel that held so many of the moments that hosted my childhood. But I knew the change was inevitable; the whole I was used to that included both of my parents and the ongoing cycles of living in that house was going away. Granny was still just a shortcut across the park away, in the old house on Elliot. I didn't go over there as much as I knew I should. I felt so guilty every time I went over there because I smelled like weed.

Pieces of home being packed away made me remember all kinds of things. When all the pots and pans and cookery were being put into boxes, I saw the big wooden sauce spoon that didn't stir sauce very often; there were other spoons for that. Tantrums and jazzy outbursts were usually met with a great deal of patience, but when I pushed a line too far, the spoon came out. I don't even think it hurt much, but I screamed like it did to escape its wrath. In the summer, when the windows were open, we had neighbors who thought I was being abused because I yelled so loud. They used to invite me over for pudding, probably to protect me from my parents.

Dad and I spent that last Christmas Eve just the two of us and Sneak, drinking Moretti's while the old man drank bourbon. After Sneak left, we hung out, eating frozen pizza, talking shit, watching *A Christmas Story* until it got late. We had to get up early the next morning. Dad was cooking spaghetti dinner at Mom's apartment: it was a somehow coordinated arrangement that Christmases would stay intact, regardless of what was happening between them. I had to put on an old Santa suit and show up at Sneak's to take pictures for his son's first Christmas. I took a lone photo that night of Sneak and Dad sitting in the living room, bottles of beer and a crumb-filled cookie sheet on the coffee table, a crystal ashtray full of butts. The pictures were still on the walls then, the plants and the four-foot house speakers in the background. If I had shifted just a little bit to the left, there might have been a scant glare from the lights of the last Christmas tree. Mom had intentionally avoided putting up any of her really nice stuff; the crystal and blown-glass ornaments stayed in boxes. I can't remember why we even bothered to put it up; it was just the two of us, neither with much concern for the holidays, and we were really only speaking to each other in short, to-the-point sentences.

They told me in one loaded sentence that they were "separating and selling the house." I didn't need any explanations. I didn't need to ask them why. All I could say was "All right" and accept it. I was twenty years old, and I knew I was on my way out. As far as dealing with any kind of shock at hearing my parents tell me after twenty-five years of marriage that they didn't want to live with each other anymore, it really wasn't my place. I was the kid who had to be bailed out of jail a couple of falls earlier. I was also the kid who dropped crack in the cushions of the living room chair. I'm sure they were plenty shocked to find a gun stashed between sweatshirts in my closet, too. I wasn't disillusioned with any notions over an indestructible force shielding their union from all the things that change people's minds about each other. I was kind of surprised it hadn't happened earlier.

After all, my father had spent much of the decade of the '90s with a gun close by waiting for someone to try him. It started with the burglary at the house during the afternoon of the great Halloween snowstorm of 1991. They chipped out the framing in the front door and took the glass out and snuck in. By the next spring the three of us were shooting at old air conditioners at a garbage dump outside of Owatonna. It was where I learned the nuance of owning and holding and shooting a gun. I took turns with every caliber, watching dust exude dry composted soil into the air as I fired a .44 or a 12-gauge at objects off in the distance. As the decade got crazier and the city transmogrified into what it had, the more common it was to see my old man with one of his thumpers, preparing himself for an enemy that didn't have a face or a motive yet. Most of my friends who passed through didn't know there was something disastrous waiting under one of the couch cushions, but plenty assumed it and gave him all the room he needed.

Mom wouldn't listen to anything any one of us would say about the neighborhood, or the park, or the fucking house. Her stuff was packed and shipped to her new place before New Year's. To her, it already wasn't ours anymore. To her the neighborhood was what screwed everything up, the neighborhood that turned Dad into a Clint Eastwood character and me into a hoodlum who went to jail instead of college. To her, it was just as much my dad's fault for convincing her to stay for all of those years. She wanted to leave long before, but Dad convinced her there was something essential in the ground and roots of that place, and that leaving wasn't going to fix what was wrong. None of the good moments mattered then, nor did it matter to her that it was the only house either of them would ever own. By the time their separation came along, she was already disillusioned with the house and the neighborhood and the church-like doctrines that came with them.

<hr/>

WHEN WE MOVED IN, it was 1983, and I was five years old. I wasn't sure then how to feel about the great big expanse of hill and trees just across Thirty-fifth Street from us, the Grand Canyon in the middle of our neighborhood. It was presented to me as being very close to an actual member of our family. After all, my dad brought me to South Minneapolis to meet her: "This is Powderhorn, she was my childhood sweetheart, and sometimes she'll be your guardian." Only, she felt more like a passive aunt with a house already full of spiteful children, where the aunt looked the other way: "Let boys be boys."

It was something different to everybody who ever knew it. It was May Day or the Fourth of July to some people. It was where people walked their dogs, or kids risked their lives on the monkey dome of the Tenth Avenue side playground or the tire gauntlet on the Fifteenth Avenue side, during the old cowboy style of childhood, where one was meant to fend for themselves to figure out what was safe and what was fun all on their own. Families barbequed and hipsters played Frisbee golf. South High students had their tennis and baseball practices there. There even used to be world-class speed skating, and before that sing-alongs on the hills. For a while it was a danger zone: for some it was where they learned how to fight; for others it was where they got their bikes stolen. Mornings were usually peaceful, afternoons mostly boring, evenings volatile, nights shadowy and suspicious. To my mom it was heartbreak.

To my father Powderhorn was the world. Most of his days started and ended at the park. In the winter, he skated and played hockey throughout entire days. They used to leave him the keys to lock up the warming house and shut off the park lights. A lifetime of days turning the lights out, skates tied together flung over his shoulder, a hockey stick, and the taste of cold numbing his face. In the summer, he played baseball with the neighborhood kids in uniforms and equipment my grandfather got for them through the American Legion. He caught bullheads and turtles from the island with his first rod and reel. Back then, he could walk across a narrow land bridge out to the island when the water levels were still low enough to do so.

Any kid who has ever lived near that park can tell a version of the legend of the Giant Snapping Turtle that supposedly lived in that lake. The stories had become mythical about a creature of almost Loch Ness Monster proportions, reputed to be anywhere in size up to that of a compact car that had been swimming around in the sewage runoff that was Powderhorn

Lake for decades. My father, not a man for exaggeration, would modestly tell anyone who was willing to take him seriously that he had actually caught it and brought it home several times during the years he fished down there. He'd bring it and anything else he caught home with him and build ecosystems in the backyard on Thirty-fourth Street and then after a couple of days bring them back to the lake. Plenty of kids swore they had seen it, but my dad was the only one I really believed. I got a sense the creature only showed itself to a select few attached to the lake through some kind of esoteric relationship. It kept itself hidden, only revealing itself to those worthy of knowing of its actual existence.

The park became his passageway to the universe, showing him the things he couldn't previously understand. He even discovered the first dead body in the pond, just off the shore at the bottom of the hill on Elliot Avenue, on Granny's side of the park. He told me the story of going down to the lake one morning and seeing the bloated mass floating close to the shore. It was a morbid example of all the things that had been discarded in that lake for years. I can only imagine how many guns, knives, and other items of danger were left there, attached to stories someone didn't want told. A friend of mine's sister drove a car into the lake once that never got pulled out. It probably drifted into the mysterious drop-off right over the edge of that side of the island and just never came back. The chances are pretty good there is more than one gathered in the junkyard under the surface in the never-ending muck.

||||||||||||||||||||||||||

WHEN IT CAME TIME for me to inherit my piece of the park, it was different: things were changing and there were more disparate energies competing for her attention. There weren't bullheads anymore. Instead there were immense schools of goldfish from people releasing them into the lake over the years. From the hills, there were large masses of orange visible from different angles. Some things were the same, though; the turtles were still there. In winter, my dad taught me how to skate and walked me across the ice behind a folding chair. The hills were filled with kids sliding on plastic sleds just down from Tenth Avenue. There were hills of every pitch and gradient, fast and slow, smooth and bumpy, open or full of trees. Back then, there was plenty of snow, and it lasted the whole winter, so the long, steep sidewalk right across from our house on the Thirty-fifth Street side that ran into the canyon of the park was like a luge run with three- or four-foot trench walls on both sides. It made it easy: we didn't have to go all the way to the Tenth Avenue hills. Years later, after the city gave everybody recycling bins, kids would use the plastic lids for sleds. Early in the mornings there would be empty hills littered with flat, green strips of plastic against the white background.

In the summer I played tennis at the courts right up the hill from the infamous forest on the Tenth Avenue side. In fall I played football for the most notorious park football program in the city. Most of the time when I was young, I spent hours with my mitt, throwing tennis balls against the steps or against the side of the house or garage. I lost so many balls to cubbyholes in the alley and to the obnoxious neighbors on the other side of the street. When I was old enough my dad brought me down and signed me up for baseball. A year later, he was the coach. It was a role that never went away, pitching batting practice and hitting fly balls to kids in the outfield with holes in their gloves. It was a natural role for a man who was one of those kids for so long himself. Even as the years went on, kids who played with us still called him Coach Mike when they caught him in traffic. In the evenings, the baseball diamonds were my Mecca. I learned how to field ground balls and left perpetual orange stains on my uniforms from running and sliding into the bases, with the Sears Building looming large in the background. Some years we were really good and ended up playing for city championships at Parade Stadium. Other years I swore at the umpires and other kids threw rocks at them.

On one of those summer days coming home from Saturday practice, when the sun was warm and present, I saw all the turtles on the island, basking in the heat. From the sidewalk we could see dozens of them, some the size of what people would expect, others abnormally large. On that day, there was one turtle that was significantly larger than the others, and I've always believed it could've been the one. I would say it was maybe three or four feet wide and at least that big lengthwise. Whether it was the same turtle of legend that my dad caught or not, or if the myth had just become something that much greater than the reality, I don't know, but I've always believed it was him. I've always wanted to believe it had deemed me worthy to show me its existence.

||||||||||||||||||||||||||||

DURING OUR FIRST SPRING IN THE HOUSE, we woke up to bad Bob Marley and Woody Guthrie covers coming from speakers just down the hill. Swarms of people were flooding into the park from Bloomington Avenue. Back then, we didn't know what the May Day Festival was. My parents had been in California for years and had no clue what to think about the procession of papier-mâché puppets and masked characters streaming into the park, in small squads shouting out political causes. I strapped on my twin-holstered six-shooters I got for Christmas the previous winter and followed my parents along the route of the masses. I was the kind of child who, without scruple, would pull out and start clicking the trigger at anything in particular.

In the midst of the politically charged, patchouli-smothered celebration of Spring and from behind giant puppets came a collective of camo-clad women and children in gas masks and combat boots, with handmade signs for WAMM—Women Against Military Madness. I didn't know what that was, but I probably thought the camouflage and the gas masks were my cue to take my six-shooters from their holster and start shooting at them, sound effects and all. I started following them as they moved down Bloomington, shooting from behind trees and fire hydrants, with my parents behind me trying to suppress my exuberance. There were people yelling at my parents to get me out of the parade. It took a while for either of my parents to realize it was me they were talking about. Even then, they didn't go out of their way to disarm me. Instead, they just turned me in the other direction to watch more of the parade, where instead I shot at the big sun and moon puppets.

As I got older, May Day became part of the cultural foundation of where I was from. As years went by, May Day became the day our whole community reunited after the shock and entrapment of winter. It always brought out aspects of the community and of ourselves that were in hibernation for most of the year. The first Sunday in May was when the whole South Side was from Powderhorn.

The Fourth of July held a similar sort of cultural relevance. The blocks around the park were filled with cars of people who came to watch the fireworks shot into the sky from the island or the hill on the Fourteenth Avenue side. When I was five years old, a police officer kicked me out of the park for selling freeze pops out of my red wagon without a license. The next year during Fourth of July I sold Kool-Aid on our front steps instead. It didn't attract the same kind of crowd that May Day did; it didn't feel the same either. There was a different kind of thump to the rhythm of its energy. There were always more police, more crackheads and gangbangers, more casual friends showing up to watch the show from our front yard. One year, some family friends showed up with a minister and had their wedding in the backyard.

The Fourth also became an unspoken ritual for late-night shoot-outs. From my bedroom, I could hear the back-and-forth exchange of gunshots disguised in between the ignition of common firecrackers. I didn't know how to process such things into an applicable reality. As a kid I still had a disconnection from the hurt and feeling of actual events and their consequences. It hadn't taken hold of me yet what bullets did; I just thought all of it was exciting, even if I wasn't prepared to do those things myself. Their effects weren't placed tragically in my living room yet. Instead, it was like watching TV from my front porch. There was an exhilaration without direct contact to the pain and suffering, the fear and trembling. They were something I just came to expect, until the police came to expect them too and started crowding the park with squad cars after the park shut down.

Early on, there was still a level of innocence that surrounded the neighborhood, an innocence for which we had moved there. There is a picture of me on the first day of kindergarten. I was on the front step, the porch and the crab apple tree in the background. I had a short-sleeved blue oxford shirt and one of the steel lunchboxes I got from when dad was a kid, with a haircut uneven in the front that Mom used to call "the Steve McQueen." And even in those early years I used to trek through the park to Granny's house unchaperoned. I used to break-dance in the front yard with wristbands and bandannas without music. I went to the co-op or the corner store on Thirty-fifth and Bloomington to play arcade games with the other neighborhood kids. We used to skateboard in the Holy Name parking lot. It would seem the neighborhood was safer then or as yet untouched by the events that started to overwhelm the local news. There were times growing up where it seemed I literally could have been the only person in that enormous park. Some were summer days where the green spread out and sloped incongruently, where there were no other neighborhood kids on the swings, or neighborhood folks walking their dogs, or young people in menacing poses waiting for a singular victim in a giant, empty park.

There were always things happening, something for us to watch out the window. There were the Take Back the Night rallies, with a parade of vocal activists marching from the park. Every once in a while there'd be the headlights of a vehicle zipping through the park, being chased by squad cars. In the summers there were life-and-death basketball games on Fifteenth Avenue. The summer basketball games were never-ending. There was always a full run and guys waiting on the sidelines to get next while drinking Old Gold on the hill next to the court, alongside all the kids' and babies' mothers who came along to watch. Every once in a while games would get too serious and someone would get laid out on the street somewhere on their way home, the red and blue lights flashing their way into the windows of our living room.

iiiiiiiiiiiiiiiiiiiiiiiiiiii

THEN THERE CAME THE TIMES in the neighborhood where dodging collisions with collections of other kids was impossible. I got hats taken off my head at the park, someone stole my skateboard in the parking lot of Holy Name, and someone else tried to take my shoes off my feet across the street from Sears. I even had a group of bigger kids try to take my jeans off me, while someone else put the boots to me. One particular time we were coming back from baseball practice and we had bottles whiz by our ears. The neighborhood became far more territorial, less mine or our family's, less the place my dad knew or I had come to expect of it.

As the '90s hit and I moved into early adolescence, it was apparent my relationship to the park and to the neighborhood could never be the same as it had been for my father. It also became apparent that my relationship with my father would never be the same as it was when he first introduced me to them. There were just too many dueling energies emerging and competing with each other at that time. It was somewhere around then when my interest in the sports that had meant so much to my identity started to go away. It was hard to tell him I didn't want to play anymore, many years and generations of equipment later. It was hard to say I wanted to sit on the awning outside of the window of my bedroom and smoke blunts instead. It was hard to say I didn't love to play the things anymore that had connected us from the beginning. It felt like I was saying I didn't love *him* anymore, too.

During the summer before high school, I started sneaking out of the house to hang out with my friends. I would cut through the park to get to the other side of Bloomington, so I would have to pass by the park building. That was when the building and the surrounding playground became a dope spot. As soon as the park shut down, the park building and its adjoining structures (the playground and nearby bushes, the pissy swimming pool) all became a wonderful setup spot where a crew of dudes stood outside in the scant light under the over-hang of the roof and pushed packs at a stream of oncoming clients. I'd roll through and there'd be a whole slew of cats in starter jackets and David Robinson's, gold chains and Chicago Bulls hats. There was always some kind of traffic. People came and went; smokers beamed up on the playground or in the sur-rounding bushes, veiled in darkness. Coming and going, I shot through quickly, doing my best to stay out of their way. Some-times I knew some of the people, an older brother of someone I went to school with or from around the neighborhood. They'd pull me up and holler at me for a second, and then I'd be gone again, planning a way to sneak back into the house. Early morn-ings there was always paraphernalia in the sand: burnt-up old lighters and cellophane knots, broken stems and brillo. The po-lice eventually figured out the game and shut it down, but even before the hustlers were gone and the park was empty, I was always more fearful some weirdo would snatch me up from be-hind the shadows of one of the trees than I ever was of anybody milling around the park building.

As I got older, the neighborhood was becoming less cen-tral to who I was. I didn't play organized sports anymore, so the park was usually just a last resort spot to smoke blunts or play drunk basketball at 2:00 a.m. Most of my friends lived in Phillips then anyway, and when we were in the neighborhood, it was at a house in the no-man's-land between Bloomington and Cedar. There was a period where we spent most of the time riding through the city on bikes we took from the old Franklin Avenue Theater. We spent whole weeks without straying much past Fifteenth Avenue.

Me and Dad didn't play as much catch then. He still had his Tuesday night softball games. The old guys my dad went to Central High with who had helped us move into the house were slowly starting to give it up. There was Dad and a few other die-hards wrapped in Ace bandages and reeking of Ben Gay who stuck around to play during those years. Every once in a while I went to watch the old man do something an old man is not supposed to do. When I was about seventeen, he and the guys invited me to play, a gesture that was special because I had been the batboy when I was little and had berated them at every loss, even though I hadn't swung a bat in several years. For an hour or two I was in my father's fraternity again, even if afterward I was right back to flunking out of school without a clear idea of what I was doing or where I was going.

Mom was more stunned by the school thing than Dad was. Her aspirations for what I would be were uncertain but grandiose and limitless. I would sit on the purple velvet couch watching *Dallas* or *The Dukes of Hazzard* and listen to her tell me how as a baby somebody swore to her I would be a preacher or a politician when I grew up. I think Mom thought that when I messed up, she could just sit me in the living room chair and drill rationality into me. I would sit for hours while she reiterated the same points repeatedly. I would zone out, and anything past the first ten minutes was a blur. I'd be hypnotized by the designs in the living room rug as words blurred and obscured in their transmission. By the time I got the GED, so many different bargains had been made; there had been so much remortgaging of the terms of my educational expectations that she was exhausted. It was in that same chair I got the talk after my drug case. And in a related tone, it was the same chair where I was told they were selling the house.

‖‖‖‖‖‖‖‖‖‖‖‖‖‖‖‖‖‖‖‖‖‖‖

WHAT WASN'T MENTIONED was how financially it had gotten so bad and that all of the cumulative expenses that were meant to make our lives what they had become, were too much to maintain. They also didn't mention how much of a role I played in it: the arguments between the two of them over the burden I had become, the loan they had to get to get me a lawyer, on top of everything else. I had hit an age where the mirage put up to protect me from all the harsh things that went into supporting a family could no longer persist.

There was an extraordinary gloss smeared over all the Christmas and Thanksgiving dinners, a gloss of security. The

ornaments put up to cover the things that almost didn't happen. At the time it probably felt like a purge, a time to break
down and start new. It had been a long time, but the two of
them had done it before—the moves to and from California, my
dad's trip back from Vietnam, and Mom's choice to come to the
city for college. I had never been through it, not as a person old
enough to feel and understand it. I had no idea where I was
going. At all the stages of packing I was asked if I wanted to
keep anything. Not realizing I would need some of these things
when I was out on my own, and not wanting to seem greedy, I
just told them no to everything.

I was the last to pack up my stuff. It wasn't because I was
hurting over having to move but, rather, because I have always
been extraordinarily lazy. At the same time, I knew something
in me wanted to believe we weren't really moving. I think I
wanted to believe the house would always be there, the root
of our cosmic tree. I wanted the assuredness that there would
always be this place for Thanksgiving and Christmas dinners.
I felt magnetically connected to the space. I hadn't learned yet
that there is more than one of those places in a lifetime, and
sometimes things went away. I was connected but disconnected
in so many other ways. The closet in my room was still a mess,
despite needing it clean so they could show the house. I threw
up Southern Comfort on the white carpet early on the same
morning they were supposed to have people see the house.
Mom and Dad were thrilled with my cooperation. It was hard
to visualize the future without the house, but I was through
trying to make nostalgic moments from the past. I was just trying to get going, even though I had no idea where I would go.
My faith in the "church doctrines" had long started to wane in
me, too.

ıııııııııııııııııııııııııı

I WAS TAKING LAPS through the house trying to squeeze every
last bit of nostalgia before we had to leave. I took a tour through
the basement: no more clothes hung from the lines hung from
rafter to rafter; all the junk my dad had stashed away was gone;

the freezer was empty; and the memories were insignificant. I went through my room, tried to catch every last angle from out the window. One time I took a bunch of acid and watched the searchlights off in the distance duel like light sabers in the sky until it was time to come down and go to school in the morning.

My dad was still looking for a roll of bills he had hidden somewhere in the house that he couldn't find, that he swore either my mom or I had taken. He had spots everywhere in that old house, with bits of money or other stuff stashed as his own personal bank. Now that moving out was inevitable, he was probably trying to recall all of the spots he had used over the years. I'm sure he was itchy to ask me if I had taken the money. I wouldn't have known what he was talking about if he had asked me. In the state he had been in, he probably wouldn't have believed me anyway.

||||||||||||||||||||||||||||

I WALKED OUT ON THE BACK PORCH. Even in winter it was just as it always had been—a view of an alley and a never-ending string of electrical wires. When I was seven we dropped water balloons from it. When I was seventeen me and my friends threw up St. Ides over the railing. There were all sorts of little angles throughout the house that I would forget as soon as the door shut behind me one last time. I came back downstairs and looked out the windows for anything lasting to keep with me. It was a long time from when Granny took on the bees, the sheetrock long fixed by then. I came back to the floor, redone and shining like the day we moved in. I was surprisingly underwhelmed with emotion. I didn't care as much as I thought I would. The feeling of the house was what I knew I would miss, the sounds and the familiarity. I would miss the creaking of certain stairs from when I used to sneak out. The sun from the summer lancing through the living room. I would miss sitting on that awning trying to blow weed smoke into the heavens, as though it was going to fix me or make a path for me to follow. I had no idea where I would go from there. I was supposed to be an adult. I was supposed to be able to take care of myself—and I felt like I was ready for it. That is what kept me from being nostalgic or from being truly distraught or sad.

Me and my father moved along separate lines. I was looking for anything sensory that might trigger a memory I would need for the rest of my life. My dad took his last tour, his senses feeling for one last time anything he might have missed. Twenty years of finding and creating small coves to hide little things had created a sense he had forgotten something. His hands felt around edges in the old architecture, under overhangs, along hidden brackets that held the staircase up or supported the world. There were little spaces behind drawers in the buffet or behind edges in the cupboards in the pantry. Going down into the basement, his hand reached into a small, hidden alcove above the door and there it was—the money. The money that was at the root of the toxic blend of mistrust and resentment that had been cooking in him for months. There it was, a roll of bills and a temporary reprieve from being poisoned to death by the mix of caustic chemicals he had created around it.

After the last tour, I was ready to go. "Let's get going." I pulled that old, heavy door open—the same one the thieves had busted the glass out of to get into during the Halloween snowstorm—and pulled it right back shut. Me and my father walked out, probably the last time we would walk out and see the park from that angle again, at least together. It was somebody else's church now, the stained-glass windows taking and maneuvering light from their place in the attic. The park stared us in the face, withered and dingy in its winter costume. It used to have such a mysticism to me. It was an expanse, the Grand Canyon in the middle of a regular neighborhood in Minneapolis. But right then it was emotionless to me, ground and matter without feeling. Without a human voice to speak for it, it was someone else's world—it could have been anyone's.

We came because it was Powderhorn. We left because it wasn't enough to keep people from changing their minds about where they wanted to be, where they wanted to go. It wasn't enough to sustain our faith in the same things that brought us here from California, that made us a regular family, that made my father a man and made me a delinquent, that kept our faith in family from being susceptible to all of the impermanence in the universe. My dad moved in with my grandma for a while on the other side of the park. He could give up the house, but he wouldn't give up the park. He still went down to the empty hockey rink and shot pucks into an empty net, its mysticism as strong in him as it ever had been. All the hockey players played at Longfellow by then. Besides Granny, there was nobody else still there: all the neighbors were long gone, and most of the kids I knew from back then were in jail or had disappeared into the streets.

I ended up in a duplex on Thirty-first and Cedar, just grimy enough to feel like I hadn't strayed too far from home. I unpacked the few belongings I had kept from the house: the TV, some pictures, and a whole lot of clothes. There were also a few boxes my mom had put aside for me, despite me not asking for them: pots and pans, glasses and Tupperware. And in a pile of silverware wrapped up in a coffee can there was the wooden spoon I had dreaded as a child, all of its spankings done and over with. It didn't look so big now that all of its punishments had been delivered.

Fourteen

FROM SEPTEMBER
TO SEPTEMBER

IT WAS HARD TO REMEMBER ever being happy. I probably could've looked back and idealized those simpler times when I was younger, when I likely misunderstood some of the complexity around me.

At that moment, though, there was nothing simple. I remember being crouched down, sweating rivers on a layer of rocks behind an air conditioning unit in a cubbyhole behind an apartment building with my gun in the coat pocket of my leather. My hand clutched around the handle, forefinger massaging an unreliable trigger, I heard the radios around me and saw the moving flashes of blue and red in the blank sky in the middle of a broken night. My chest was heaving; my heart and lungs were yelling at me. I was thinking that this is what happens—at the end of a chaotic year and a half of personal deterioration, the slow feeling that I was dying, and that hopefully it would come before catastrophe. The only question that really mattered then was, *What the fuck am I going to do now?*

Only a few minutes to make the decision I had spent a mini-lifetime trying to envision, built an entire ideology to justify: the die-young narrative, the burn-out-fast, shoot-out-faster storyline. The depression that had become a canyon didn't matter anymore—the money I never made, the girl I never met, the person my family hoped I would be didn't matter at all.

I could stay there and let the adrenaline suffocate me and accept that at the end were steel doors and a promise of prison. All of the things that wrench and seize the systems of my body— the fear of entrapment, being stuck, watching everything that is comfortable shut a door. I had been in jail before, just enough to know it was a life I didn't want. It was something I had spent most of my life trying to avoid, the impersonality and the voices that screamed and went on forever from inside locked doors.

I hoped they'd go away, that the swarms would move on and I could run off into the night, that this moment would dissipate into nothing. Then, maybe, I could change my life. There was another voice that talked louder and more aggressively to sound stronger than the others did, that said to go out blasting: *This is your moment, go.* But I didn't know what I would've been trying to say. It just made me feel stupid for not being prepared, for being scared, for still having an unfinished life.

Mostly, though, it felt like the end. It was a moment like this for which I owned a gun at all. I kept one in case the consequences became too obvious or overpowering. There's something dark and morose about boys and guns. But at the exact moment, with the sharp edges from the stones beneath me poking and slicing their designs on me, I had to decide if I wanted to live or die. Part of me said I had prepared for this my whole life the black would one day just be too black. I would have to put the gun to my head and push the button—there wasn't a way out after this. Anyone who still loved me would have to understand, would have to grip the things I was too scared to face. That part of me just said I was delaying what was inevitable. The other part just wanted it all to vanish.

Every second my grip grew tighter, hoping the right answer would appear in the swirl of polluted thoughts. A year and a half of being miserable that turned into the closest thing I'd ever known to desperation. I hoped solutions existed, that the fall could somehow be clearer than summer had been, or spring, or any of the time before that had become so hazy. And there I was, backed up, trapped in that corner. I was too far gone to be sentimental or sad. I thought to myself in that instant how stupid and naïve, how young I really was. I had never taken the time to think about what the world should do with me after I had gone.

|||||||||||||||||||||||||||||

MY PARENTS had always been clear in the decisions attached to their own deaths. They made it clear that they wanted to be cremated. They said it was a waste to have a ceremony where people showed up to be sad and were reminded that their day was coming too.

Dad had always said he wanted his ashes spread in a beautiful stretch of Lake Alpine in the Boundary Waters, where he and his oldest friends went every spring for as long as I could remember. But he changed his mind. He decided he wanted his ashes to be laid along the first base line of the baseball diamond at Powderhorn. The sentiment brought tears when I was told, part appreciation for all the best years of our lives that were shared there, and part guilt and regret because I had never given him anything other than hour-long visits coming through metal detectors at a Minnesota state prison.

Mom had decided that she wanted some of her ashes sprinkled in the Pacific Ocean. I would take the rest to the fire tower at the top of Buckhorn Mountain, where I would toss them into the air to become a part of the geologic sediment at a crest in the earth's skeleton where she overcame her lifelong fear of heights. Later, she would hold steady to her wishes to be spread out on Buckhorn but changed her mind about the ocean part. Instead, she wanted the rest of her ashes incorporated into a mix of gunpowder in fireworks so that we could shoot her into the sky and she could explode for one last time for her friends.

I was just then starting to recognize something happening to me at certain times in my life and how it affected the decisions I made: a never-ending succession of highs and lows that was killing my soul. I was never completely sure how I felt about what would be the end of my own life, but there was always a strange darkness that held on to my moods as far back as I could see. I should've expected it. It was most treacherous in the fall. When I was young I didn't know what it was, just an overwhelming hurt that stole much of the beauty in living. It would leave and then come back. I forgot about it until I was back in the darkness again. Nobody told me it was depression—nobody even knew. If anything I was just strange because I smoked too much weed. It came every fall in different disguises with varying degrees of severity, looking different, feeling the same. It would start in late August as anxiety that played at my nerves like a violin, and after crossing over into panic at times, bundled with a whole variety of off-balance side effects, made me mistrustful of everyone around me. It made me question the value of my friendships, made me sabotage friendships and relationships I didn't trust, even with my family. A short-circuiting that scrambled everything I believed about the world. I lived with it like I lived with my migraines, the latter's debilitating power a metaphor in scale to the melancholy's power in my life.

This is what September was in my life—a beginning, as though my world was a collage of fragmented little pieces out in front of me, and I couldn't touch or control anything. They were the instruments in the orchestra of my life, and I couldn't play any of them. I had forgotten it was coming. September always reminded me how things could fall apart in my life. It felt like some years the cycle just got longer and longer until there was no break from it. At its height it manifested itself in the explosions that would determine my life. I could look up in the middle and without fail see the colors changing and life migrating. I ended up seeing a psychologist who gave me something that messed with my whole equilibrium. I think I was unconsciously getting myself ready for the explosion that was going to shape my life.

The previous fall should've made me ready for that final blast. It seemed like the darkness just came charging up from behind me, chased me down at an unrelenting pace from the spring before. It weakened me enough to make me incapable of fighting off the future. It was such a stark period of instability—wispy and really absent of any joy. I remember not wanting people around me, but they were, constantly. At work, I put the smile-mask on and sold shoes I couldn't afford myself. I made good money, and the people treated me pretty good. I had a pretty good job, but it wasn't the gateway.

It came after a spring and summer where I really was starting to feel renewed and reenergized. It was a time abounding with metaphors of rebirth, renewal, new love, new outfits, with new lighter colors—new frontiers after the psychological war of a Minnesota winter. I was back on my feet with a better perspective of where I could go. I believed I was out of the fog. No more petty hustling, no more bottom-of-the-barrel grinding—fuck a street corner, fuck being a lowlife, fuck being dirty and unrooted. I knew I wanted more; my New York experience still had its fangs in me and clouded how I looked at people and their intentions. I still felt very small; it wasn't humility, more an insignificance that made me thirsty and deliberate. I could be a wolf or a shark, never a sheep again.

I always believed in a Golden Gateway that came through opportunity. It was supposed to mean that whatever I had to do to be the man on the other side, it didn't matter. Even if it was created from grime, it was a belief that if we could steal enough, stay dead long enough, maybe there could be rebirth somewhere else. I also thought it was what made you. It made so many others I knew. Then I could be the soul-controller of my own universe.

<hr />

BY FALL I HAD FILLED MY LIFE with all sorts of new distractions. I was selling shoes, and I fell into a side scheme that made me more money than I ever had before—even though I was falling behind on all the customer service stuff. I was so preoccupied with getting through individual days. At night a paranoia crowded the moments right before sleep—that somebody would figure me out, figure out I was behind, or that a customer would end up livid and call the boss, then another and another. I was failing at being a shoe salesman. That would really make me look stupid. *And my scheme: how long before someone noticed it, recognizes something isn't right? Did I cover myself up enough? Probably not. It's probably an indictment waiting, and what about that other thing with that other guy?* And I was still getting high every day—drunk too often. An inner dialogue started where I began to tell myself I knew I was missing the corners: *You're slipping Zeke—really.* Another dialogue would start in: *It doesn't matter; you're too smooth to fail.*

My landlord had his police scanner hooked up in my living room. Throughout whole days and nights I heard CB beeps and chatter over a radio. I couldn't help but always feel the police nearby, coming to get me. *Did you hear that? Was that my address?* It took me weeks to unhook the thing.

I got a baby pit bull that I had no idea how to train. I named her Crook because that was what I felt I was, a crook, and her name was emblematic of how I felt. We never had dogs growing up; I just thought she would be a great accessory to wear alongside the rest of my lifestyle. I was very attached to her, but I found dog shit in the most obscure places, and she chewed on my $240 Allen Edmonds shoes. Anything at dog level got it. I couldn't leave her out during the day because she would terrorize the place, eat out of the garbage, shit in closets. Sometimes piss would dry on the carpet or in the cracks of the wood floor in the kitchen, and we'd never know it happened except for the smell that hardly went away.

When there's more money around, there's more people, more activity, with more schemes and conspiring. It seems like in movies and in real life there is usually a crescendo that hits when bad stuff starts happening: perceptions emerge, a door gets kicked in, or someone across the street with a long-angle lens is taking pictures of the house. And if it wasn't me, it was somebody else dragging their dirt with them. Nobody else was going to stop; so even if I did, it didn't matter.

September was back. It started to become what it always was in my life: the sly transition into more confusion. I spent money like I never had before, on things that weren't concrete, that turned to smoke and went into the sky. I looked around at a house full of people—some I'd known for years—but I didn't feel like I knew any of them. I was in it again, and I didn't realize it.

October came, no different from September. Mounting energies built up to the crescendo I couldn't see or hear, only felt in my shoulders, or in the headaches and the fatigue and the continual activity around me, conspiring with me. Maybe if my head were clearer I could've weighed the risks better, I could've had a better idea what to do. But it wasn't clear. I woke up one morning after another, and I was in a blur.

When I tried to tell a couple of my friends about why I felt the way I did, they yeah-yeah'd me, as though it were something that would go away, something people didn't suffer from until someone came home and found them hanging from a rope or in a corner with brain matter pulverized against a wall and a gun in their hand. Even though most of them had their own brushes with melancholy, this was something detached from them. I probably shouldn't have expected much from my guys. Most didn't understand that these periods weren't always incident-oriented, but, rather, just came, a wave in the brain's ocean, sometimes one greater than another. *I* didn't understand. I was in it—I couldn't see anything but what was there then—and I couldn't expect them to fix it for me. I didn't expect they could fix *anything*. I just needed to deal with it by myself.

While I had felt like this before, it was never this grotesque. It might not have been so hard if I wasn't trying to hold everything together—the stuff normal people dealt with—while trying to avoid the unknowable physical and spiritual entity of prison.

〰〰〰〰〰〰〰〰〰〰〰

IN THE MIDDLE OF EVERYTHING, I turned twenty-one. We did the midnight madness thing at Fowl Play in Dinkytown, and I drank as much Hennessey and any other junk as could be laid in front of me in the hour before closing. I got my birthday beatdown on the boulevard outside of Second Foundation

School. I ended up passed out on the money-green carpet in my place with a pool of Tanqueray drool next to my face. When I woke on the morning of my twenty-first birthday I was alone, dizzy, and dying. In the midst of that hangover something clicked, or snapped, or changed its rhythm abruptly, and the next day I quit the job that was so much a part of my reincarnation, my shucking of all the adolescent shit I had declared dead in my life.

I told the boss I got a different job. I hadn't, but I still told him my last day would be at the end of October. I didn't really know what the fuck I was going to do. I didn't have a plan. I had a little money that I thought would last me a while but not forever. I told myself I would get another job, that it would give me a disconnect from a lot of the complexities building to this numbing uncertainty. It would be a way out of the drudgery, but I needed something life-changing. I'd made no changes in my life except giving two weeks to my boss. When the last day came, most of the people I worked with didn't even know I was leaving. Even the ones who did know looked at me suspiciously like they knew I was fracturing: a circuit had shorted and the rest was crashing. I couldn't even come up with an adequate answer when asked where I was going. I could've told them all, "I'm going into hiding."

I ended up messing with a hood-rat that Sneak brought over in the middle of some random night. I just kept thinking; is this the kind of hook-up I've got waiting for me forever?

I was detaching more and more from the people and things in my life. For a while I tried to keep the lights in the house low so people didn't think I was there. I would sit in the dark, smoke blunts, and drink beer. I moved my PlayStation into the bedroom so the glare from the TV was not noticed from the street. People still came over, though, tapping obnoxiously on the front window for twenty minutes at a time. I hoped they would go away after a little while, but even when they did leave, usually they came back, again tapping at a steady peck. Some of the more cunning ones—who were more likely to sneak in and rob somebody—figured out the whole bedroom thing and came straight to that window, hidden by bushes and overgrowth on the side of the house. The blinds, even at full closure, still had enough of a crack to see in just a little. "Come on, man, we see you in there!" I'd have to let them in.

"Fuck you doing? You're getting weird, Dog. You didn't hear me knocking? I been here for a half-hour."

Sneak wouldn't even wait. He would knock a couple of times and a couple of minutes later I'd hear squeaking and the thump of his body hitting the floor coming through the back window he'd intentionally broken so he could sneak in on such occasions. He would just pat himself clean and stroll to the front of the house to let in some chickenhead he came through with. Sometimes it would be three in the morning and I felt murderous. He'd be stumble-drunk coming from the Quest or Tropics or Club Extreme and want me to get up and drink beers with him.

My hiding didn't last long. My friends all just went on like they were supposed to. I got a few looks of diminished appraisal, but it didn't stop anyone from coming by and drinking from the bottles in the cabinet and criticizing how I kept my house. The house was a mess. They'd come over, the place would get fucked up, and I was too zoned out to care.

But the immediate part: after I quit the job people started to find out and wonder why. I didn't see the dropout as part of the darkness. I just needed some relief, a break. I started to sleep most of the hours of the day. It was the beginning of the pattern; I stayed up most of the night, and when I did go to sleep, I slept until it started to get dark again.

After a few weeks Mom found out I quit my job. She called a few times before finding out, but I intentionally didn't answer. My caller ID overflowed with familiar names or numbers diverted from familiar people calling from different lines. After finding out, she started calling at least ten times a day; I just ignored them. I knew she'd want to talk about it, look for an explanation. But I really had no explanations. I had nothing rooted in rationality to say about my self-exiled expulsion from life, and I had no intention of revealing my failures to her then.

She would come over after work and knock until she was convinced I wasn't there. For a while the wires from the phone got
yanked from the jack so I didn't have to hear the ringing; it was
actually very peaceful.

I fell into a dreadful daily routine of getting up in the afternoon and noticing the sun was already going down and
that another day had gotten away from me. I looked at myself
in the old, stained three-foot wardrobe mirror that sat in the
bedroom, about bed level from where my head hit the pillow. I
looked at how the cave-lit room and diminishing sunlight were
starting to make me look. With a shrinking, yellowing face
with marks from the wrinkles in the pillowcase—the darkening
rings of Saturn around my eyes—I would stand and try to shake
the dread I wore as pajamas from my exhausted body. I would
take a few dollars and slide out onto the street, down Cedar.
By then there weren't many leaves of any color anywhere, but
in the gutters it had become mulch under the onslaught of the
fall rains. The trees moved, and any sun left was going home
for the day just like all the cars moving in the direction of their
lives. I'd stroll down Lake in a straight shot to the liquor store.
I'd come home, turn the lights on, and pour beer into a cup,
mostly out of ritual. Then I would sit and make up a scenario,
hoping something would come up that could take me from the
place I was.

I daydreamed scenarios of wistful worlds not so different
from what was usually happening, only with me being a little
stronger, a little more composed, and a whole lot more prepared for things to happen. I looked out of the old green blinds
wishing I were in one of those cars, trying only in my mind to
get back on, wondering about how desperate someone could
get, feeling and knowing I wasn't there yet, feeling but now
knowing that something was coming. I just needed something
to happen.

llllllllllllllllllllllllllll

ONE SUNDAY MORNING Dad stopped by unexpectedly and
took me to the bar to watch the Vikings. It was the year they

were supposed to win the Super Bowl. We went to Whiskey Junction and then Mortimer's to watch the game. He asked what was going on: "What happened with the job? Your mom is worried." I told him I was tired. I needed a break and I didn't know what I was going to do.

"You should just call Mom, though, whatever you do."

"I don't think I want to deal with that lay-on right now."

Somehow, though, I ended up with my parents that night for dinner. (They were split up but still did family dinners together on Sundays.) A welcome of tears and concern, worry that came out in the plain language of "Hello" and "How are you?" For me, I knew there would be beers and food that wasn't in a wrapper for the first time in a while; my dad made a roast with carrots and quartered potatoes. We didn't share much conversation, though, outside of baseball or football. It was uncomfortable because I was dreading the eventual conversation that would have to happen. But I had already told Dad that I wasn't ready for the lay-on yet. Right after dinner, I had one of my guys come get me. "You're leaving?"

"Yup." I promised I'd call her in a couple of days.

We went to some bar, then ended up at someone's house where I mostly just stared at a wall for a couple of hours, then ended up back at home, walking into the dark and empty apartment, with the sound of my dog's tail wagging profusely against the plastic of the inside of her kennel.

It seemed it was like this every day, a blob of days stuck together by the gunk of irregular hours and a diminishing sense of time and equilibrium. There was just no enjoyment in anything anymore. I managed to make it out enough to end up at parties where I sat in corners doing my best to conjure interest in the jovial greetings of the people in the community. Or we ended up in bars where the bustle of people I didn't know who had been on the scene for years already ran around me and drank to all the multiple reasons for why people drink to anything. I wondered if I would be one of those people sitting at the end of a bar as I got old—at the place everyone knows to find me yet no one really ever looks for anymore.

I got impromptu visits from Mom at random points in the day, to drop food off or scented candles or anything as an excuse just to remind me to come through on Sunday. Dad cooked; I drank beer and pretended there weren't any motives for the visit. I pretended there wasn't going to be a sit-down, that the conversation would be a dialogue. Her sit-downs were just tellings, declarations from Mom to me, that typically were in response to the times I fucked up. They were tellings rich with guilt and emotional layers. She laid it on thick when I was in school and I had a bad report card. I had to sit in the living room chair and just absorb it all.

"Don't you know we love you more than anything in this world? Do you think there is anybody else out there in the world who cares about you the way your father and I do?"

I shrugged.

"All we ask is for you to go to school and perform."

It repeated itself in a loop for hours, where there was nothing new I could say to add any explanation to my mother's mania.

"I'm sorry—I'll work on it."

"You say that. You don't mean it, though. You're a good liar. Oh yeah, you're a great liar, because you say you're sorry, tears come out, but you really just want to escape."

I did want to escape, especially as hour one became hour two became hour three. I spent most of my adolescent energy trying to avoid these talks. After them, what I usually needed was a nap. Then I'd get a period where every day I got my homework checked; agreements were made between parent and teacher I wasn't included in. Then I would burn out and go back to the places and things that germinated into what had previously led to the last living room shellacking.

This one was different for a few reasons. The big one was that I didn't *have* to stay; I wasn't a kid anymore, so the trap-in-the-corner method didn't work as well. And she was scared— scared to make things worse, scared to push me away and back into isolation. But I was still in isolation. It was a break from being met at my front door whenever I came back from anywhere at all. It was an escape from being awakened at 2 a.m. so that Sneak could knock down some bigheaded girl he met at a club inside a mall somewhere. I was in a constant juggle of dodging my family at times and my friends at others.

This conversation started basic with, "What are you going to do?" I got that question from a whole lot of people in my life for kind of a long time. I still had no idea what that meant, in the short term or the incredibly obscure long term. I felt what she meant, but I could only see in front of me a few yards, let alone understand the direction I was going to take with the rest of my life. I had no idea how to start. But the talk was inevitable; the moment and the face-to-face report card talk. The chair was different, and the tone was a lot softer. The motive and intention were the same, but instead of a declaration it was more of a plea. It was her reach into the darkness in an attempt to yank me out. She looked me in the face—not standing over, but eye to eye, a couple of feet from me—and told me:

"I just don't want you to die. . . . Is that what you want to do? Are you trying to die?"

"I don't know."

"I just don't want you to die." There it was.

I sat there, trying not to absorb what I had just been told, trying not to accept my feeling that this might be what I was doing. Instead, I thought about my death. I thought about the decision they had made about the ends of their lives and I thought about my own death.

I always agreed philosophically with them. But the little king in me had always thought that if I was going to die young, that maybe I deserved that one last display of my relevance, no matter how much I actually had left. Shouldn't I get to look down and see the tears on the faces of all these people who just couldn't muster enough commitment to care about what I was before? But then I just got sick to my stomach thinking about how stupid that sounded. Instead, I thought about looking down at an empty funeral parlor, with my parents and my grandma—my mom the only one with tears in her eyes.

My mom told me she wanted me to go back to work. She

also talked about me maybe going back to school, maybe a community college. But that wouldn't have worked then because I wasn't ready yet, and I didn't want to. I couldn't go back to that dependence; school had been such a failure the last time around, and I didn't want to be reminded of that failure again. I had to get back to sitting in my window waiting on a million dollars to fall down from the sky, in front of me.

llllllllllllllllllllllllllll

THE GUN WAS ALWAYS THERE. A piece of shit, cheap from its start, a misfit, like I felt, sitting on the cable box, always present. Still, it sat on top of every episode of *Friends* or *Seinfeld,* a piece of furniture like a centerpiece with fake flowers poked into foam. Sometimes, when people weren't around, I held it and paced around the house. When I slept it was just in reach from where I laid my head. I was the boy and it was the other half, soothing, dark, and morose. And jagged. There was also a Mossberg that sat in the corner. I thought about people coming in; it wasn't an unrealistic possibility that if someone was going to come through the darkness, they'd be a bad motherfucker to stick around after they heard the chick-chick.

I kept playing with the notion of taking that pistol out with me when I left—just in case some sort of otherworldly opportunity arose, something magical opened up in the fabric of the universe for me. I was hoping for something life-changing where I could miraculously be something else, a "break out of the prison of this house and this neighborhood" event. But I was a felon, a reality that meant any fluke pull-over, pat-down, jump-out, block-sweep, party breakup, crowd control, or tackle after fighting in the parking lot of any bar in the metro would get me five years in the joint—five years of wall I couldn't see over. I told myself it made me feel safe, but it really brought me closer to the line between a false sense of security and disaster.

When I did take it out with me, I knew I was always at the cosmic entrance to something unknowable, unforeseeable, always enacting scenarios around corners or as people stepped onto the bus. There becomes a window where something

viciously unpredictable sweeps in and the unpredictabili-
ty alone owns your future. It was the thing that scared me so
much, but on some level I felt like I needed some reshaping,
some redirected momentum.

I kept it at home, even though the faceless object whispered to me to be invited on those late-night walks with Crook.
It sat on the coffee table next to an ashtray full of cigar guts and
cigarette butts from the friends I told not to smoke in my house.
I watched TV with the dog sleeping on the couch next to me.
The three of us were as dysfunctional a family as there could
be, until naturally someone showed up and set the dread and
anxiety back into its loop again—a bottle would come out of a
backpack of one of the b-boy kids. Then I would get dropped
off again, alone in the dark, listening to the same Tupac dub
I had been wearing out for months, thinking I should maybe
write some of my life down before the end comes. I went to
sleep instead.

I still went to those Sunday dinners with my parents, staying a little longer each time. It was an escape for me, not from
the internal but just from the circular revolutions of routine
that got smaller and smaller. I was virtually out of the money I
thought would carry me until my next lick, and my confidence
and the energy I needed were shattered. Getting up was a task
that dominated me. It overpowered and dictated my life. Some
mornings I would put on the suits I used to work in, and I'd go
out with the front on, and I would apply for work at Niemans
or Saks. I could usually get an interview right away, but I was
hardly composed well enough to sell myself. I certainly didn't
exude the confidence these kinds of places were looking for. I
felt almost like I was begging for a job—a vagrant in the nice
suit with all the grime and soot visible just under the surface.
I'd just go home, not knowing where else to go or what sort of
work to look for. I always thought there would be somebody
with somewhere I could go, but there wasn't.

I found myself lying in bed, promising myself that tomorrow I would get up and something would happen. But it didn't,
and the day would be over and another night would be right

there for me to face again. I remember feeling an ache, a pulsing hurt and confusion that ached so bad; I remember hoping I wouldn't wake up. I was through with what I had to do on Earth. I was ready to die—empty and dulled with anything I had left to live with. I had contemplated this at several points prior to then, but there was certainty to it just then. I wasn't going to kill myself, but I was ready to cross over. And I felt if I didn't, something was going to happen—I didn't know what. I just knew this was how things exploded.

At some point in this fuzzy period the winter became actual winter, where things froze and snow suffocated what was left of fall. The sting in the wicked whip of cold winds met me at the doorstep. It made the outside world all the more unwelcome. The air bit me and I had no idea what I was going to do. I even went to the plasma center off of Bloomington and Lake Street. It was a crackhead move done in the dark, and I was hoping to God nobody I knew saw me walking in there. All around me were hypes and the prostitutes I saw every night in the back alley. I got all the way until I realized my ID was expired and I needed my birth certificate. I called Mom to see if it was at her place.

"What do you need it for?"

"I just need it," I was ashamed to say.

"For what?"

"The blood bank."

"What? Just go get a job, Jesus! If you need thirty bucks that bad, just ask for it. Jesus, just get a job—anywhere."

And the humiliation I was hoping to avoid from the world boomeranged back at me from her instead. I just abandoned the whole idea. I ended up in the window again until the sun left.

With my defenses shattered, my pride dehydrated, I somehow got my old job back, and I went back to work, a few steps down from when I left. I hadn't been up that early in months and came in after being up the entire night because I knew if I did go to sleep when my body wanted to, I would never get up. I'd have opened my eyes at some point near dusk again. I probably looked like shit, with the pale of winter escalated by the hibernation and the long night. I had to fight to stay awake to this point.

I had a job again, so appearances were better. Christmas was uneventful but sidetracked me enough not to think about the darkness. I dressed up in a Santa suit and went around taking pictures with Sneak and Dennis's kids with a beer in my hand. It offered the traditional euphoria I got during the holidays. When it wore off, usually the same shit was waiting for me. Nothing had been fixed, none of the personal mysteries had been solved, and the confusion was as active as ever.

The same people came over every day to remind me what I felt. I was just back to scuttling from place to place in the cold, from one warm escape to another. The problem was that every time I got inside from the cold there was a mirror to remind me of what I was. New Year's came and I was in a house somewhere that was supposed to be a party, sitting amongst people who were supposed to be my friends, but I had nothing to say and ended up staring at the walls again. I went back home and sat by myself, coming to the conclusion that I didn't want people around me anymore. I was becoming less and less comfortable trying to figure out these other people. I stopped feeling attached to the kid I used to be who hogged everyone's attention and budged into conversations to hear himself speak. That kid was stupid to me now, I felt ashamed I was ever him, even if it was that kid who endeared himself to the people who cared about him. I started holding on to this sort of resentment for those people who were somehow disappointed that I wasn't that kid anymore.

Sid came up with the idea to move to Phoenix, of all places. It was his way of getting out of what was to him the trap of the Twin Cities, and a sincere attempt to take my sinking ship with him. It would only be a temporary out, but nonetheless it was his out, not mine. And as much as I needed a way off of Thirty-first and Cedar, I couldn't foresee running off to the middle of some strange city as the fix to any of the things that were wrong in my life. I did what I did most of the time: I said I would go, then didn't.

After the holidays, things started to feel like fall again, only colder. It got harder and harder to get up in the morning again. I fell into the habit of coming into work whenever I woke up. Sometimes I just didn't show up at all. I almost shot Dennis one morning for pushing the wrong buttons when I absolutely couldn't handle it. I came out of the room with the gun, Roscoe, fully intending to shoot Dennis in the leg or somewhere else nonfatal. I didn't want to kill him. He took off and smoked with Sneak on the front porch, both laughing as though something awful didn't almost happen.

It felt like the people I knew best didn't take the things breaking down in my life seriously, that what I said really didn't matter. I just needed them to know I was serious, that this was serious, that the impending doom I had been sensing was going to happen might happen to them.

There wasn't much of a future floating in front of me, but the looming something I had envisioned happening was subverted for another day.

||||||||||||||||||||||||||||||||

I GOT REUNITED with an old friend from Powderhorn who had recently found Jesus. He kept trying to get me to go to church with him, but I wasn't prepared to confront the things that were happening in my life with him, because I expected it would lead to him telling me I needed to be saved. Somehow he did get me to go to a service at this enormous church in Golden Valley, where the choir outfits matched the carpeting and there were giant projection screens of the preacher in the pulpit, just in case any of the congregation couldn't see him from their balcony seats. On the drive there I was tortured by a Christian rap CD the whole way.

I think he thought it would be transcendental for me; it was not. It just seemed like church. When the preacher asked if there was anyone in the audience who hadn't been saved who wanted to be, to come up front and say a prayer asking for Jesus to come into their life, he started nudging me, a normal nudge that became almost violent in its urging. I declined, just to avoid the public display. I was more preoccupied looking at the girls in the audience, young and glowing as if untouched by the dirt swirling around the universe.

I couldn't help but be intrigued by the whole idea of rebirth. It made me think about reincarnation—that I might take on a new life or new shape. It was the same as the Golden Gateway: I pass through and I get a new life on the other side. I could start over and be something different; a splash of water or a new set of clothes, and I was someone else. It just seemed the brand of reincarnation being sold to me in that church/auditorium talked in the language of freedom but really just had all sorts of new restrictions. And while I understood the whole "submit and the New Life will be brought to you" thing, it didn't keep me from walking around in the same body, sleeping in the same dilapidated place with the sinking kitchen floor, walking the same route down Cedar to get Jucy Lucy's. I had a hard time believing it was going to stop me from feeling the brutality of those unquiet hours in the night lying in the dark. It looked like once you scratched the surface a little bit, they were just the same scriptures that were on the tracts the guy in the dusty trench coat passed around outside of Chicago–Lake Liquors, which were usually attached to declarations in bold lettering about the coming apocalypse in the year 2000.

Summer was coming again, and I had nothing shiny to show for the previous stretch of my life. Everyone was coming back from school or had just finished, starting to find jobs in whatever they got their degrees in. A lot of them had left Minneapolis for a bigger city and were coming back to show off their new lives. Some were chasing lives as artists, or rapping, their own kind of Golden Gateway. Even all the grimy characters we ran around with were either moving on or were starting to compile felony points on the criminal justice grid, doing stints in the joint. The ones who had already established themselves had saturated such a substantial part of the market it was hard to start from nothing anymore.

The days of opening a crackhouse in the zone between Bloomington and Chicago and Lake and Franklin by dropping a piece on somebody's coffee table and watching lines form around the block were over. There were just way too many police and special task forces, and there weren't as many addicts as there once were. But there were just as many thirsty motherfuckers out there with cheeks full of nothing special driving down demand. As people my age started to think about their lives, the petty hustler as a concept became less and less interesting to them.

The extra sun that came with spring helped a little but didn't create any sort of stability. I was still immobile, at the whim of others. I was riding a city bus to work with a Walkman that played cassettes. I had a dub of all the songs I would have wanted played at my funeral. It was a mix of Biggie and Mobb Deep and Gang Starr and Tupac, playing on a loop while my head rested on the glass at the back of the 19. I saw so many people, at every age, suited up for the grind—the grind of living, getting on a city bus, and working somewhere they never thought would be their future, wearing clothes they never thought would be their uniforms. So many people hauling groceries or a bag too heavy with the things that weigh down a person's life. At only twenty-one I was one of them now, the people they told us we would become if we didn't go to school. It was the trade-in for who we were just to be someone who survives all this shit. There were mothers as heads of households, where every penny was accounted for, every bite consumed. There were men and women living second or third lives after coming home from prison sentences, trying to be anonymous enough to stay away but couldn't help recognizing all they had lost. Heads rested just like mine, with stone gazes out of a window that cycled through blocks, with houses like memories coming and going. I watched kids riding bikes in groups, waving middle fingers at occupants who didn't even care. *We'll see your little dumb asses with us on this bus in a few years. Those kids will get their chances to share in some of this regret.* And I started to feel less like Tupac or Nas and started to feel more like a sucker, like someone I used to have to push from the dope spot for hanging around, or more like the guy who hangs around the cipher waiting for somebody to shoot him a possible puff of charity. And I daydreamed again, pretended I wasn't actually on that bus, that I hadn't actually gone broke, listening to bad dub tapes on a Walkman. I thought I could pretend this was just reflection, meditation time to get back on my feet. But the longer it lasted the less I was sure I had ever learned to stand up.

I started going out most every night then. We went to the Red Sea and drank Red Stripe and Hennessey and berated local rap acts, disregarding all the smiling faces of the people I grew up with who were just trying to be friendly.

"It's so good to see you. What have you been up to?"

"Nothing. To tell you the truth, I've been on some bullshit. Things have been awful, and I have no idea what I'm going to do with myself."

"Oh, okay."

Then the fellas would start throwing beers and punches, and we'd be out on the street looking for something else to entertain us. We had a guy rolling real tight with us then, the type of lowlife who comes around too much when things aren't going well. People like him seem to attach themselves to the regress. As long as we'd known him, he lied and exaggerated.

"I'm fucked up right now. I'm broke and they are about to cut the gas off."

"Don't worry—we're gonna get you back on your feet."

"You—you're gonna get me back on my feet?"

The outrageous alternate universe he lived in was even more delusional than mine. Then a bottle shattered over somebody's head and the chaos began again.

And then I would have to get up, slap my face against the glass of the bus again, hit play, and imagine how I could go back for another day. It was hard to gather, but something offended me at work that I can't even remember now, and I just stopped coming in, except to get that last paycheck. They wondered why I didn't come back. I told him I was better off running around in the streets. It sounded stupid. It *was* stupid and rooted in fattened ego, which was the only thing that spoke for me anymore, besides beer and dollar-night rum and Cokes. So I shed that uniform again and put a hoodie back on. I knew then I would have to live a lot more uncertainly, jump onto opportunities whenever they arose.

I started middlemanning any transactions I could— skimming thirty or forty dollars whenever I could. Any lick that popped up, I was in; if I wasn't, I was disappointed I missed it. At parties or the bar or birthday barbeques, I was watching for someone showing off too much, whose watch was too shiny, or had a backpack full of weed he thought was cool to let everyone see. I was conceding to the notions I had been negotiating after coming back from New York a couple of years before—that people would always see me for how they wanted to see me, that it would be better to be this guy, constantly disconnected, constantly thirsty, dark, and foolish, living in an abstract present, devoid of future.

When summer finally came I didn't feel the same strandedness I had spent an entire fall, winter, and spring trying to escape from. I did feel something, though—more of that impending doom lurking, a feeling of walking blindly toward something ugly and not caring, thinking this might be the last summer, without an exact reason to believe it was, as though a whole lifetime of fatalism was trying to fulfill itself. The fellas around me didn't think it was; they ran around like every day was a party and went out from one spot to another every night. We drank Coronas at Augie's, and one night we saw a pregnant woman dance on the stage at the Skyway Lounge, which was a pretty provocative moment for me. I wondered if that girl felt the doom as I did, I wondered if she cared. Then we went and shot dice at the spot on Twenty-fifth and Columbus; a house full of crooks and hustlers, hats cocked, with money and worry from who knew where, passing it around through the lottery of nominal tosses of ivory, whose order and allegiance are drawn in the stars somewhere. Any love I ever had for gambling had mostly gone away by then. I would shoot for a few cycles and duck out again. I did enough gambling in my life every day as it was; I already couldn't afford the kinds of losses that came with it.

And home was just as cavernous as ever. I was certainly aware of the dark recesses I was walking into, but I didn't understand their depths yet. I couldn't quite recognize that there was a point where crawling back out was impossible. I still slept close to Roscoe—ugly as ever, getting his chance to be a part of something, however insidious that was—saying to me, "See, I told you I was worth something—I can make things happen." I still had that felony, though—invisible most of the time, but attached to my name in a database somewhere I wasn't trying to go—and Roscoe didn't understand he could take me there.

I still had the fog in my eyes, but I had accepted that it might not ever go away, especially doing the things I was doing.

I couldn't tell Mom what I was doing, or about the doom. There was no way I could tell anyone without sounding a little out of my mind. I think I believed if I could make enough money and become self-sufficient enough, the feeling would go away, that a little security would keep me alive, would allow me to shine enough to not give a fuck about the generational transition going on around me, or the deficient levels of serotonin and norepinephrine moving through my brain. There was always supposed to be a Golden Gateway on the other side of the dread. If there wasn't, then I stood no chance.

I would watch the sunset every night—smoke a blunt, tug on a beer, watch yellows turn to oranges to purples to blues. Then night would come and the urgency of the lifestyle would swoop in and pull me amidst the hysteria of each individual night. A girl I knew brought me home one of those nights.

"Doesn't it get lonely in that house by yourself?"

"Yeah, it does." And I walked solitary into the unlit black of the haunted house.

I'd wake up, face on a pillow looking at myself in that dirty mirror again, funny sun looking in from indirect angles.

Time is running out. Moods and ideas were changing. If I didn't get on quick, the whole prosper of the decade would go to waste. My entire hustle would be a piece of shit on a sidewalk somewhere. *I'm going to end up as one of those people whose generation zips by on the freeway,* thought I was running *fast until someone got a car that left me behind.* It created in me a sense of urgency that only metabolized the anxiety more profoundly. *And the end of the world is coming—Y2K—am I ready? Get on, get as much as you can.* I could've only been so lucky as to have the world end then. I felt the doom as chemicals oozed over neuroreceptors, and I just knew the end of something was coming. I tried sounding prophetic quoting parts of a copy of *Behold a Pale Horse* that was floating around, just to speak a language that sounded dark and apocalyptic, to speak a language that sounded edgy, but that I didn't wholly get. I began to think people were starting to wonder about me:

"What's the deal with Zeke?"

"I don't know. He's depressed."

"Depressed? Shit, we're all depressed. What is that supposed to mean?"

"I don't know. I don't know what his deal is."

||||||||||||||||||||||||||||

I STARTED SEEING GUYS I went to school with riding around in new trucks with gigantic wheels. Was it hustle or opportunity that made that kind of money possible? I hadn't figured it out yet. So I made the mistake I so often made of telling myself being as grimy as I could be was the only way I could get back to the Golden Gateway.

Somebody put me onto a way to make some money. When we got back, we divided shares and went our own ways. In real life, numbers got obscured; people said things and amounts were taken, stories were told even when they weren't necessarily true. That's how beefs start, and I had to figure out who my friends were in the situation.

In a murky moment, the next thing I remember was having somebody tell me he was going to kill me—and that changed the entire landscape of my financial situation, my summer, my mood, my future. Now when I was out on my own, I felt like I had no choice but to bring Roscoe with me. I knew I was more likely to get snagged by the police than I was getting into a shootout. The likelihood was greatest that we'd run into this guy at a bar or a party and maybe a bottle would get busted over somebody's head . . . . But that's not what I heard. What I heard was, "I'm going to kill you!" And that meant, *No, you're not. You're not going to kill me and/or embarrass me in any way where I couldn't go back to the community with my pride intact.* And for that, Roscoe came with me.

All sorts of scenarios went through my head: What would happen if . . . ? It just created more imbalance to the summer. I started looking at things through the lens of street people and the dilemmas they've shared for a thousand years—the accidental beefs, the cross-outs, the front-offs. Not being on my feet made making decisions harder, made it obvious I didn't have the resources to pick from a limited set of choices. There was a lot of sitting in the dark waiting on an idea to come that was different and more powerful from the ones that floated around at the surface. Rarely did they come.

⁙⁙⁙⁙⁙⁙⁙⁙⁙⁙⁙⁙⁙⁙⁙⁙

ONE OF OUR GUYS came back from boot camp right before the Fourth of July. I rode with a friend to pick him up at the airport in all of his Marine stuff, skin-tight, spouting all the rhetoric of his brand-new indoctrination. In the car he didn't stop talking about this guy or that guy, or some obstacle course, or his scores on some drill, a gun with a billion rounds. He kept saying, "Hoorah!"

"Look, settle your ass down—you're in South Minneapolis now, not Camp Pendleton."

When we brought him to his grandparents' house, his grandpa asked us if we were ready to sign up now. And while he was a very gracious man, sincere and genuine, there wasn't anything that would get me to sign up. I grew up in a household where it wasn't an option. Mom would have shot me in a leg to prevent me from signing that paper. My boy emphasized it as a way out. It *was* a way out, but it was *his* way out, not *mine*.

It was hard to take him seriously sometimes now because he had run around the streets with us, drank and did dirt with us. We were dumbstruck when he told us he signed the paper that made him their property. He had brought the idea up and we laughed at it. I never expected one of ours, after all those years of contriving government conspiracy theories, secret organizations with worldwide plots to keep us in a gutter somewhere, would ever end up in one of those outfits with a mouthful of all that propaganda. A lot of us tried talking him out of it, before and after he signed up. We thought he was selling out, falling into a classic trap. He told us we didn't have anything better for him here. He was probably right.

As the Fourth got closer, it was more apparent most of the fellas had no intention of laying low. And especially with the newly born Marine in town the intensity level of the group was more pronounced, and I wasn't trying to be part of it. With every venture into the world, every return home was a potential beef, a potential life-changer, a never-turn-back moment with prison or death possibilities. I bought a cheap ticket to Phoenix to get a break and see Sid for a few days. He looked at me, head full of working parts maneuvering around this latest instance of burrowing deeper into an abyss. It was the stuff that motivated him to stay away. There was always a cash register scam, or a stolen goods ring, or a hunk of dope I had stashed in a cereal box in his cupboards—and he wanted no part of it. I don't think he could understand how so many of us who came up together hadn't shed our adolescent skins and moved on. He had been trying to stay as far from the impending indictments he knew would come someday.

I was in a pool in Phoenix on the Fourth of July drinking beer and watching fireworks. It was nothing special, but nobody except a few people on the planet knew where I was and that was fine with me. I met a bunch of people who would forget my name and that I had ever been there at all. Sid suggested I just stay. I probably should have, but that wasn't going to happen. I had too much money tied up in things at home—it really wasn't that much, but without it, I would've been on the brink of starvation. He knew it wouldn't happen, but at least he knew rather than expected. I could have easily made another commitment to him that I wouldn't have upheld. So when another new start that I told myself and everyone else I needed was offered, I still chose to walk past it. There were just some things I couldn't run away from, because they were the problems that were part of me.

On the plane ride home the anxiety started coming back. *You know it's not over. It's back to the grill again, and nothing's changed.* I had only been away five or six days, but it felt like the gap of uncertainty had expanded to something unrestrained. The first night back some of the guys came through when they saw the light on.

"I thought you were gone—like gone forever. Like in that movie—what was that movie?" one of them asked me.

"*Good Will Hunting?*"

"Yeah, we just show up one day and you're up."

"I wish," I responded, still getting used to being back and what all came with it.

One of the guys was trying to load the Mossberg right in the living room, for no particular reason but to mess with something. I was only a few feet away when a Boom! roared through the house. My adrenaline zoomed through my body. Next to me, maybe a foot or two, a quarter-size hole was smoking through the arm of the couch. My landlord came downstairs, revolver in hand. We told him what happened, and with an irritated but accepting smirk he went back upstairs. It was a grand welcome home. If I had illusions about what was waiting for me, they were dispelled with the thunderous wake-up call of bird shot that came in small and blew out the back with pellets and upholstery scattered everywhere under the couch.

I got another job selling shoes, but after a few weeks I got fired because I didn't tell them about my criminal record. I guess I hoped if I pretended it never happened it would just go away. I hit the point again where I was starting to worry about where money was going to come from, and working again eased that a little. I was so much more manic during that time—manic and paranoid. Long days, with longer, depressed nights by myself. A lick was going to come that would dress me in a new uniform of confidence and success. It would be a lick that would put me on, get me through this period. I knew they were lies, bold obvious lies that only a delusional person growing more and more desperate would tell themselves to avoid an immediate panic. The Gateway seemed more an imagined part of my daydreams now, and not even a real possibility.

So I started descending again, getting trapped, looking for any come-up I could. And it made me sad because I wasn't getting anything that changed my life. I got crackhead money. It sufficed for a little while, then I was back lurking, looking at angles of the city I never noticed before. I was looking around me. People back from college for the summer, re-networking, and starting to wear their new identities, were even less impressed with the hoodlums who were still running around grinding knuckles with nothing to show for it. It was bleak. There had to be ways out, but there just wasn't enough serotonin flowing through my head to push me forward, to see past the next blunt. I was on the backseat of cabs, or buses, or a friend's car: I was at the mercy of where these forces took me. Instead of steering my own destiny, someone else was driving my life. So much for that whole soul-controller-of-my-own-life stuff.

I went where the car was going. I was watching out of a window, watching my life disintegrate, and I saw all the kids I had tried to be so much cooler than redirect, make long-term plans, let the horrors of the midnineties be history, where all the kids who died could rest and be free of what had happened. They would be able to blame all that madness on being young, trying to be free—and "Whew! I'm glad I escaped that." But I was so far from even fathoming what I would be or escaping from anything. I was still waiting on the lick, still teetering between wanting something and expecting to die, expecting it because it felt like the obvious exclamation to the way things had unraveled. It felt like the alternative to not getting through the Gateway.

Everywhere I went was potentially the last time I would ever see some people. I went to the cabin my family went to every summer. It was where when I was twelve I met a girl from Wisconsin who I always wished I would end up with. The few days I was there, she wasn't. I figured I would never get the chance to tell her how I felt or what was happening in my life. She couldn't possibly have understood what I was going back to—I didn't even understand. I was on a farewell tour and didn't realize it.

The doom I had been feeling started to accelerate, its pace quickening. We went right back to the same kind of work, looking for that lick, the get-me-out-of-here lick. But the universe doesn't work like that; it has its own time, its own reordering. I got a job working with Justin at a telemarketing place selling long-distance. Everybody in the building was on some kind of parole or probation, trying to get paycheck stubs to show the law. It wasn't much money, but I had to get on again. September had come back and the heat had been shut off. I wasn't even sure if I would be able to pay the rent that month.

Justin brought his three kids over to the house and played video games. I smoked blunts with Sneak, who had another baby on the way. I stopped through all the spots, gave dap to everyone, even the dick riders and the lames. I was borrowing time, because it was coming.

I even sat on the grass on Nicollet Island and watched the Dayton's fireworks show with my mom. They were spectacular sculptures alive in the sky. Mom still expressed all the ooh's and aah's like a kid. She never stopped loving the little explosions into the atmosphere, even if they were just for a few fleeting moments. I could understand then, maybe I already did intrinsically—about how lives are just moments. We think we understand the terms but really we just want to leave enough of an impression so that someone might remember our moment. Some lives are just duds, don't even get their chance to be seen. When Mom said she wanted her ashes put in fireworks, she wanted her friends and family to see what she saw—she understood the moments. I did not.

I was back in September again. It knew me well. It was hard once I started to fall to believe I could fall any further; then it happened. Something that was supposed to mean rebirth became something so much other than that. Then one of those acts that shouldn't happen, that almost doesn't—the almost moment, the almost-stayed-home-played-video-games moment, the almost went-to-sleep-woke-up-and-went-to-work moment. It is the moment that was going to happen, that was always going to happen, with all the tassels of possibility that trail behind it. The what-the-fuck-am-I-going-to-do? moment. I could stay here in the dark, options getting smaller, reality closing in. I did find the Gateway, but there was nothing magic or golden, just hard feeling and a sobering sense of time. It was the Iron Gateway, and it locked behind me.

"Is always be" is what an old poet with graying dreadlocks told me in the joint once. *What is will always be*—there was always a better choice for what was, but what was really was. And what I was and did I really was, and I really did—regardless of all the other things I might have been once.

Then the opportunity came, and everything I knew to be true in the world came to an end and I died. The kid who was Superman or E.T. went away. The youngster who dressed as Santa for his friends' kids went away. The smooth cat with the sag and an acute fear of imprisonment got locked up, this time for real, this time for what felt like forever. For the kid who was Zeke—who was chasing after the lick that would change his life that never came, who instead found something that changed his life to a perpetual series of opening and closing of cell doors—old and new disappointments weaved together in a tapestry of sadness and good-byes.

III. Death: Putting It Back Together

I became a blue shirt, a ghost
hovering through hallways.
I am atoms collapsing, but it's okay
baby new year, on the cusp of a baby new horizon—
it's okay I'm still the abstraction
that will maybe write that poem,
or change the last one.
Tell a story
or write my way back to life.

—from "Before I Was Anything"

Fifteen

THE LAST VISIT FROM THE
GIRL IN THE WILLOW TREE

SHE CAME AT A COMPLEX TIME. We all knew it, and she did too. She made the trip all the way from Boston, had bundled it with her summer plans to go back home to the suburb outside of Milwaukee where she grew up. She took a hammer and busted off a chunk of her summer just to come see me when my life was on the line, behind glass in jailhouse oranges. It was a time when part of me was so very scared to death that my own apocalypse was coming, while another part of me held on to just enough hopefulness that I could still go home, that I *would* go home. I needed to believe that I could reinvent my dreams, still young but wise and triumphant. I wanted to think I could be with her—even though it was becoming clearer that I *was* going away; I just didn't know for how long.

Now she was here—the real person who drove with my mom over an hour from Minneapolis to the small jailhouse in the middle of the plainest town in Minnesota, where I was being held before my case came up. I knew she was coming, but I could never be prepared. My hair and sparse beard that sprouts in odd patterns just couldn't be right enough. We had been writing letters during the whole year I was in the county.

I had a friend go and find her. I couldn't help but tell her about the Hennepin County Jail with the green roof, old and rotten little corners that felt haunted. I told her about the nightmares I would have: waking up in sweats, realizing I was still there on a bunk, in a dorm that smelled like bologna and orange peels. It was a sober experience that humbled and reconfigured me. She sent me a picture of her in the red graduation gown with her university degree. It was evidence of the obvious contrast in the directions the two of us had taken in our lives. It helped me create a delusion that somehow even in my delinquency I could live vicariously through her light. The background had changed dramatically from when we used to drink whatever beer we could steal from our parents' refrigerators and sit in a cabin throwing abstract teenage philosophy in the air and letting it float with the cigarette smoke.

I got her high once, and she had to leave to go freak out in the bedroom of her parents' cabin. The next day she looked at me like I had sold her a bag of bricks in a TV box. She would smoke the cigarettes she had packed away for the quiet, sophisticated moments on the swing by the lake, or on the porch of the lodge after the lights went out, underneath the electric bug zapper. She called them *grettes*. I teased her about how she manipulated the word so naturally, so cool and matter-of-factly, even though I came with an entire lexicon of word manipulations that I know she couldn't help but think were a little silly sometimes. But she put up with me just like I would've put up with anything she brought up there with her. I might've playfully flirted with her about her slang, but there was always this genuine comfort I had around her, this relief I didn't have to be the character I played in the hierarchy of the world I came from. I had lots of friends, but even though my guys were my guys and the girls were my people, I didn't really like all of them. Some of them had been forced on me through alliances in grimy friendship politics—compared to this girl, who felt like someone I'd known for many lifetimes. I often wished I could have up and left with her, leaving all the politics and treachery behind me.

The first time I ever spoke to her, she and a bunch of the

other kids who came every year to the clusters of cabins in northern Wisconsin were jumping off the float in the lake. I was trying to navigate an old paddleboat with a friend who had come up with my family from the city. The whole group swam up on the paddleboat, and she swam up with the rest of the young strangers. She asked us with the most genuine smile if we were "Straight Edge" kids, maybe because my friend had long bangs that came over his eyes. We told her, "No!" despite not really knowing what being Straight Edge was; in fact, there was definitely nothing straight edge about us. But despite the question, there was a magnificence that was obvious about her, that made her that much different from the rest of the kids hanging on to the edge of that paddleboat. We weren't sure about some of those kids, but we wanted to know *her*. We started going there every year after that.

We would take these walks through the odd trailer park that was strangely adjoined to the resort, walk slow, and listen to each other talk about all the stuff happening in our lives. I used to get these weird butterfly flutters before we went each year, scared to death she wouldn't receive me the way she had sent me off the previous year. She was good at keeping in touch, did her best to keep things constant—at least for the first couple of years. I wasn't so good at writing back, though. I may have written back once; I always had a whole lot I wanted to say to her, but I was so worried I would sound stupid and less cool than I was trying to be. I was worried I wouldn't sound like the rebellious and dangerous city kid I tried to appear to be.

We used to sit in the lodge, a little older than kids, a little too inexperienced to be grown, with the same songs on the jukebox every year. It played a catalog of cornball country I didn't otherwise know really existed: "There's a Tear in My Beer," or "Mr. Bojangles" or anything by Garth Brooks or Alan Jackson. One year "Achy Breaky Heart" played over and over along with a cache of the commercial oldies meant to be apolitical, not meant to drive anybody crazy, but did anyway. Every once in a while "Stand by Me" came on. "Don't you like this song, though?" "Yes—of course I do." When it got cold at night, she used to tuck her hands in the sleeves of her sweatshirt and fold her arms across her body to stay warm.

|||||||||||||||||||||||||||||||||

NOW HER ARMS WERE FOLDED in a similar way, not for warmth, more likely to protect her from something else. We didn't know how long we had. It could be an hour, it could be twenty minutes—it all depended on how many visitors showed up to see their people. There were only four visiting booths, so there was always the possibility for congestion. She came with a smile, soft freckles, and a light emanating from her eyes. She came in with a familiar summer sun in her hair I hadn't seen for myself in so long. Most of my day I would be somewhere in the jail, playing cards or reading, windows frosted over, blocking the sun and everything else in the world. My body was taking up space, but I really wasn't anywhere at all. I was transporting, getting ready for a crossover in time and space that I didn't yet understand. But here behind glass, locked in a box, squished between walls with the love of my life sitting across from me, I was trying to recompose myself. So much of my summer had centered on this visit. And she was the pretty face she had always been, the something beautiful we all want, we all envision for ourselves when we are growing up, sitting in front of all the ugly I had made out of my life.

Her smile changed fast. Only a few sentences in, after the basics of "You look good," "Yeah, you too," "How are you?" "I'm making it" were through, and she and I had to start saying to each other what she had come across an entire country to say. The tears started to come to her face, the genuine heart-wrenching tears I only knew in the privacy of my pillow. They made obvious how badly I had fucked up this time. Those tears meant that the game was over for me. They meant there might be a life waiting for me separate from a jail or a prison—even if it only were to exist in the alternate universe of hopefulness. They were cried about who I used to be, someone who *was* rebellious but not so dangerous at all, scrawny and kind once.

We tried to talk about the people in our lives—the ones we

both knew and the ones the other only knew from the other's letters over the past year, or from a phone call or on the lodge porch years before any of this. One of her best friends came with her and was outside with my mom. My mother had made this very same trip at least once, sometimes twice, a week for all the weeks I had been here. She believed that's what you did for people you love: you support them when they're in turmoil. My mother and father both understood it—and the girl who was sitting across from me did, too. I did, however, wonder what her friend waiting outside thought of this trip, about the person she never met who her best friend came to a jailhouse in the middle of nowhere to see.

I told her about my friends, the ones she had met the last year I had been to the cabin. There was the one who had joined the Marines, and my best friend who just up and moved to the East Coast to get away from all the things that were happening— the explosion whose force was too great to keep him and his new family around. And I told her about all of the others who had figured out for themselves that the bonds they had with me weren't strong enough to keep them from running off.

I told her about what I was reading—Hermann Hesse and Jack Kerouac, Dostoevsky and Steinbeck, anything I could get my hands on. I thought I was the shit, that I had become in ten months the cliché of the convict who found himself in books during the grind of doing time. She had already read them all by the time I got to talking about them, so she was amused by my sudden enlightenment. I told her I started reading the Bible, and how I was mad at myself for ignoring it all those years. In the panic of being locked up, I had no idea what I was supposed to believe; I was just absorbing anecdotes and phrases as they flowed into my world. I used to show off when we were younger by puking out the small bits of Nietzsche I understood and free-styling off the so-much-of-him I didn't understand. She had told me in a letter a few months earlier that maybe I should've read Nietzsche *after* I read the Bible—she was probably right. It was probably another example of outsmarting myself, skipping a step to have what was on the other side, missing context while trying to nuance the subtext. Before she left, she would leave me a stack of books: Kafka's "The Trial" and "The Metamorphosis"; Faulkner's *Absalom, Absalom* and *Light in August*. And she left me *Farewell to Arms*—there had to be the tragic love story snuck into the pile waiting to be discovered.

She told me about her family, her parents' irreconcilable differences, how she wouldn't take sides. She told me about her sister in Germany, figuring out things about her own life. And she told me about her grandma, the woman I had hardly ever seen, sitting in the cabin out on the point. How she was able to spend some time with the woman she called her idol—precious moments of reflection during her most recent trip back to the resort. They were reflections I could still appreciate, that came to me sometimes in confused rhythms and patterns obstructed behind two-inch-thick glass and the click that recorded everything I tried to say on the phone to the people I loved.

She told me about how big some of the younger kids at the lodge were becoming, how the ones with *Little* as a prefix for their name weren't so little anymore. She also told me about the girl we both knew from that itty-bitty town in Illinois that could be hard to pronounce after a few beers, the one who didn't quite live in the same universe as we did the other fifty-two weeks of the year but who genuinely had a big heart, and for the most part kept most of her particular small-town judgments to herself. She would sometimes look at us funny when we drank beer or smoked cigarettes. The year before, she had come up to the lodge pregnant, married to a guy in one of the armed services. This year a divorce was imminent. She said that maybe she should have given that girl the birth control speech instead of the one she had given me the year I came up and was on the phone every day waiting on pregnancy results from my girl back home. I sloshed a whole bag of quarters in the pay phone just to get the news that she wasn't pregnant. Back then I never expected circumstances could make it where being a father might be impossible: it's tough to make babies in jail.

We reflected on that for a moment, and then she told me out of the blue that my English teacher from high school was waiting outside. It was a huge surprise, but more anticlimactic than anything. Normally it would have generated a pleasant sort of excitement that this man who hadn't had me in class in six or seven years remembered me enough to drive the hour and a half to see how I was doing in the tumult I was in and to drop books off for me. It would have garnered much more appreciation on any other day except on the one when this woman—who had been a girl most of the time I had known her, who I loved and compared every other girl I ever knew to, who I was fatally in love with—was here face to face with me from across the world, many realms and dimensions separating our realities. I needed every minute I could get with her when the pieces of matter that connected us were breaking into infinitely smaller pieces, and we had no idea where either of us would drift. Neither of us knew what was going to happen—in her life, in my life, with us—or who we would be in the overall contexts of our individual lives. Especially after years in a cage made me into what it would, or how kids and real-life success would make her. Or how either of us would transform when family died, priorities changed, and we all had shuffled on down the line in each other's worlds.

She asked about the case, but I knew my mom had already told her everything there was to know. I had been beaten emotionless from all the dimensions of fear and uncertainty, the life or death, the right now or forever. I was digesting it, numb from all the emotions. It was hard for me to dredge up the kind of feelings she may have been searching for. I didn't know how to tell her what happened—just that it wasn't supposed to be like this. I told her bad things just happen even when you expect such a different outcome. I told her how ready I had been to find some different directions, that I had just pushed it a little too long. I told her I never intended for it to happen, that it was never in my heart to let it happen. It just did.

||||||||||||||||||||||||||||

WE USED TO GO ON THESE "BEAR HUNTS." All the kids who could still be out after dark would go out on the lone two-lane road leading to the resort, without flashlights or adult supervision, out past the scant light of the cabins or where the trailers couldn't light the road. We walked on asphalt in the unrecognizable black void. None of us knew what was out there, watching and waiting. Talking about the future and shucking our shrinking attachments to our lives as kids. She was more bound by them than I was—at least my dumb ass thought so—but her vision for what she could be was much greater than I was prepared to consider for myself. I had started playing with the fatalistic notion of dying young, shaking the things that were hard for me to grasp about getting older, having kids, paying bills—being not so cool—having to be what I was going to be instead of just talking something into reality.

There was always someone who would run up ahead and wait. It was an exercise in blind faith, trusting there wasn't a crew of foraging bears cutting across the road or waiting in the brush along the side. After a few minutes people wouldn't notice the missing person crouched down waiting for everyone else to catch up. Then bang!—he or she would jump up and startle the shit out of everyone. This happened for years, from one group of kids to the next group of kids. Sometimes there would be a few other kids, but mostly it was me, my friend, and her. Then eventually it was just the two of us, and the allure of confronting a bear took a backseat to sitting at the kitchen table in one of the cabins. Or else we took walks to the dump and sat on large rocks or a broken air conditioner, and she smoked those "grettes" and I smoked something else. She told me her favorite trees were willow trees. I didn't know a person could have a favorite tree. I don't think I was even sure exactly what a willow tree was then. I thought I knew everything else, though. And she listened; nobody else was watching, judging how it sounded or if I was full of shit.

One year, a month after leaving the cabin, Justin got shot in the neck, dropped on a boulevard in front of some of the guys. He stopped breathing, his heart stopped beating, and they told us all he was dead. But he came back to life. He was a little wobbly, but he could walk, a little spacey but not brain-dead like they said he might be. It changed all of us. I know it especially changed my life. And when I came back to the cabin the next year I was different; I saw the world a little darker, and a little less merciful. She was different, too, though: her world got bigger, and she knew more people, had new experiences that made her perspective all that more interesting. The strictures that bound her to her youth were starting to break off. But out of nature, we gravitated back to each other, had new stories to tell, new people to be.

And that week, like so many of those vacations, insulated me from a relentless, unforgiving world outside of them. At home I was starting to feel stuck, starting to worry about the crew and how long it would be until the next inevitable fragmentation. Where would we all end up? It was something I had come to expect. Feelings changed and throats got cut—and truthfully, I had been one of the worst cutthroats of the bunch sometimes. And what would happen at school? The pattern of failure already in full swing, what was waiting at the end? We had already been through this so many times. At the cabin it didn't really matter: it was mostly about being with this girl who read great books and listened to cool music, who had a perspective I'd never listened to before—gentle and well-intentioned and meant for me—which I had too much pride to say how much I appreciated.

The people at the jail started ducking in every few minutes, sweating us to start winding down because there were a lot of people waiting. And I still had my English teacher waiting his turn, who I'm sure didn't realize he might be stealing a half-hour from the visit I'd waited to get my whole life: the "you meant something to me" visit, the "what you felt wasn't imaginary" visit.

And the tears came from the gut again and overwhelmed her as she tried to say what she had meant to say, what she came from so far away to say. But the tears shocked even her, interrupted what was supposed to be her declaration—tears that no woman besides my mom had ever shed for me, genuinely shed out of love for me, even as wretched as I had become.

They shocked me especially, suffocated my cool. I had never seen them before. They embarrassed me, and I didn't have an adequate response to the emotion. I had scripted so much of what I wanted to say, things that had to be said, but I had no script for this. Even after the blunt hammer of sorrow and consequence had busted me down and broken me open for what I was, I was still trying to play that cool, like her wet face didn't affect me in the earth-shattering way it actually was. The water started gathering in my eyes, too. But for one of those reasons I couldn't understand, after I had already cried so many life-changing tears into a pillow and broken down into the innumerable pieces I was only delicately holding back in place, instead of sharing my tears with hers, and breaking back down into pieces, I started laughing. It was an insecure, unprepared laugh, embarrassed at seeing one of the strongest people in my life show her vulnerability in my presence, vulnerability for me—because of me—and I was too afraid to reciprocate. I was too afraid I might melt into a puddle and not be the person I wanted her to see. And after I got past all the prepared "See, I told you how dangerous all of this was—I told you how real my life was," I was left simply with the fear to say I was scared—of going away forever, of getting old and dying, and of everything about the madness that was in front of me.

She told me she loved me. She told me I had taught her so much, that I meant so much to her, that I helped her become who she was. I should have let her help me become something other than what I was, learned more from her. I was crushed because I had lived as though there would always be enough time for things to happen. Now I was teetering on the world ending, and the beautiful correspondence we'd carried on over the turbulent months before, where she had been so honest and full of heart, had come to this moment. And I was still too scared to admit I wasn't so cool and unaffected. At that moment, as tears gushed from her face and the reality of the moment became clear—a visit that might not ever come again—we were face to face at the precipice of our young lives and at the most profound levels of uncertainty over all the dueling entities in our universe: freedom or a cage, sanity or madness, and life or death were laid out in between us, taking our cumulative inexperience and trying to make sense. We were trying to offer hope to each other and say good-bye without actually saying it, or giving in to it, without admitting that was what we were doing. None of the ideas or proclamations either of us ever made on a bear hunt or drinking a beer on the porch of the lodge ever added any insight to right now—in the physical separation between her, only a few steps from the sun glaring off of cars in the parking lot, going in one direction, and me making the trek back deep inside myself where I had already been for so many months, going in the other.

We sat for a couple of tough minutes, plenty to say, no words to fill the space, just still snapshots of the other to take with us where we went. They were vivid and lively enough for me to internally negotiate with while my high school English teacher talked to me about Gatsby and the irony of my tenth grade how-to project about robbing the nearby Burger King. I would take these shots back with me—still dim to the reality of my destiny—to a bunk I had only kind of made into a home. She would take her last glimpses with her on that return trip to Minneapolis and would soon be on an airplane and from the sky see the green roof of the Hennepin County Jail, the building I had told her had haunted me for so many months. Then they would go with her on her life-changing pilgrimage through Europe—London, France, Monaco, Barcelona, Italy, Austria, Germany (with her sister)—the places too endless to encapsulate, when in the midst of exploration, the snapshot might get lost, obscured, or refigured in the chaos of her self-discovery.

I remember feeling sick, gagging on reality and the toxin of jail, looking in the mirror, seeing someone look back who was starting to understand the world that might exist had he seen himself as anything other than doomed for so many years. Even the earlier version of that person thought doom just meant crossing over, escaping. Now the doom had an actual physical result: it *was* something to dread, something about the things he loves, and full of the terrifying possibilities he had always done his best to avoid. And there was the realization that nothing he ever put in was ever enough to hold him up in that water, heavy and violent, falling in sheets from the sky. People may hold him up for so long, but soon their strength just wasn't enough to keep him from submersing.

Walking out, I couldn't tell her I was in love with her, that I needed her to love me.

It was the love I could never admit but had secretly always hoped for. She was the girl I wanted, who wanted me, too. My obsession with tragedy always seemed such a profound thing that gave meaning to the melancholy I felt my whole life, until I got right up to it and realized the limits to those choices— the no-way-out end of the story hurts. The narrowing existential platform aches; it says that someone else is going to marry this girl, is going to have the huge party with all of his friends. Someone else is going to have the pretty babies who look up at them, who have no fathoming that this moment, this visit, ever happened, or that the tears flowed so gracefully and bruised so easily, or that they had ever come to their mother's face over someone or something other than their dad. I guess it wouldn't be tragic if it didn't hurt so obviously.

She sent me a letter she had written a few hours after the visit. It was the letter I had always wanted her to send me. She told me she would take me around the world with her, that to all of the places we had talked about going she'd take me with her in her heart. She said she'd see me in her dreams. She said she hoped I would be able to find some peace. She said it seemed like I was almost there (I probably wasn't; I'm still not). She told me she was a better person for having known me. I knew she would have done all right without all of the bullshit I distributed in her direction. She told me how her emotions after the visit came in waves, like a surreal rush of feeling. I wanted to tell her that meant she was doing some of this time, too—that realizations come and aren't necessarily even rooted completely in any sort of reality. I had brought her into the cyclone with me, and I knew that was unfair. It was more bullshit she didn't deserve.

By the time she came back from Europe, renewed and reborn, getting ready for life to start, I had been through a wringer. I was trying to figure out if I wanted to live like this or die, whether I had done enough with my life to make the statement I wanted to, or if any of it really mattered anyway. A gavel thundered and a number too great for me to hold on to exploded at me, blackened both of my eyes and swelled them shut in darkness, hiding the future from me. The number would be my burden—it would be my life, a rebirth into a world I didn't know yet. I had been reincarnated so many times throughout the course of my life on Earth, and this would be the most profound thus far.

The next time I heard from her was a letter I received after I was already in prison, doing orientation at St. Cloud, switching in and out of a real-live cage, moving in the tide of human bodies, trying to figure out how I was going to adjust to all of the things I would never see or experience again. I was acclimating myself to the not-so-subtle aesthetics of living in hundred-year-old buildings and being just another soul crushed under the force of a deteriorating penal system. She was in her own transition. She ended up back out in Boston, figuring out where she would live and where she would work. I was glad to hear her voice. She wrote, "I hope to hear from you soon." And she gave me an address to send my next letter. I wrote a numb letter back. I told her about the time I got and the thumping I got from the kitchen sink, and about how crossing over into the new world that was going to be my home was going to superimpose itself over all the other places I'd been in the universe. I wrote believing there would be a reprieve, that the decades the state wanted from me would be shortened and that I could be Lazarus. I told her it wouldn't be the last time she heard from me, that I would tell her more as my new life unfolded in front of me. I took the letter and sent it out, waiting on its response.

I always knew it would come, even for several years afterward. I thought, and then hoped, I would come back from my prison job one afternoon out of the hundreds and then thousands of afternoons, and I would see it next to one of the letters from my grandma. I thought I would get something, something that spoke to the abruptness of her disappearance, but three years later it never came. Five years down the road she seemed just another figure off in the distance. Ten years, and it was like she never was, except for the purple scribbles on the letter she wrote the few hours after she left me in the county jail, which sits in my footlocker next to Faulkner and Kundera, under the bunk in my cell.

⸻

AT MANY DIFFERENT TIMES during the stretch that became the After Death period of my life, I would daydream about things. It became a complex world where people I knew were only capable of being how I could conceive them in my imagination. Trying to stay relevant, usually I would place myself at some prominent point, but the physical universe would always morph reality into something completely different from what I imagined it. It was as though I were trying to wish things into becoming what I needed them to be. Regardless of how I reconstructed things in my mind, old girlfriends still ended up married, or with babies, or in strange relationships with people I couldn't stand. I still had the grand constructions of a miraculous reentry, where the world wouldn't have a choice but to recognize my success. I could come back stronger and better than I ever was—instead of just older and punch-drunk from all of the years. It's crazy to think how people who could have been so central to who you believed you were become almost imaginary figures in the ethos, become characters in a book you read once, who go away and never come back but are somewhere at the same time we are here—wherever here is.

Is the reflection worth anything? Just because I was the dopey somebody she had a crush on once, when youth made it all seem a more serious fire within her than it turned out to be? Even if she was the girl who for some strange reason wanted to know me, even after only giving her the parts of myself I wasn't too scared to show her? I couldn't possibly have expected her to stay. I just wanted her to. It just was amazing to me that she couldn't smell the decay, the insufficient future like most of the other girls in my life had: she couldn't smell the descent. And I got those butterflies because she was that girl I was afraid would one day find out how out of sorts and ready to fail I was, that she'd get that great realization and move on. And then I would see all the pretty girls on TV letting dirtbags—filthier and more ragged in their approach to life than I ever was—get them pregnant, bring them to tears, and then move on to another pretty girl just as shook as the last one.

I started to realize a long time ago it was never fair to call this person the love of my life, especially after all that time passed, but maybe it's because it's so damn hard to see things different from when I left them—like the views of the city I'd seen growing up, from random angles on top of abandoned buildings, or from windows of houses I only ever looked through once, or horizons from hilltops that made colors move like I never saw again. I can remember the images, even rustle up feelings associated with them, but I have no idea where any of them are now, or if they even still exist. And of all the teenage crushes that grow up and dissipate into the air, why should this one mean anything other than it did? Probably because I went away, and no one else took her place. Life went on for everybody but stayed the same for all of us who got our feet stuck in the concrete of these institutions.

But I still think about her, even as others have come through my life. I always have. I wonder where she is now—who she married, what she became, what her kids looked like. Did she still go to the cabin? How would she act if she saw me again as the person I was now after being where I was all these years? I was told once about someone we grew up with who went away for a long time when we were young: "He's always gonna think the world and everyone in it is the same as when he left it." I wonder if that's how those out there feel about us. Maybe that's why so many people out there don't return letters or pick up the phone when I call. I wonder if some of those people would rather we just stay the same person, the same image as they remember—that way they can love or hate us or stay as indifferent as they ever wanted to.

At that last visit I remember her asking me if I remembered what her favorite tree was. I didn't; I was too preoccupied with my own world, my own persona, to remember. I was ashamed of all the things I *could* remember—names, dates, times, and contexts—but I couldn't remember something I'm sure she wholly intended me to. Maybe if I had remembered she would have stuck around. Maybe if I hadn't turned down that certain street or gone out that particular night; maybe if I hadn't quit that particular job; or maybe if I hadn't protected my pride so much or had been tougher and less afraid; maybe if I had just been braver. There would always be something else I should have done, the do-over that would never be done over. Things happen all the time, and I catalog them as things she might've laughed at—songs I wondered if she would like, if by now they probably just reminded her of other people or experiences. In the darkness, I had run up ahead hastily to see what was there and came back to where she was waiting, just to tell her there was just more darkness.

Sixteen

WALKING INTO
THE REST OF MY LIFE

I SPENT HOURS on the transport bus watching the green pan-orama move by. I saw things I had never seen before say hello and good-bye forever. I had a guy next to me who told me he was from the "Hundreds" in Chicago but had lived in Minnesota since he was twelve, telling me his entire criminal history. I had my hands in cuffs, locked to a chain at my waist and the shackles on my feet. The metal on my wrist was already starting to cut and bruise. Although I was already beginning to harden myself to that sort of entanglement, my body was still soft and sensitive to the discomfort of steel on flesh. It was like this in every jail or prison I went to: there were always voices that never stopped telling me their gangster-ass life stories. They were sometimes heroic, sometime notorious, but always incredulous to me. They were talking, but none seemed to understand I was walking into the rest of my life; at least I told myself that. There was no looking beyond thirty-plus years. "I woulda never got this much time at the crib, Joe," the guy next to me told me as though I was still listening.

It was a sunny day at the beginning of fall, as we rode past grass and old, very full trees—until all I saw was old red brick and rifles poking out of guard towers above us. The dungeon doors closed as the bus rumbled through. It was like driving through a ghost town, with shut-down factories and warehouses. Decaying brick and lime buildings—Old World symmetry and symbolism. When the bus touched down, a procession of bodies leaked out in single file, strides shortened from the dig of shackle at our heels. I came off the bus into the new world of Stillwater Correctional Facility, the ancient building that was going to be my new home. Seeing these walls made me believe all prisons were like this: old, majestic, mean, and a little nasty. The mean and nasty part was probably true everywhere, but these walls were the only prison walls that mattered in my life now. They were the ones that blocked off the future. A guard said to one of the transport officers, "They just get younger and younger every year, don't they?" I was twenty-two, but I looked like I was fifteen. There was fresh fall air but no sun, just more invisible straight lines pointing toward another cage.

I spent hours in an old warehouse area in the back of one of the many old prison buildings that stood on the grounds where they stripped us down in steel holding cages. The routine this time was done by a woman walking around with her hands on her belt and an eighties-style part running through the middle of her hair. People were still talking. There were always enough men who had been here already to do all the talking for the rest of us. I just let the mercurial winds move me in the direction they were headed. Some of the men clearly had to talk about something, just to fill the empty air. There seemed to be a need for them to vocalize the bargains they were making with themselves over the rest of the time they had to do. Some guys broke their bids into pieces, from closed to medium to minimum to work release. Other guys swore their lawyers would get their case thrown out: "I won't even be here by next summer." When they asked me how long I had, and I told them over thirty years, which meant I would have to do at least twenty-three years, they all asked how old I would be when I got out. I told them I'd be forty-five. "You'll still be young. You can still have kids." It was a usual response, as though having kids was the litmus test for what a person's life was worth in here.

We sat there for so long that guys started reusing their material or reignited something that had been exhausted hours before. They name-dropped people I had never even heard of or rode down on the young kid with all the awkwardness and conspicuousness of someone with some kind of sex case. Anybody trying to push attention away from himself had an easy time driving down on the kid wearing extra-tight state jeans and Velcro shoes. Everybody had opinions as to how the next several years would be for that guy, without really knowing anything at all.

When I finally got to the dual steel doors leading into my block, there was a wall of men in state blues and grays, as though waiting for us. They opened the steel doors and we were walked through the wall of people. The block was a spring of activity and movement. All I saw were trapped mosquitoes in a glass jar, standing there, leering, trying their best to project an air of entitlement of having even the most basic experience here versus those of us who were seeing all of this for the first time.

I didn't recognize anyone. The guys walking in front of me were greeted by what seemed like every other person who came by us. I sensed there were eyes in the weeds somewhere looking for something vulnerable, but I was too numb to care or notice. I just tried to stay as emotionless—and with as little expression as I could—as I moved in slow motion in a time-lapsed whirl of running lines of light and bodies. We got stopped at the desk to get a bag of linens to take with us to our cells. They told us it would be a day or two before we got the rest of our property. I didn't have much of anything besides maybe a few pictures, some ramen noodles, and notebooks with stress-filled poems of desperation that were meant to be my manifesto. It wouldn't matter much if I went a couple more days without them.

There was a strange little man with a red beard and potbelly standing at my side when I was waiting for a key and room assignment. "Hey, I'm such and such. I'm not a pervert or anything but . . ." This might've been the first test. Everything I did was for the first time; my whole life was brand new in an extremely old place. I was brand new, but this world had always existed. It had its history and stories that preceded anything I understood about it. Real men had quarried the limestone foundations with me in mind a hundred years ago. This wasn't orientation or intake: it was my life now. At first I thought I might have to take off right then, but I tried to stay stoic, not show any feeling at all—after all, I had been hit with a sledgehammer. There was no more feeling left in me, except devastation.

I went up to my cell on the third tier, right next to one of the guys I came on the bus with and down a few cells from another. They were the only people I even sort of knew. They both had guys at their bars, catching up with who did what and what happened to whom. I walked into the cell, mostly empty except for the bunk, the toilet, a desk bolted to the wall, and all the unnecessary junk left behind from whoever was here before me, toilet paper rolls, crumpled papers with inconsequential scribblings on them. There were a couple books left on the counter. One of them was *City of Anger* by William Manchester, a novel about number running in Baltimore. It was all I had in the emptiness of that first night. I went to dinner and sat at a table with a guy I didn't know who came with us on the bus. Neither of us said anything to the other. We just kept our heads down and ate the turkey ham and macaroni and cheese.

I went back to my cell. Since I didn't know anyone, I didn't have anything to do. I didn't have a PIN number yet, so I couldn't call my family to let them know I was here. I opened *City of Anger* and started reading, hardly following anything because I was too obsessed with the scenarios in my head that took me away from this place. After the evening count I heard my neighbor yelling to all the other people with TVs to turn to specific channels when something came on. Then there would be dialogue, running commentaries on what "that bitch was really trying to say." At one point I shut off the light and sat in darkness.

I looked out the windows at the yard, envisioning myself walking endless laps around the track. And I thought about being propelled from the womb of my childhood into this

world I didn't understand, without any of the friends I counted on, no property of my own—just a physical body that hadn't
completely grown up yet, behind bars that showed no mercy
in sight. Summer was over. I didn't know what seasons meant
behind those concrete partitions. All the hopefulness, the
prayers to reemerge, the metamorphosis in concept were cold
and dark and mostly quiet by night, but busy, filled with clanks
of doors being closed and different kinds of bells, with muffled demands through old loudspeakers by day. It was a steel-
reinforced cocoon that suffocated instead of transformed most
of its inhabitants.

This would be the natural time where I would spit out my
visceral reactions to all of the cliché initiations of prison. It
would typically be the time when I would describe the sound
and feeling of a cell door closing behind or of walking back
from a visit where I couldn't follow my people out the door—
but I don't remember that stuff. I remember being a robot that
moved mechanically and emotionlessly from one space to the
next—my cell to the phone, to the yard, to the gym, to the chow
hall, back to my cell. Everything existed in compartments. I
worked in one room, I slept in the cell; I went to the gym in
another compartment, the yard in another. It made the place
feel that much smaller. As time went on, I would get used to it
shrinking slightly more all the time. I went to the yard and was
sick by how small it was, thinking it would be my only perspective outside of the buildings forever.

The next day my neighbor gave me the info I needed to buy
a TV and some of the other things I might need, like sweats and
thermals. This way he could yell over to me at two in the morning to switch the channel whenever *Thong Song* or *Like Whoa*
came on. He let me use his PIN to call home to tell my family
I had moved again. I had another new place to get used to and
try to understand. When I got the TV, I watched baseball, as
though I might attach myself in some way back to something
that meant so much to me as a child. I stayed up all of most of
every night for a while, trying not to miss anything I had missed
over the entire year I was in the county. It was like a whole new
world had sprouted since I'd been away. Out in the world my

friends were having babies and getting new jobs, moving into new places where addresses and new phone numbers were no longer passed along. People told me they would all go away eventually; I just prayed a few would hang on, though, for a while. Mom came out. She still believed, still premised much of her optimism on an idea that relief was coming, that something unfair had happened and some sort of energy source in the universe was going to right it. She swore that this wasn't our fate, that this wasn't the end of our journey. The length of those first days started making things feel like maybe it was.

I would go back to my cell, which after a while had developed a little more personality. I had pictures taped to the gray square on my wall designated for such personal things. They were pictures of friends and family, of the strange months before I got locked up, with that hurt, strained expression on my face—a futureless child. Now I felt like a dead man, pretending to myself that it was temporary.

||||||||||||||||||||||||||||

I APPLIED for a few different jobs and ended up with a job as a tutor for men with reading and math levels between fourth and tenth grades. It meant moving to a new cell block. My guy from the streets was over there, but he only had a couple more months left on a year and a day bid. They moved me into the cell closest to the guard desk, and it was probably the worst group of guards in the joint at the time. They asked if I would position my TV on Sundays so that they could watch football. I didn't even respond to that. It was also right by the phones so as people waited to get on, they stood outside my room. There was always someone asking to use a pencil or a pen, or a piece of paper, or all three at once. They'd ask what I was watching on TV, ask about scores and about pictures on the wall. The unit was always so packed, so I never got the chance to move into another cell on a different galley.

Waking up in the morning and being in that classroom was just about as unbearable as anything I had ever endured. I was new so I got all the guys the instructor considered to be the most difficult. I was assigned three students in the morning and another three in the afternoon. Most of the time they didn't want to do anything, so they just talked about videos and fucking. Mostly they just talked about fucking the woman who was the instructor. One of my students was a young Mexican kid who I got along with pretty well, but he didn't have much of an attention span or any kind of scruples either. When the instructor would turn away for anything, he made not-so-whispered comments, certainly loud enough to vibrate far enough for her to hear them: "I bet she's got good pussy."

"I can hear you—I know it's you because you're the only one with a Spanish accent in the class." And I'd be sitting next to him, with my head lowered as if complicit in the absurdity. He'd briefly go red with embarrassment at his exposure and then defensive as though it was not him and he was hurt by the accusation. Then she'd suspend him for a few days, and he'd hold his head low and have me fetch him his workbooks so he could do problems while he was off to win back her favor in hopes of not getting fired again.

He was by no means the only one pushing boundaries—it was the entire classroom, even tutors, too. When she used the board to work through math problems, there were students who would jump up to a few feet behind her and go right into humping motions with facial expressions until she turned around and the humper bolted back to his seat. This was not a one-time thing: it was constant. At least once a week she would have the talk—about how "things are getting a little carried away with the sexual harassment stuff." She'd call out names and threaten to fire people.

I had one hefty student who wore a red beard like he was Amish, even though the hair on the top of his head had mostly escaped him, and he was still in his early twenties. He spent an entire afternoon explaining to me about his plans upon release to transgenetically crossbreed bovines into a sort of Super Cow. He went into all sorts of ridiculous details: from insemination to milking to beef yields that farmers could expect. It was *his* daydream, while most of the people in the joint had kingpin fantasies. My other two students sat on the sidelines making bestiality jokes.

It was way too heavy for me to endure. I already felt dead to the world outside, but now I felt like I was really dying, days and hours just wilting at the start of winter. And everything from that job, the cell, and most of the people in that block just seemed stuck. I would get a cringing burst of Uh-oh, thinking about being in that room as years evaporated. It made me cry to think about it, even though I thought all my tears had been cried out already from the months before. Thinking about becoming this place, the trap, all made me ill, and locking myself in at night still made me gag. I got lucky, though: one of the applications I put in when I first got there got me into the computer program and got me out of that class and out of that unit.

My parents and their friends would come to see me and ask me what living here was like. I was so numb and had nothing personal to share. All I could tell people was that it looked like Alcatraz, the tiers and the bars, steel married to concrete. I told Mom to dig out the old pictures from when we visited Alcatraz. We could take the same picture now.

Every morning there was a procession of condemned men walking in the same direction in royal blue coats and navy stocking caps to take their place in a slot that had always existed for them since this place was born. The first building here was a twine factory where men stood in rows and pumped out product. Now the products were different: upholstering furniture instead of rolling twine or picking cotton, folding balloons instead of shoveling coal. It was a machine, and any sense of individuality or human worth didn't exist. But it was hard trying to explain these things to my family without getting a heartbroken reaction that I was becoming too jaded and nihilistic. Guys were telling me these places are what they are: they would always exist, but we were the ones who came and went— lived and died. It was unceasing. I didn't want to believe that any buildings or ideas could outlive the human will. I thought it was a slave mentality. People were always telling me things as though letting me in on a secret. It was more that they just needed someone to hear what they thought they knew, because once people got to know them, they stopped listening. They were always looking for someone new to listen to their ideas. It was all something separate from me. I was different from them. My tragedy was different from theirs, I thought. My eyes were still too swollen for me to see.

I started to meet people, though—people whose eyes had opened after the swelling went down. There were also a whole lot of people who had given up and instead lived through their stories, exaggerations as large as the walls keeping us in. Of course, everybody had angles that with a little light stopped being so sharp and stopped seeming so dangerous. I linked up with an old stickup artist named K, who was also in the computer program. He was the grandson of Pretty Boy Floyd, the legendary pimp who was famous for once buying a Cadillac that he never shut off. This wasn't his first bid: he had an entire career of points in the criminal justice grid. He had fallen down so much, but he seemed to believe this was the last one. At thirty, he had a whole lifetime of self-inflicted disappointments. This was just another. He told me once, "I've robbed hundreds of people, and I don't mean snatching white people's purses. I mean real motherfuckers that will kill you."

His presence showed me some of the hidden angles of this place. He was just enough of an enabler, and just smart enough for where I was mentally then. I found out from him and others that a lot of times it was the ones who had been through the most who had the most realistic perspectives on suffering and perseverance. They are often the ones living in the dark corners we fell into. When he was locked up the first time his dad died, and during this bid his mom died. It made the climate of these experiences feel that much harsher. It was my first example of the things I could lose on my bid, but I still felt detached from them. They seemed like somebody else's burden then.

And even after seeing so many similar examples of how people fell down and tried to get their asses back up, or just stayed in the dirt, I still had those feelings. They were the feelings that I was sinking, or that the bombed-out crater I had created in my life was filling up with falling rainwater. I would wake up, and it felt deeper than it had the night before. I went to a psychologist, but they didn't have anything for how devastated I was at that point. Night became my time to meditate, a cold space to get dizzy from thinking about how I was going to gather what I could of myself and put "me" back together. I felt empty, again. It's not a feeling that I didn't care anymore; it's just that life and all of its components just started to seem hollow.

Young men tended to coat real-life with a layer of hip-hop excess. An older mentality seemed to overdraw lines of an old convict code. Some of it was respectable; other parts of it seemed like more sickness. I felt plenty sick already; I didn't understand yet that there are so many more levels to it. So I just let what was going to happen anyway go on without my interference. I let the sun come up and I let hours meld into one another until they were weeks and then months.

And then one afternoon I was sitting with K in a cell smoking weed, trying to feel free again, every so often looking at myself in the mirror saying, "Yeah, I remember you. You're still alive. I thought you were dead, but you're still there under a few layers of change and circumstance." We were laughing at something that probably wouldn't be funny again, the room still laced with smoke, getting ready to light up again. We were absent of any concern over the cops or anything else other than what I had done most every day of my entire free life, weaving in and out of these social ciphers. I started to drum up all sorts of the things my senses had forgotten, the subtle taste in my mouth, a nuanced unease that always came, and a basic human experience just like sitting in a friend's living room watching episodes of *Jenny Jones* or *Ricki Lake*. Things were still, and the world hadn't fallen down on me. I was intact and the "before" and "after" didn't exist at that moment.

But on an unexpected round, a guard passing out daily movement passes snatched us up. It made sense: we didn't even have a spotter. Handcuffs clicked around my baby wrists, my eyes red from mystery. I knew it wasn't anything real serious, but there would be a trip to the hole, a brand new experience for me. I failed the piss test and went to segregation. Segregation was the back half of one of the cell blocks, partitioned by a wall and an electric sliding door that opened and closed all day and night. The only thing that made it different was the black caging that dressed the tiers all the way to the ceiling to keep them separate, with bodies bouncing around in their boxes like the zoo, with nothing to do but yell and screech at anything moving, or at any of the other noises that responded back. Men glared from their cells, but nobody really gave a fuck. New people came back every other hour, sometimes more. People just wanted to see if it was anybody they knew, to have something to break their monotony. It wasn't a zoo, and these weren't animals; it seemed like the cages confused that distinction, though. And it was so much darker there. Even at 3:00, the afternoon sun blazing in, the cages made everything seem dark.

They stuck me in a cell—empty but for a bed, sink, toilet, and some linen. Long hours in a naked cell, it was prison inside of prison. I got looked out for and thrown a book, a romance novel no less, but it was there, and I needed something to read. I needed something for minutes to go by. The guy who gave it to me made sure I knew to get it back to him. A Danielle Steel paperback was a highly sought-out item back there. Everything felt cool until my high went away and the before and the potential after started to matter again. So I went back to one of the prisoner's most basic coping mechanisms: I slept. I was trying to time-travel through vast hours of mostly solitary time.

There was an inmate swamper, or janitor, on the galley and the officers made rounds, but most of that time it was just me and an empty cell. There was a peace in it that was most often disrupted by voices from outside ricocheting off of everything. People had homemade chessboards drawn out on sheets of paper with makeshift pieces made from anything random. Men, separated by bars and often by galleys and many cells, would yell out their moves. It never stopped, from breakfast until breakfast, someone was calling out "Move 24 to 31, move 7 to 13."

In the middle of the night the voices just kept vibrating. They played Drop Off, where one person created a scenario where another would get dropped off somewhere in the world with a set of items and conditions and given assignments. It was like 'hood Dungeons and Dragons. "What would you do? Say you get dropped off on Franklin and Portland at 4:00 a.m. in your prison clothes, but you ain't got no money, only a pen, and you have to get to Selby and Dale to take your driver's test at six. What would you do?" It was a series of never-ending scenarios with feedback and assistance from a whole gallery of faceless but very vocal opinions, coming from their own individual segregation cells. "First, what I'd do is take the pen and rob one of them boys at the red brick house, then take the weed and sell it to my guy who lives on Tenth, then borrow his car. If he don't borrow me his car, then I'll steal one, then break into Montgomery Ward's, get me some shoes, smoke me a blunt, and then take the test." Scenarios would meld to another and another, until the sun came back.

I would sit in my room, try sitting meditation, try lying-down meditation. I walked the eight feet on my floor back and forth in meditation for hours, my shadow moving in rhythm over a bare slice of light pointing into my room. It was the part of time that is most universal, that is most representative of the human being's capability to cope with it—the time by yourself when there is nothing outside of you physically to occupy you. It made me remember one of the voices on the tour at Alcatraz that explained how in the hole there, with a closing steel door that sealed off any light, they played a game where they took a button from their shirt and flicked it up in the air and then spun themselves in circles until they were dizzy. Then they would scour the cell until they could find the button. Then they'd start again.

I was trying to be mindful, trying to concentrate on each breath, but I couldn't stop thinking. I thought about girls I knew, or kids who were still babies being adults when I got out. I thought about names for my own unborn children. I thought about my generation and what our time was in relationship to those before. Mostly, though, I thought about a world that had no problem forgetting any of us ever existed. They built places like this so that they could do that. I thought I was kidding myself to believe people could ever feel empathy for a person in these places. It led me to think about being alone at the end of my life—wondering where all that time went.

I was only in segregation for fifteen days; guys I met spent months and months, sometimes a year or two, back there. There was a guy who just stayed back there until they released him into the world. They tried several times to kick him back out into general population, but it never lasted more than a day or two. I don't know if he was afraid of somebody or just weird around people, but he stayed until they took his Segregation Grays away and pushed him on out of the gates. Guys would get these mind-altering chunks of time, and I'd be salty and fucked up about it. Then the time would come and they'd get out, and within a few weeks or a month, it would be just like they never went away—compression, decompression.

I got out and went back to the computer program. I was ready to stay focused, even if I really didn't know why I was supposed to care so much. I figured it would all be obsolete by the time it mattered. I watched TV and ate a lot. I took pictures with a friend who came out to see me, and I noticed how chubby I looked. I was fifty-five pounds heavier than I was when I was originally arrested, and there wasn't much muscle to coincide with the fat. Instead of becoming better and more capable, I was becoming a slovenly mess. It was the real start of the bid. Any hopefulness I kind of had was smothered; there was no magic formula. I read *Executioner's Song* by Norman Mailer, and it only emphasized the anxiety I was reading to get away from. It solidified how far I actually was to getting back the old Me. It was hard to tell myself that old person didn't exist anymore. At other times I was glad because that person was pretty well broken and full of shit. I wanted to be this new person, with a chance to start my life over. But that wasn't real, and I had to figure out what I was going to do with my life if I didn't plan on going crazy. I looked around and everyone had a story about getting fucked by the system, or by their best friend, or the mother of their kids. Everyone had some loophole in their case that was supposed to set them free; they were all waiting

to get the old "them" back. They all had something better waiting on them—if they could just get out of this place. Only, some
of them had been relying or waiting on these things to happen
for many years. It is an early symptom of the disease. The disease of encagement.

Every day I hoped for new reaffirmations, a new burst of
identity and changing energy. There was the belief that as part
of the classic prison narrative I had already "found" myself and
was thus ready to leave. But most of that idea was just a part of
the bargain I made to get through a day or a week. Time was
showing itself to be much harsher. I didn't really know how
much yet. It wouldn't expose all of its intentions until the pain,
the time, and the loss got heavier.

Eventually, my world became a mostly never-ending succession of sleeping and waking, going up and down the same
hallway every single day. Holidays would come, and I would
call home and talk to friends and relatives. They would all have
encouraging things to say: "We hope you can be here for one of
these soon." And I would respond with my own hopeful affirmation, but my environment told the truth: "You've got thirty
years—this is what your holidays are." Everything lived in con-
tingency of the day I got out—which was a long time away. It
was time that even people who had already lived through that
kind of time didn't want to have to look that far into the future.
Then there were the people I talked to where I would mention something not so far off in the future, and there would be
an awkward pause; I knew then that even they knew all the
things I knew of the world were over. The most common question was still, "How old will you be when you get out?" When I
told them, I'd almost always get the same thing: "Oh, that's not
so bad, you'll still be young. A lot of men at that age have kids."

There was a feeling when I walked in that this was my future, getting used to something that was alien to me. The daily
meditation I had that doors would open and the nightmare
would end was fading. There were years in the way now—a
sense of permanence in that empty cell with the dust bunnies
living on the edges and in the corners.

Seventeen

THE ONLY ONE NOT THERE

I WAS TOLD ONCE that the two moments that matter the most are the birth moment and the deathbed moment. With grandparents, they are usually at our birth, and we hope to be at the other for them. My two grandmas were very different people who played very different roles in my life. One, Granny, I was just getting to know again. The other, Grandma A we called her, I was saying good-bye to. For both women, I was the only grandchild—later than hoped for, but certainly the answer to mutual prayers. Both of them were very doting, and who these women were in my life mostly had to do with opportunity, their involvement varying mostly due to the distances from me. Granny was the ball of energy I spent great chunks of my childhood with, the nearby emergency option for any kind of turbulence in the city, staying put just across the park. Though always close by, time and circumstance sort of obscured the bond between Granny and me. We were getting to know each other again through phone calls and the letters she sent every day.

Neither was much different from the other: both were small-town women who came of age in the era of the Great Depression, and much of the essential decisions in their lives was squeezed between the two Great Wars. Grandma A had a sense of humor, Granny did not. Not that Granny was so serious

all the time; Grandma A just had a timing and subtle delivery
Granny lacked. In many ways they were two different parts of
the same era. Granny was solitary; Grandma A was at her best
with family. Because Granny was so close, she was the one I
went to if I locked myself out of the house, or needed an emergency ride somewhere, or just felt like stopping by. Her house
was the cluttered time machine through which I could access
my father's history. It was a whole museum full of fifty years'
worth of gathered ephemera most people might not find much
value in: boxes of old stationery and ashtrays, decades of Cool
Whip and Country Crock containers hoarded in corners with
gallon water jugs and paper towel rolls. For a kid there was
endless wonder. Granny was the secret keeper, and if you were
one of hers, her house was like a vault you could crawl up into
and hide. Since I was her flesh and blood, I was in.

Grandma A was just as doting, even more affectionate. I
know she would have been as involved as much as she could have
been allowed, but she was anchored to her life with my grandfather in a small town on the border of Wisconsin and Iowa, a
place where the world moved a little slower. So her role as grandma was limited to a few days every several years. She wasn't
used to having very many choices in most aspects of her life.

She was now lying on a bed set up in her living room receiving hospice care, preparing herself to cross over. It was a
posture she had been accustomed to for so much of her life:
a ruined back from lifting old folks up and down at the retirement home, a broken hip or two, giant flat feet. Most of her
adult years were a succession or overlap of one illness to the
next—COPD, pneumonia, diabetes. She had been on disability
since she was fifty-two, and she was eighty-four now. After that
many years it wasn't so much that she had all of these problems; it was more that she thought she did. She was a classic
hypochondriac, and after a while it seemed like she had just
talked her body into really falling apart. Even as she was lying
on what was supposed to be a deathbed, the lines were blurry
as to what exactly it was she was dying of.

My mom had been making routine trips to see her, antici-

pating that the end was probably soon. To me, it was all something happening in another world, because even after three
years of my being locked up, neither she nor my grandfather
knew where I was or what had happened. My mom had been
slinging a narrative that I was going to college in Arizona, or
selling shoes, or trapping lizards in the desert, exactly where
the details came from I have no idea. In fact, there were narratives all over the place that filled in the gaps for relatives
or friends of my mom's who didn't know. She would bring up
names and tell me they said hello, and I would counter, "Do
they know where I am?"

"Oh no, they think you're working in New York."

"Why wouldn't you just tell them?"

"I just don't really want to have to start from the beginning
and explain everything again. It really is difficult having to tell
people you're in prison. It takes a toll." I think I could understand a little bit.

So her entire side of my family was completely oblivious
to what I was doing. Some thought I was in school, others believed I was volunteering my time in Jamaica working with un-
derprivileged children. There were so many other stories that
sprang up in defense of not having to say what was real. And
so there was my grandmother, mostly incapacitated, probably
wondering a little bit where her only grandchild was. I'm sure
in all of those visits from my parents she asked about me, and
my mom told her I was somewhere but was too busy to come
back. Instead I wrote a short letter for my mom to give to her. In
it I told her I was sorry I disappeared, and that hopefully soon
enough she would understand why I couldn't be there. Mom
hand-delivered it so there wouldn't be any proof as to where I
was sending it from. I guess I understand trying not to add any
unnecessary confusion to a time when they were looking for
some kind of closure.

I was expecting a visit from my mom. I was turning
twenty-four that day—another inconsequential number that

got obscured and blended in with the rest of them. It had all been planned: the meal, pizzas with crust made from loaves of bread, a jug of something we brewed into something nasty, and something simple to smoke. I came back in the afternoon from the vocational program I was in, ready to smoke something, ready to accept the inauguration of another year in one of the last places on Earth I wanted to be. It was the first birthday since I came down where I had friends to celebrate with. The previous two birthdays had come at points of transition where I was left to meditate on getting older inside these kinds of confined spaces. And while some of these friends were just meant to pass through without leaving anything indelible, I did have Cuzzo and D from the block, who were also trying to figure out how life was going to carry on now that they were here.

When I got back, there was a stack of mail sitting on my bed. There were naturally the birthday cards from my parents with the "We'll make it through this" stuff dripping from it like it were just common homesickness from being away at summer camp. My mom usually went back to the "I can remember the day you were born" theme. On the bed next to them was a card and letter from Granny—of course there was. (Unlike Grandma A, Granny knew where I was and what I was doing.) They were there with the familiar mailing labels for every day the Earth rotated. They were usually no more than a single page telling me about her day. Often they would just be about the weather or calls from telemarketers. At the bottom was the always comforting "Granny loves you!" They were probably not unlike the letters my dad and grandfather got from her during their trips to Vietnam and World War II. I'm not so sure she expected she'd be writing these notes for so many years, though. I knew she was probably sitting by her phone waiting for it to ring so she could give me her personal version of a happy birthday.

I was leaving to call her when Cuzzo and D and an old-school crook/megalomaniac showed up at my cell and snatched me up to give me the honorary birthday beatdown. It was a peculiar tradition that at least for a few years survived the dramatic lifestyle changeover. It was a usual sneak attack; I was alone in my room reaching for something. I turned my head just long enough to get slid in on and held on to for the other two to take licks to open parts of my body. D held my legs and gave me Charlie Horses. Cuzzo, just like every other birthday beatdown I ever got, picked out his spot on my left arm and doled out twenty-four hard and straight blows to that same area, leaving the rawest and most colorful bruises the day after. I struggled to fight back, but I just didn't have enough to fight off all three of them. Afterward they lifted me up and gave the hugs and expressions of love that usually come after. I never really understood why we were supposed to be touched by someone putting hands on us as some kind of ceremonial rite of passage. We'd done them so long and by then had just accepted their inevitability.

Other than the ass-whooping, I enjoyed the nominal attention I got because it was my day. People streamed in and out of my cell pretty much nonstop, bringing things and offering others. One of the guys was running around collecting stuff for the meal. There was a frenetic energy zipping through everything, even though I just sat in my cell as it was all happening, I looked at my mail again trying to get every last emotional gasp out of it before I put it away in a box somewhere.

I wanted to see if I could catch my family on the phone, but there was no answer, so I called Granny. Four rings and the voice of a little white-haired old lady answered with a hello. When the recording didn't pick up right away, she followed up with several more hellos. Sometimes she would talk to the electronic recording as though it were an actual operator, and if a call didn't go through right away, she would ask it questions and thank it when it did go through. I told her several times over the years that it wasn't a real person, but it was all so new to her that it took a while to accept it. After all, a lot of these kinds of things were new to her; it was the first touch-tone phone she ever owned. My parents bought it for her just so she could accept calls from me in jail. It was quite an adjustment; all the other phones in her house were still landlines with rotary dials.

When she answered, she started with an overemphasized "Happy Birthday!" and just as fast transitioned into a more somber voice. "I'm so sorry, honey, but your folks aren't going to make it out there to see you today because your Grandma Agnes passed away this morning." There it was. We all knew it was coming and here it was, nothing overwhelming, just the truth—just the first hit—but my armor was strong enough to withstand its inevitability. My first thoughts were about my mother losing her mom and all the complicated dimensions of their relationship. My mom told me in the weeks prior that she had the chance to tell her the things she needed to say to her. There had always been the divide that had existed between them. Grandma A's meekness had always bothered and eventually exasperated my mom. Defending her against my grandfather became tiring and too overwhelming a job, sticking up for someone whose defenses had been undressed from her long before any of us ever existed.

I absorbed the information and tried for a short second to figure what it meant, how things might change now that she was gone. My physical world was exactly the same, and emotionally I felt less affected than I thought I should. I thought she deserved some tears. I never actually saw her in those last days, so I was able to detach myself—or at least so I thought. I shot back up to the tier, somber-faced and disconnected—from my environment, family, and even to some extent my past. Somebody gave me something warm to drink that tasted like death and burned my chest as it went down. When they locked us in for the afternoon count, I sat and tried to process it all. I tried to absolve myself of the natural guilt of not being around, of not being able to help out or even show my face. I had been trying to transform myself but couldn't even help out a woman who was so kind and gentle with me during all of those surreal trips to see her in Small Town America, which was always so alien to me. A realization hit me that I hadn't seen her in five years.

The last time was the fall my great-grandmother died at the age of 101—a remarkable life that most of the family needed to have extend a few more years in order to keep all the pieces connected. My great-grandmother was probably who my mom modeled herself after most—a strong, capable, independent matriarchal figure. Grandma Nana exuded the same grace, strength, and family leadership my mom exuded on our side of the family. To my mom, those were the things that were admirable in a woman. Grandma A, though so kind and so loving, was reduced to a subordinate place under my grandfather, and the passing of time and social norms of her childhood were the wedges that split who my mom was from who Grandma Agnes was. It was the same fall I nearly crashed the family with my drug case. I was eighteen years old then, getting a quick start to the messing up of my young adult life. I wonder if even then my grandma could sense something, could smell the potential for failure or collapse in me. I can't remember what I might have told her when she asked me what I was doing with my life. "Are you in school? Are you working?" No, I wanted to tell her, I'm truly failing.

I sat in my cell and wondered how the story of Grandma A's life would be told. She was the oldest of three kids. One was the star, the opera singer with all the glitter and personality, whose star searing through the sky exploded and burned out early from electric shock treatments at the state's insane asylum. Her other sister found a man in a neighboring town and they escaped, got out of McGregor, Iowa, and extended her sanity by creating a life outside of the twilight zone of that town. Anywhere would've done. But like me, Agnes got prison. It was prison in a life as the obedient wife to a man who always believed he was right by God, and that she could only be right as the wife of a God-Fearing man—the Missouri Synod Lutheran kind of God-Fearing man. His voice spoke for the both of them—two bodies but only one mouth. She did all the domestic things: cooking and cleaning and bending at the whim of the overtly masculine figure who shared a bed with her—a figure who made the rules and paid the bills; a figure who went off to two wars, the Second Great War and Korea. She got to fight along with him through her submission, the great socially granted responsibility to wait on the man until he gets back (if he gets back), moving to wherever it was he was stationed.

And she got the great socially granted responsibility to be the mother to the man's kids. She ended up with two, adopted as babies—adopted because in the years after the man, tall and rooted like an oak, came home from Po Valley to start his family, there had been other babies. They were babies who just couldn't make it through the violence of Agnes's womb. Something wasn't right, but they kept trying; some were given names, but most never made it that far. Finally they chose adoption, my mom and her brother from anonymous universes spread across Iowa. And still I thought about all of the individual hurt that came from losing those children, the individual tragedies to be relived through the loss of one child and all those expectations, the cosmic connection between a mother and her child. And then to have to gather those emotions as another is lost and then again for another try. What could be left for the kids with somebody else's blood who came to her after all of those horrific disappointments? I wondered about her courage: was there enough? Or had it been suffocated from all the years of having to be the subordinate? Or was it an abundance of courage that kept her from falling apart from them?

I couldn't help but try to imagine before she was ever a mother or a grandmother—when she was a girl and the young handsome serviceman came around asking about her, what it was that made her love *him*. I wonder what he said or promised that might have convinced her to give her life to that one man of all men. There had to be something syrupy sweet in the things he said or wrote that made her want him. I envision as part of the story of her life a fist wrapped around flowers handpicked from a backyard garden that sat in a vase until they wilted. It was the great gamble of that generation that when that ship left, he would be the man she needed him to be if he came back—what you got is what you get for a lifetime. And the things he must've said in those letters while he was away—the soldier's story of writing with brutal honesty and need because he knew he might not make it home. Those letters never romanticized that if he came home she would live her life at his hip, be the housewife without any say, be the grown woman with a spending allowance. Granny's life could be told similarly, but any dependence on her husband was snatched from her when he died in 1980. We might say her independent nature was left to thrive or die at that point, and who she was was anything but helpless.

I wrote a letter to say good-bye to Grandma A. In it, I said I loved her, but I knew that just didn't mean the same thing as it once had. I told her that she had always deserved better than what she got, and that soon I hoped she could understand why I couldn't be there. It was a letter with her deathbed message, hand-delivered so that the wording on the envelope wouldn't decode the message mom had so adamantly hidden: that I had been locked up for the past three years. She was probably right: it wasn't the time to mash-up a complicated admission of closure with more injury. I wasn't sure if I said enough, if there was enough emotional compunction she deserved from me. Mom read it to her as she reclined with oxygen tubes attached at her nostrils. My mom said Grandma A cried. Maybe she did; I wouldn't have been offended had she not. She may have just been crying because she forgot I had come up missing again when it mattered. I could imagine her asking where I was, and my mom having to react instantly with the most current explanation. I just wanted to talk to her on the phone one last time to say, "Look, I fucked up. Otherwise, I would've been down there." But I couldn't, instead I was in my cell with that first taste in my mouth. It was the taste of loss and failure—a dish cooked with the reality that this place really does injure, takes away things you never get back. Even if I were to come back to life, not everything else could. There was the reflux of booze at the back of my throat mixed with the flavor of knowing there were some relationships I would never get the chance to rebuild.

I reread Granny's letter, listening to her voice tell me about the cool October temps and colorful leaves falling from the elm tree out in front of her house. "Granny loves you." Her classic exit—she could have just written those three words on a blank piece of paper and I would have been satisfied. Most of the rest of what she said was to fill space. And the Granny who loved me was eighty-four then, about the same as Agnes was, a whole lot fitter, though, a lot more alive and energetic. A whole lot more equipped for the future. We expected she would be one of those women who lived well past a hundred. But unless a miracle came, I expected an end would come one day to those letters as well. I thought about her doing pirouettes on fifty-year-old figure skates on the frozen lake at Powderhorn. The little old lady in the sundress with the two cans of Raid, walking into a blaze of bees without fear. I wondered how long she could stay that fearless. And how these two women, who had given much more than they ever received from me in return, were still sending their love—one reminding me of how little more time I might have with the other. I wasn't sure if I had the kind of endurance to go through more of these kinds of losses. If I didn't get out soon, I would have to live with the likelihood that Granny wouldn't ever see me on the other side of these walls either. That was a loss I knew I wasn't ready for. I was always protected in areas I just never had to worry about because I had them. Tears came to my face—difficult, hard-fought tears that were probably mostly selfish, mostly planted in my own regret. They told me how dumb I was for thinking I could coast through these years unaffected.

I knew there would be a funeral in the old Lutheran church with the old wooden pews at the end of Main Street in that little town in Iowa, the same place where my great-grandmother's life was celebrated after her body was put into a plot at the family cemetery. Naturally there would be a reception in the basement where Grandma A and Papa Arno celebrated their fiftieth wedding anniversary. And just as I am sure about anything in this world, I knew there would be a gathering of a lifetime of family and friends eating slices of ham on buttered rolls and drinking thin coffee from the church cabinets. More than a few aunts or uncles or cousins would ask my mom, "Where's Zeke?" "Where's Agnes's only grandchild?" She would tell them with unwavering eyes that I was in Phoenix, or in North Carolina, or in the Peace Corps in northern Africa. It didn't matter. I was the only one not there.

Eighteen

JUST PICTURES
||||||||||||||||||||||||||||||||||||||||||||||||||||||||||||||||||||||||||||||||||||||||

IT WAS JUST A PICTURE, two friends certainly not aware our faces would be stuck on that piece of celluloid forever. I don't even know who took it. My face was flush with blood, my eyes bloodshot; the pink would get richer as the photograph got older. I was in a rented tuxedo that only made me look silly, emphasized I was too young to be the best man at my best friend's wedding. I was ripped from drinking moonshine from a plastic flask the bride's father had given me earlier in the day. And the inebriation showed from the second I showed up. I was sort of expected to show up this way; I was the cantankerous one who had been opposed to the whole thing. There had been discussions and meetings with the priest as to how to deal with how I might show up. But I had no intentions of screwing anything up, and I was by far not the only one who had questioned the necessity of the night.

Bruce was supportive of our friend and was glad to be there. The rest of us thought it was just plain corny. Bruce was next to me at an angle to the camera where his left shoulder took the brunt of the flash. He wore his usual smile, only mildly disguised at the angle with his head cocked back and one mischievous eye visible, likely trying to appear smooth. He had on a light gray herringbone sports coat none of us even knew he owned and a tie that was perhaps a generation past its peak. He was visibly having fun, and it was evident he still had a bit of that childhood light—not a lot, but enough to notice it. I don't remember if I was, but the red eye from the camera on my blue eyes just made me look evil. The inner light in my eyes had gone away long before. I kind of even remember feeling a little wicked that night, for what I'm not exactly sure. It was probably the low-grade liquor I'd been drinking since early afternoon. There is a red line on my forehead from early in the day when I tripped on the top step going upstairs in the house I grew up in and split it on the light fixture in the upstairs hallway. It was one of the last weeks we lived in that house; mom had already moved out a couple of months before. It was our home for most of my life, and it became stacks of empty boxes and empty rooms; its part as a member of this family was over.

The picture is a relic from a strange time, a time before Bruce decided he was going to be a Marine. He was twenty years old, and it was just four years after losing his mother with nothing else going on in his life to give it the purpose he was looking for. He spent most of his life crafting an identity as one of the only black kids in Apple Valley. When she died he had to come back to South Minneapolis to live with his grandparents—bad timing. When he told us he was enlisting, I was in the middle of the worst depression of my life, but even in the darkness I couldn't understand a decision like that. "The Marines? He said he was going to be a Marine?" It didn't seem real. It seemed like a whim that could be steered in another direction if we hit him hard enough over the head with some sense. But tackle football games and dinner with a recruiter and his grandparents caught the kid in the snare before he could ever grow up and see some of the angles for what they were. I remember asking him, "What if there's a war?" I hardly believed it could happen. Our generation had been insulated from that reality; I was more concerned about the indoctrination of my friend. He said he didn't know, but he'd go anyway.

That night, without recognizing all the other flashes, we drank Hamm's beer and smoked blunts in the parking lot. The

winding of a disposable camera and the push of a button became a photo of two people going in different scary directions.
He could've easily stayed on the same road as I—later on with
shackles and wide eyes—but I could have never walked into his
life. I grew up in a different environment, where the prevailing
attitude was that since my father went to Vietnam and both of
my grandfathers were in World War II, my mom's only child
shouldn't have to go. She would have shot me in the leg before
I ever signed that paper.

Bruce's grandfather came from a school where if you're lost
and without direction, the military will find one for you. They
had Bruce before the end of the first sentence that recruiter
spewed from his lips. His grandfather, a very thoughtful and
sincere man with the kindest intentions and a big heart, suggested that maybe a friend and I should think about it for our
own lives. He brought it up in his kitchen after we picked Bruce
up after boot camp. He was in full Marine Corps uniform: the
navy shirt and light blue pants. He was one of the few and the
proud of where he had recently been, and they were sure to
have told him just what he was accomplishing, doing pushups
and crawling through obstacle courses. His grandfather asked
us if we were next. "Probably not."

||||||||||||||||||||||||||||

I NEVER THOUGHT about friends and family members running
around taking pictures. I never thought that one day I'd be
sitting in a prison I couldn't get out of, looking at this photo and
trying to envision all the paths that got us to where we were.
What the picture didn't say was that some of us would go away;
come to lives that stole much of what we thought we were.
And it was before 9/11. The two towers fell, and as I watched
it on TV, over and over and over again, I thought mostly about
Bruce and the likelihood he would have to go to war after all.
I didn't get to ask him how he felt about it—if he was scared
or ready, if he was ready to die. At the time asking people how
they felt usually generated figureless ideas and abstractions.
He was living in San Diego instead of coming back to South

Minneapolis. He found a girl in the city, where finding a nice soldier boy before they shipped off was as old as the city itself. They were planning to have babies when he was given the word he would be shipped off.

For a while we only heard about him, never anything from him. We knew he was overseas; there was a picture of him and someone else in his platoon sitting in a bunker next to guns nearly as big as his grown-ass body. He wasn't smiling in that photo. He looked tired and serious with the smoke of life in his eyes. The photo was attached to an article in the *Baltimore Sun*. In it they talked about an ultrasound picture of his son taped to the butt of his M-16. He was there, he was really there—and we were really here. It felt like the world was spinning out of control, but it always had been. I started to get letters in the mail a little while later. The first one that came was obviously several months late because in it he was still training in the Kuwaiti desert. He talked about being excited that he was going to have a son. He didn't say much else; he was just waiting. The second letter was after he had been in combat already, and he mentioned he thought the article that had been written made him sound afraid. They were letters written by a different Bruce, someone with no choice but to recognize his new world around gunfire and sticky bombs, with conversations about friends who would come home without a leg or in a flag-draped coffin.

APRIL 23RD

Sup E-Z

How you doin homie? I hope as well as you can. I'm doin OK now. I got two of your letters and 1 from your mom. I wish I could have wrote back sooner, but we were still real busy. Plus we could not send or receive mail while we were doin the damn thing.

I have to say, I was not expecting the amount of action we got. My machine gun team even made the papers after we got ambushed. The story was not that great: the reporter messed up a bunch of facts, and he made me sound scared. Whatever though, a pic in the paper ain't putting cheddar in my pocket so fuck em. By the way this paper I'm writing on came from an Iraqi soldier. I ran outta paper and he did not seem to mind me borrowin his. Come to think of it, he was havin a hard time breathin when I last saw him.

That dude was at a fight we call the killin fields. It was ugly, we ran up on a compound that terrorists from all types of different countries trained in. It surprised us, luckily it surprised them too. Them dudes were ruthless, fakin dead then jump up and start licking shots, takin off their uniforms so they looked like civilians. They even rolled up in a bus with a white flag, we thought it was just another civilian bus, but then they started jumpin out and sprayin with A-K's. Somehow my company only had 1 wounded and 1 dead. A good friend of mine. God bless the dead.

We even had a few small fights in Bag[h]dad. We thought the fightin was over but it wasn't.

Everything has been real cool though now this last week. They even say I might be goin home on the 9th or the 10th of May. That would be cool. I'll be home in time to see my son's birth.

But on to something else. I hate to hear what the state is tryin to do to y'all. I hope they don't succeed. I wish I could just say do your bid and get the fuck out, but I know that's a lot of time to just do. All I can do is pray and hope that nuthin but good things come about for y'all, from here on out.

Peace and love

Ontime

I remember reading the letter and feeling a sense of inevitability—the sense that he would be one of those people who didn't come back, because life and especially war showed themselves to be so merciless time after time. Even though he said they were going to let him come home. Even though his four years were almost up, I couldn't help but assume it would catch him, because wasn't that how it was conditioned in us?

It was in the movies we watched and in the music we listened to. Wasn't it always the guy on his way home to see his child be born, the person with the most to lose that gets caught by *it*? It was hard not to hold such a pessimistic outlook, but I was filled with ugly at the time. It was so hard to see through all of the complicated layers when it felt like everyone I knew was catching the disease of life.

He did get to come home. And he did get to see the birth of his son. There are pictures of him getting off of a flight in his desert fatigues, with his classic smile, almost childlike again, with his white teeth glowing and the American flag draped over his shoulder. It was his hero's welcome photo that is supposed to capture the emotion of that single moment. I think it did, even though it spoke very little about the before and the eventual after. There was another photo in the same group of him with his very pregnant wife and her family, who were just a bunch of strangers to us. He is the lone black figure embraced at the center of this strange white mob. He's the guy who knocked up their daughter before he left. There were two little boys, no older than ten, each waving cheap little flags on chopstick-thin wooden dowels. They smiled uncertainly for the camera. In that same bundle were pictures of the newborn child while Bruce was in hospital scrubs with a face that had shed all of its baby fat; now it was all sharp edges that softened for moments like that. It was an evolution from all of the earlier photographs meant to say something about his life.

It could be any picture plucked from any certain night, any of the nights we wandered around in the wilderness looking for a way to get out or screw our lives up. They were pictures about divergent paths; both sets of eyes would get to see ugly incidences of the underside of the human experience. His smile still had the celebration of life in it; mine did not. My serious, unfeeling mug; the shadows the flash created in silhouettes behind us—they were shadows that were part of us. They may have been the ghosts of what we used to be. There is a secret hand that snuck into the frame, probably attached to somebody we knew once, whose magic doesn't work in our lives anymore.

It looks like four fingers coming to snatch us up and push us in our separate directions. My shadow looks like a different person looking another way, already yanking at me.

||||||||||||||||||||||||||||

AFTER HE FINISHED with the four years he owed to the Marines he was able to de-enlist. He had done his duty. They wanted him to stay on and go back, but he had his son now and that made the decision different. He was fortunate to have left when he did because soon after legislation passed that would have kept him. He was able to be a father. He thought he would get to be normal for the first time in so long. The trick was there's never normal after coming back. He started feeling some of the things other people who had been over there talked about, the same things people he knew who came back from Vietnam and Kuwait. He started having awful nightmares and streaks of rage and sadness that came unannounced. He had traveled across the world to get away from it, but he still wasn't spared from the violence and destruction that shaped all of our lives growing up. His wife told him he was different from before he left and signed them up for couple's therapy. Of course he was different; of course there was an effect; of course there were parts she couldn't understand about what it was he had just come from.

He got a job as a security guard at a nuclear power plant. I didn't get any real details, except that it was work and he needed it. Things weren't any better when I talked to him. He said he and his wife argued constantly. They got into an argument and he tried to disengage, and she threatened to call the police and tell them he was beating her up. So he locked himself into the bathroom and didn't come out until a police officer knocked on the door. Apparently he moved out after that. That was the last time I talked to him. I heard since that he ended up having another baby with the same woman. It was a long way from his hero's welcome photograph and those undivided smiles of that pregnant girl and the family that welcomed him back. I guess being the Hero only lasted so long, and only meant so much in contrast to what he had to trade of himself. And so he got his own taste of life after the explosions—a lifetime of reminders that he chose one over the other, that neither life would spare him or me from the harms of living.

That picture of the two of us could have said to the world: we were young. It could have said we were naïve or confused. It might've even said something elemental or profound about our lives, spoken in a language neither of us understood. But it doesn't say much about what we were before that click, or what either of us became after the flash. We weren't young: we were just pictures.

Nineteen

NO MAN'S LAND

O NE DAY, several years into my prison stretch, I took a look around and realized the world had gone on without me. It was something all the convicts told me to expect. I was lucky; I still had both of my parents coming out to see me every weekend, and my grandma wrote me letters every day. I still had some friends who found time to come out and see me when they could. There was even a girl I came to dig a lot who stuck around and stayed in touch with me for a few years, but there were so many others who just figured something else out for their lives and decided there wasn't that much intrigue still left in keeping up with their people in the joint. It started to feel like the self I had spent years trying to understand had finally died, and the realization hurt.

I tried to look behind me for more of that hopeful energy that got me through the years I had already done. I hoped maybe a parole board would come along, or maybe an appeal would relieve me. The lawyer I hoped would save my life just told me to save my money. I was starting to see I was too far in to act like this was only temporary or this really wasn't happening. It happened—the judge said thirty years, and it was. I had become too much like so many of the people I had been doing time with: waiting on something great and life-changing to happen, and being miserable when it didn't. They waited, just as I was doing, for the years to go away, and they did—they just didn't come back. It started to become unrealistic and almost harmful to daydream about the future anymore. It got hard trying to expect anything, except the next memo, with the next exclamation point after what would be taken from us next. After so many years of that, the people here start to become like robots moving in different directions, spouting angry speculations from bits of abstract information.

It was even harder to look forward because there were just too many years out ahead of me, and everybody around me had the same kind of time, or worse, on their backs, too. So many of these guys had already been down for so much longer than me, in increments of five, eight, ten, and twenty years. I wasn't even halfway to the door, but I already felt dead to the world. It was impossible to see myself after two more decades of this. It was like a whiteout in the middle of a snowstorm. I was in the no man's land of my prison bid; I just hoped I had a rope to follow myself home—even though any home I might have envisioned didn't exist anymore or wouldn't by the time the storm was over. Many of the people I knew were moving in a gradual deterioration that led to a spinning, which ultimately led to going stir-crazy, sitting in the ever-shortening cycle of their sentences. It seemed there was an ascension that came with hope and good intention, and at some point it didn't matter anymore.

⦚⦚⦚⦚⦚⦚⦚⦚⦚⦚⦚

GRADUATIONS WERE TWICE A YEAR; they were our big, fat congratulations for finishing something, anything. We were lined up and patted down on our way into what is usually the visiting room. There was a whole group of us, sparsely associated to one another, who had committed our days and much of our nights to the idiosyncrasies of the particular education programs we'd completed. It was a gathering of vocational school and community college–level students, as well as three columns in the graduation program of men who earned their GEDs. Some of these men were young and had just missed an earlier opportunity, while others weren't so young and had endured quite a bit working toward the accomplishment. For a lot of us there was a substantial gap in years and experience between these kinds of recognitions. For the most part we were all there at a prison graduation ceremony, at least in part broken or misdirected people with a far-off projection we could put ourselves back together and increase our self-worth along the way. These are the good kind of times. They are the "I'm getting there," life-affirming moments of a prison bid, when the world feels conquerable and possible. Our families and friends start to look at us as something other than the great big disappointments we had come to represent.

I had finally earned a degree, just a two-year accomplishment. Not a huge deal and not the tip of any life monument either. But it was significant after all the frustrating years of underachieving in the Minneapolis Public School system, and at just about every other aspect of my young life. I was in my late twenties, an age when people stopped accepting me as young, and when my life choices could no longer be given that excuse. The people on the sidelines were starting to look and see if any of that young promise could ever be fulfilled. This was not *my* first graduation. My mom and dad were coming and were most likely outside the gates waiting to come inside. They had become quite familiar with these kinds of events over the past several years and had come to expect seeing a lot of the same faces of the families who were coming to see their loved ones, too. It seemed to me they were gatherings of mostly the same people, trying their best to fight out of a succession of what felt like never-ending years in a dungeon, with what seemed the only plausible weapon we could use: an education.

People got sucked in by their bids—too many years in with too many left to go. We saw it with lifers who got themselves pumped up for visits to the parole board, only to be given another date years into the future. I would sit back and watch the guys who had unwittingly gone stir-crazy—a weird glossed-over look in their eyes with a jittery disposition and conversation that wasn't usually connected to any particular place and time. It was something we ultimately accepted in them, enjoyed it as though it were harmless amusement, but something I damn sure didn't want to foresee for my own life. There was an unspoken truth that existed in this place and in those glossed-over looks that said there absolutely was an expiration date for how long a person could hold on to his faculties. But it wasn't a magical formula. One day we would catch a glimpse of some-one going sour: a temper tantrum over a call during a prison dodgeball game, or a plain difference in opinion that spouts an outright leap off the proverbial deep end. We'd look around and ask, "What happened to what's his name?" "He's going nuts"—generic for something complicated and overpowering, not a choice but a succumbing. It was something that was probably chasing after all of us. I just prayed to God I could outrun it.

I was seated right next to Cuzzo, a long way from when we met at Andersen Open, and an alternate universe to the kids we were when we found all that crack in the abandoned car a few blocks from the homecoming dance. It certainly wasn't a thought the night Justin got shot, or the possibility that Cuzzo might have been, too, standing right alongside the flashes when it happened. After all of the jobs, school camping trips, and house parties, we'd shared so many experiences—now we were sharing this. These were the times when we could look over at each other and say, "We're gonna make it through this. I wasn't so sure for a while, but now I know." We got a little positive affirmation, and it felt like we had wills strong enough to move time out of the way. The flip side to the incarcerated coin: the very plain moments seasoned with equal parts hardness and madness, which wander around these hundred-year-old build-ings. Earlier that day, me and Cuzzo laughed at the guy with the long black hair and Jesus beard, who every day lowered his head and held his arms tight against his wafer-thin body and sprinted to and from the dining hall. Then we watched as he would go table to table as an unpaid busboy collecting as many trays as time allowed. He aligned them on the cart in a sort of tray matrix that only he knew the meaning to. The gate would open and he would shoot without hesitation, full-speed, postured aerodynamically back to the cell block and disappear, only to reemerge to organize the book cart according to another kind of magical sequencing not even remotely discernible to anybody else.

Watching some of these men only reinforced how unreliable our footing was; lose a step and a person might not be able to get back up again. It became impossible not to be punched by a realization that the joint was more clinical than criminal. It felt more like an asylum than any image I may have previously conjured up about American prison. I started to fear that, after deciding to not give up—that I could conquer this bid— that maybe I was taking the first steps toward going crazy, too. I could see it in all the medicated and equally nonmedicated bodies moving and speaking in circles around me. They walked around in Thorazine- and lithium-laced conversations with or amongst themselves. A few of us laughed about it, but with an unspoken, cautious undercurrent moving with it. It was insecurity with a carefully sliding pride, knowing, or hoping, that none of us had gotten to that point yet.

||||||||||||||||||||||||||||||

I MET KERSHAW when I was working as the clerk in the education department, helping guys apply for financial aid to hopefully continue their schooling. He was very opinionated and had an emotionally charged voice during the morning computer lab. He shared a history with a friend of mine he spent a bunch of time with at a juvenile facility in Iowa. He was a guy in his twenties as well; he may have been a couple of years younger but not many. At first glance he had this enormous head and eyes that bulged and bugged out with long pauses in between blinks. He came with a backpack full of moods and attitudes, running around within dramatic and elastic manic phases. Sometimes he would run down a list of everything he had been diagnosed with, a lexicon of terms and medical-speak I had mostly never heard of. He spouted off these super-multisyllabic names for obscure medications that were constantly changing to catch up with every new diagnosis. He also told me about how sometimes he would have psychotic episodes where he did things outside of the way we typically expect people to think.

When you got past some of the initial layers, he really was very charming and well-intentioned, on top of being peculiarly intelligent—almost hyperintelligent, if there is such a thing. He had an exceptional grasp of complex ideas and theories, more sophisticated than most of the people I had ever met. And with them he had many credible and often profound countertheories and arguments. Sitting in front of this strange cartoon character, I had conversations I never had with anyone else I ever met.

If a person didn't already have enough background on Kershaw, they might believe him to be some kind of misdirected genius who understood something about the world that meant for us to follow after. But there was enough background, and because of that nobody was going to follow him or look for him to bring any sort of enlightenment, simply because he had too peculiar of an energy about him. It was energy of darkness and unhinged mischief, kind of like a young Charles Manson, without the devout following or charisma, but with a similar kind of sensationalism. He wanted people to understand him but knew they never would.

He was writing a novel with endless plot twists and subplots, which when he explained them only confused me. It sounded good, but how much of it was on paper and how much of it existed only in one of the compartments of his mind was unclear. I always had an inclination to write, too, so I hung around mostly just to see where he was going with the pen. I always believed I would write a novel one day myself; I mostly just filled notebooks in handwriting I could hardly understand when I reread it later.

𝚒𝚒𝚒𝚒𝚒𝚒𝚒𝚒𝚒𝚒𝚒𝚒𝚒𝚒𝚒𝚒𝚒𝚒𝚒𝚒𝚒𝚒𝚒𝚒𝚒𝚒

ME AND CUZZO were sitting in the back row of the "offender" side of the ceremony, watching as visitors arrived. We were able to kick back in what were our best clothes: T-shirts and jeans with maternity-like elastic waistbands, ironed with creases as though it made them more formal. We watched as mothers and fathers, girlfriends and wives and kids came in and sat down in the opposite section from our own. My mom waved to both of us when she came in. It had been so many years already, with her coming to these things, in and out of this very visiting room and all of its entanglements and impersonality. I know she was just hoping they might end once and for all and that I might be able to follow her and my dad out the electric sliding door one of those times. But we all knew there were a lot of years and confusing movements in the way of that dream.

A heavy black woman came in with her face a mess with tears. She was just then finding out that for the pettiest of reasons, something insignificant and otherwise not even worth noting, her son was on some kind of disciplinary status that would be over in a couple of days but was just untimely enough to prevent a moment that was supposed to be profoundly healing, cathartic, and enduring from happening. She took a bus from Chicago to see her son, forty years old, receive his GED: it had been close to a decade since she last saw him in something other than a photograph. She made the trip because she knew it would be the closest thing to a graduation she might ever get to see from him, and that if she waited much longer she just might be too old; her diabetes and high blood pressure may not let her come see the man with a life sentence who used to be her baby. He spent several years of frustration and obstacles trying to pass the last of those tests. We all had to sit there and watch it get whitewashed over, played-down as though the universe hadn't once again fucked everything up—as though it weren't another classic example of the kind of alienation this place had been cultivating since its walls went up into the sky.

While we watched this excruciating moment, I was taken over by the grim powerlessness of being one of many inconsequential bodies moving in space. Most of the other family members probably didn't understand why this woman was so overwhelmed with distress. The people sitting and standing closest to the disaster watched as, eventually, the truth was laid out as clearly and as brutally as it could be: the ceremony would go on without her son in attendance. She was escorted out. She could have stayed, but with no hug, no catharsis, no healing— just another blatant truth about prisoners' families and the fragility of hope.

They started the ceremony with introductions. Precursory congratulations were offered to all of us who made it. We were guided through the program. A few inmates with guitars comprised a band that played classic rock covers before the guest speaker from Metropolitan State stood up to the microphone. Her speech was mostly addressed to us in the romanticized language used for these kinds of events, about breaking free and liberating our minds and spirits. She spoke about the inalienable accomplishments that now existed forever, were untenable and unbreakable testaments to what we've done so that no matter what happened in the rest of our lives, they could never take this away from us. The cynicism in me understood that there were other things we'd done in this world that would never go away either. I wondered how all of those things balanced out over the course of a lifetime. But I also still believed at the time in a perpetual ascension from the low, subterranean places I found myself in. I felt like I had fallen so far and hard that there was nothing else to do but get back up and start running again, and that eventually I'd be fast and sure enough to be able to fly away from everything.

It was uplifting language, if not reiterative, presented to us by someone separate from our world. It sounded more genuine from her than when it was recycled in a different package and tone by the warden, who came up to speak right afterward. I just remember the emotionless delivery to us and our families, there to try and discern what these accomplishments might mean for our future. We got a bland, splattering of words about how education was the key to knocking down the rate of recidivism.

"These men here today made a choice, a choice to not give in to all the noise and distractions in their everyday worlds to take a step forward in this world." Yeah, it sounded good. It sounded like we were the cream that had risen to the top, the blaring examples being held up against the masses. But I thought, "No shit, education is the key to reducing recidivism." They had been telling us this for years at these ceremonies. But I looked around me at most of my friends, and it was the same cluster of lifers and long-termers that I was used to seeing here with their families. They were the ones who kept these programs stable and churning out certificates and diplomas, so far removed from what it was they did when they were younger. There wasn't a *key* to open the gates to freedom for any of them. There wasn't an action-based parole board for nonlifers in the state, and they hadn't let a lifer out in years at the time.

All the rhetoric about recidivism, phrases about choices and the future, stopped meaning what they once did. We sat through the semantics, ever more discontented by the fact that we had sought after an education that was supposed to be a gateway to the rest of our lives, but we were still here—educated but stuck. The slick suggestion that we were somehow any better than those sitting in the cell blocks while we were here was amusing, considering that the higher-education program and several of the vocational programs had just been slashed. At the end a nominal applause was expected, but our section remained mostly quiet. I was at least happy to notice my parents' hands stayed remarkably still while people who didn't know any better applauded.

Only a few weeks prior to graduation, a man whose name would have been on the graduation program hung a sheet into a noose. I talked to Cuzzo about how I wondered if during those awfully personal moments, the brace and the surrender, while his body kicked and fought, if he ever changed his mind. Or was the line drawn too sharp, his resolve too dark to rinse away? I wondered where that line was, where one more day became too unbearable for this person to endure. Was it the bid? Did he just wander so far off until he couldn't make his way back? Once the last breath of oxygen was extinguished, it didn't matter anymore—it was done. And it didn't matter that the people carrying his body out of the prison dropped it on their way down the stairs. There were the usual subjections from all the different angles of opinion. Some said he was weak, probably because it made those people feel that much stronger and less afraid for being able to endure this. Others would call it brave, because they were too scared to face what might be waiting for them on the other side. A good many others called him a punk or a faggot or some other adjective to describe what they couldn't understand and to place all the more space between themselves and the disease of it. When Cuzzo talked about the guy, he didn't understand why anybody would care: "If he wanted to die, let him die. There's enough broken people running around here." It came with an insensitivity that didn't come from malice; it came more from privacy and knowing it wasn't his business. "Everybody is standing around now, crying about what they could have done to save him, knowing nobody gave a damn what the fuck he did until that moment. People manufacture tears. They need to save themselves."

He wasn't the first since I'd been down, and there were many after him; usually it happened at exactly the most unanticipated times. I woke up one morning and a body was laid out on the floor of the cell block across the hall, and it just sat there for hours while the rest of the joint went by. It was just a body, I guess. Eventually they put a partition up because they got tired of telling everyone stopped in the hallway to move along. Rumors spread, but people could hardly understand their own lives, let alone process an entire life of heartbreaks and disappointments outside of themselves. I knew I had no personal attachment and that soon he would be just another footnote in the timelines of everyone else's stories, but I knew how easy it was to get lost in the pain. I knew I wasn't exactly happy and secure, but I was glad I had this moment—with Cuzzo and my parents sitting across from me. I knew I wanted to live, and I was glad I never put the sheet up when I thought the future was too overwhelming to adjust to. I also knew there was a lot of time left, a lot of empty space to fill between then and the door, and a lot of things were possible.

When it came time to hand out awards, they went name by name in as constant a stream as possible. There were token bursts of applause from individual family members set on not missing their moment. The GEDs were the largest group, and it was the last group of the vocational programs to be pushed through with actual college accreditation. The machine shop and cleaning programs had just been cut entirely. It was their last graduation, period. They were part of the cuts, just like the guys getting AA degrees; everything was in limbo, hoping for a return off into the future that was no less certain than any of the other things that had gone away in our time here. I went and received my degree and a handshake. I spent several years chasing after it and all of the honors associated with it. In a way it empowered me, but it didn't make the time seem any more manageable. In another way it made what I was doing just feel ludicrous and useless. I felt like I was training for a make-believe future.

Mom cried a little, even though she is not really a crier. I knew it was associated with never being part of any kind of formal graduation before. I missed the rite of passage the first time in the self-sabotage of my life. But it was what *she* wanted so bad, and it made me wonder about how many mothers and their sons or daughters shared something similar to this during all the prison bids through history. How many got this exact kind of bittersweet suture on some of those deep wounds and broken hearts? It was something I had inadvertently attached myself to, something attached to history and suffering, to prisoners and their devoted families. I just thought about the woman who came so far to get refused her moment, who missed her chance to see her son receive his piece of paper. Just as some are given some of these things, others get them taken away—without any feeling or regret.

Afterward there was a period to socialize and talk to our guests. This time Mom got the hug and the photo with a cap and gown that she missed out on the first time around. She finally got it—almost ten years after her refusal to accept my GED as a binding document of completion for my years in school. They were years hiding report cards and erasing unexcused absence notices from the answering machine before either of them got home from work. It was even more time from the first of so many lectures in the living room about underachieving and failing. It was a long ways from completely healing what was hurt back then, from the grief and disappointment of my parents' only child going away to prison for most of his life, and without ever leaving any grandchildren for them. It was a brief respite from the madness that seemed to infect the joint with its poison. It told me for a moment I was doing well, and that things were going to be all right, even if it was probably just kind of a mirage, even though we would go back to the blocks and walk amongst zombies again after it was over. I would start something new to keep from being pulled deeper into the drudgery of the bid. And just as was customary, they lined us up again and strip-searched everybody on the way out.

||||||||||||||||||||||||||

NOT LONG FOLLOWING THE CEREMONY I came back from work one day, where I was planting snap dragons and New Guinea impatiens in one of the gardens by the industry buildings. It was spring, and color and light were starting to come back into our days. There were a bunch of guards clamoring around on the galley by my cell. When I got closer I realized it was Kershaw's cell. He wasn't in it, but there was a crew there with gloves and respirator masks doing their best to clean up a blood-soaked room. There was a lake of red flooding the floor. An instantaneous blast of chemical disinfectant hit my nose as I got close enough to see all the blood, a puddle with suds from the industrial-strength cleaner being used to cut it down. Blood was splattered in thick layers of paint all over the walls and bed. It was a brutal scene that made me a little sick to look at. A friend of mine who lived between us was the one who found him, locked in his room, his wrists cut in multiple jagged lines, pacing back and forth as the blood leaked from him in thick ropes of viscous liquid. It was that same person who went and got help. There was a mess of red saturating Kershaw's clothes and his skin, and he talked incoherently and without direction as he walked the length of his cell, back and forth. In the middle of a sunny afternoon in spring, the accidentally charming, secretly brilliant madman was bleeding to death by himself in a cell.

It wasn't until a few days later we found out he was still

alive. He spent some time in the hospital ward and one day popped up, his head bobbing and his eyes bulging out. He said he didn't really want to die: he had just got stuck in one of those psychotic episodes and left reality for a while. He never did write that novel. He said the pages got lost somewhere when he got out the last time. He did however have fresh new slash marks he wore like new tattoos alongside all of the old ones he had. His scars probably could have written that novel if only they understood their stories more clearly. The time and place were starting to feel like no man's land again—empty and purposeless. So I decided I should probably start writing again, too, before so many years went by and it never got done, before these moments were erased and I forgot how they made me feel. And before that thing, the madness that was chasing after so many of the people I knew, could catch me and I wouldn't have documented anything. Only collected more sadness.

There were plenty of things that had been mended, but the rest of my life was still waiting for me and my family. Certain accomplishments made us as a family feel stronger and more hopeful, but I was never so sure things would ever be all right. I was never sure that I couldn't be the guy with the Jesus beard who stacked the trays in the dining hall, or Kershaw with the unintentional artwork on his wrists, or even that I wouldn't go stir-crazy and confused over what really mattered. And what really mattered was walking out the door, wits and self-worth intact. The truth was, time had passed and things had changed, people had changed their minds about their allegiances and their feelings. The people I cared most about were getting old, and expectations for what life was supposed to be seemed all the more abstract. I knew acutely what a cell felt like, and I was starting to understand how the rejection from the world and displacement of family and friends felt, too. I didn't know, however, how much of this I would have to keep as part of myself and my story—and how much I would have to pry from my heart and mind when the doors finally opened.

Twenty

A HOMECOMING

ㅤ

AND THEN IT HAPPENED: the last explosion, deafening and unannounced. For years I've seen men put on the orange jumpsuit and shackles and take baby steps out into the world with shock on their faces. Now it was me in the orange jumpsuit with my hands and feet shackled, leaving the state facility I had already been in for eleven years, in the back of a state vehicle, seeing everything I had forgotten about how green Minnesota can be in the summer.

It started with the phone call I never expected to get. I still get caught by surprise at how many times the important news in our lives comes from the unintentional phone call. They came and got me out of my cage right after the 3:00 count to see a lieutenant. I didn't know if they were going to shake me down or something, or what the break in routine was supposed to mean. It was the hottest part of summer and we were in the middle of a state government shutdown, so everything was being run uncertainly. They sat me down in a cubicle in the empty lieutenant's office, alone with a buttonless phone that rang—with only my mother's voice on the other end trying to speak in bouts of composure. I thought it must be my grandma—after all, she was ninety-four years old. But I had talked to her only two hours before and she sounded fine, alert, and comfortable. But it wouldn't have been her; she was the obvious one. This was too abrupt to be her, and the force of an explosion is never as great when you expect it.

In my mother's voice was a tremble—breaks in the sentences, a waver in her voice that she was sorry she had to tell me this, that the world was crumbling and our sky was falling. It was the dread that fell on her—like all the things like this so naturally since the beginning of her burdens—to tell her son, their only child, in the midst of her own shock. And the burn wounds, from being so close to the ignition and having to say the words that my dad was dead, packing the car on the way home from vacation. His heart attacked him, killed him before he even hit the ground. She knew it was the worst piece of information she could give me—one more smoldering disappointment for the two of us to share. Just two months into the retirement he had worked an entire life for and eleven years short of watching me walk out the door. And here it was, one voice speaking from a hospital hours from home to the other one alone in a cubicle— years and years, miles and miles from home—knowing that the dreams that had been reworked would have to be reconfigured again. And again, as it was in the beginning, she tried to convince me that we were going to make it through this—even though just like the times before she had no real idea.

<hr />

IT IS THE STANDARD UNIFORM: one-piece hunter orange. A Velcro strip from neck to waist, with belt loops for the chains attached to the cuffs, there in case they want to chain you in a line to the man in front of or behind you. But it was just me that day.

They came and got me on a plain Wednesday morning, quietly and impersonally. The temperature dropped ten degrees the day they brought me to see him. I sat in the backseat of a state-owned Chevy Blazer with a cage obstructing my view of the two officers they sent to be the chauffeurs to take me to see him on the other side of these walls. I still hadn't decided how I felt yet. I knew it was going to hurt me, but I didn't understand it yet.

There was a time seven or eight years ago when it became way too obvious he was withering away, losing thirty or forty pounds from his untreated diabetes. Mom said it was his expression of grief over my leaving him. My friend said people wear their pain in a lot of different ways. I really thought he was going to die then. There were interventions and, finally, something in him changed and he started to eat better, tried to be more active, and began to treat his diabetes. A few years later and he was healthier—a little older but healthier than he had been in probably twenty years. The mission was to get to the end of my sentence, to reshape our friendship, and it really felt like that was going to happen. We had an agreement: "I'll take care of myself if you take care of yourself, and we'll meet up at the end of the bid."

Part of me was just so overwhelmed with the world as it spread out coming through the gates. Seeing the way things moved, things that I hadn't seen in more than a decade, surprised me. Just watching people cross the street was sort of strange. As we moved farther and farther from the complicated workings of the place that had held me in its belly for so long, I watched for the first time how the sprawl had spread so far. It was something that for certain didn't just happen in the past eleven years since I last looked out of a car window at the traffic around me. It was something I could have only noticed now, overgrowing out of what was once just beautiful nothing. Everything was unrecognizable but also familiar, like an old room with a new coat of paint. There were signs for everything— everything was for sale, mile after mile of flat spaces and parking lots, billboards, and every kind of superstore. I was hypnotized by how fast the world moved, cars on the freeway around me with their own stories and destinations. It was a ride filled with incomplete thoughts, scrambling and changing with all the moving stimuli around me. So I just let it move and show me everything it had to show me.

Downtown St. Paul came up in the distance like a mirage, a digitized image outside of the caged window with still blue sky and buildings in the panorama. In a short passing of moments its buildings were on top of me, looking down at me as the truck moved through. I couldn't help but remember trips to the farmers' market or that last Andersen field trip to the Science Museum. It just felt strange to see things that stood higher than the five stories of the tallest of our cell blocks. It just verified how small my world had really been; no wonder so many had done their best to move on and be something greater.

St. Paul slowly spread out in front of me until the high-def image became Minneapolis and 94 crossed the Mississippi. There was the vast opening of space, and there it was: a powerful river larger and greater than I remember, with the Tenth Avenue and 35W bridges off in the distance. On the other end were the tall buildings of the city I grew up in. As we crossed, I saw Riverside Park, the great Bermuda triangle of South Minneapolis peaking out of its obscurity of trees and overgrowth. I lost my breath for a second; I didn't expect such a visceral response. I didn't expect to run into such familiar images, and watching the park pass by—which had been so much of a recurring energy in our lives that we came back to long after most everyone had moved out of its neighborhood—surprised me. Now everything off in the distance was something I needed to see, things I hadn't seen since the beginning of this ordeal, the ordeal that was my apocalypse.

Up ahead, the Cedar–Riverside buildings stuck out ugly as ever, fingerprinted with those obnoxious yellows, blues, and pinks in the sky. The whole West Bank world came back to me: from sitting on the trunks of cars in the parking lot of Hard Times to getting my toes stepped on by little kids for crack sales in the vacant lot in front of Twin City Cycle. It brought me to the time we crowded the Cedar–Riverside intersection with protesters for Mumia, and Shiz got maced, or stumbling out of the Red Sea back into my real-life conundrums. And there were all the tensions of being young at Cedar Fest and trying to dodge any life-changing conflicts that came from those kinds of energy coming together in one place at the same time. Those disgusting buildings had become just a symbol for all of those experiences. I'm sure they were a symbol for a lot of people's experiences passing through them in the seventies, eighties, and nineties. I'm sure they symbolized something for the current generation of kids running around in them now.

I saw the Cedars 94 building and the walking bridge that crossed over to the Augsburg College campus. That freedom summer of 1996 in front of a register of the Dairy Queen was so far gone now, and the place looked broken down and insignificant. Past Cedar, 94 made a dip and it was hard to see the things I wanted to. Chicago Avenue came up and all I saw was the underpass. If the freeway were higher, I could've seen a stretch of world that was part of so many different people's stories—many I'm sure would want to forget them forever. I could have seen Franklin Avenue and Peavey Park, old Green Eyes selling dimes on the corner if he was still alive. And despite how indifferent I was back then, I would have liked to see the mural on Eleventh, with the bold statement in the first panel that said, "We Claim Our Lives." But even had we passed by it, I knew the building had been torn down years before, just as so many of the claims we had all made for our own lives.

The merge onto 35 gave me a short chance to try to see in a flash what had changed on Franklin. I saw the old record shop on Fourth, but there just wasn't enough time to register what I needed to. Soon it was Lake Street and then Thirty-fifth Street, all the places I knew were still there but were just glimpses, still very much out of my reach. I remembered in an instant how much we believed all of those places to be ours—part of our right and inheritance. They were all just blinking images now, meant to hold the frame long enough for us—me in the orange jumpsuit and the two officers bringing me home to see the body of my dead father. I'll take care of myself if you take care of yourself.

I was still trying to figure out what this visit was supposed to do. The surprise good-bye, an offering of closure on any hubristic notions he would survive the final eleven years of my bid—the abrupt end to the daydreamed plans of fishing or throwing the ball around one last time. It was *I'm really dead, Zeke. I really am dead. And now I brought you from the dungeon*

back home to South Minneapolis for a far too short period of time
to show you that I was really here on this earth, but now I've got
to move on. I stayed in the euphoria that took hold as soon as I
started seeing the world outside of the prison. It only got stronger when I started to see the city and realized it hadn't burnt to
the ground when I left, that it was still there, an actual place in
the actual universe outside of the walls. I was unsure how any
of the things I would see on this trip were going to affect me.
I really didn't have the nerves I thought I would at that time. I
hadn't had the sort of emotional breakdown I expected yet, and
I was just waiting for the right trigger for it to take over.

We pulled into the parking lot at the Cremation Society,
right next to the flower shop on the corner of Forty-second and
Nicollet. It was the same lot, the same building that cremated a girl I went to school with. It was the same building, same
neighborhood, but it looked different even though it still felt
unmistakably like the South Side—the green of the trees and
overgrown lilac bushes, even the lean and dip of the concrete.
It wasn't even close to my neighborhood, but the alleys were
the same; the sidewalks and the trees were just like they had always been. There were buildings and businesses that never existed, weren't even conceived twelve years before, when I had
last been here. I stayed in the backseat while one of the officers
sorted out all of the logistics.

They pulled me out of the truck, hidden in the alley behind
the building; my feet touched the ground in the city I grew up
in for the first time in more than a decade. I was a little dizzy
from not being used to the motion of the vehicle. They walked
the shackled man in an orange jumpsuit through the back-door
entrance by the alley. I took baby steps in the leg irons at my
feet through what was essentially a basement and garage at
the same time. The head of the Cremation Society brought us
to the room at the end of the corridor with a waiting room attached. One of the guards checked it to make sure there weren't
any ways out, then the two men left me alone in the cold room
with couches along two walls and a gurney with the lifeless
body that used to be my dad lying down on it against a third

wall. There was a blanket draped over him to his neck; only the embalmed translation of his face was exposed. No make-up: he wouldn't have liked that at all. It was already beyond what he would have wanted, to have his body embalmed for a viewing that could only make more sadness, which was why he wanted to be cremated in the first place. But there would have to be a reviewal, just so that I could get this trip. The day before my mom and Granny walked through this same room. My mom told me Granny sat stoic next to my uncle on one of the couches—no tears, just steady reserve that hid all that it meant to lose her oldest son.

It was his face, but pale and dead. It looked younger than it did when he came out to see me a couple of weeks before, but it was his face. It had his beard, the unmistakable brush of whisker I knew from the day I was born on that mountain. It was his most distinguishable feature—in my entire life I only saw him barefaced twice. And there he was, still eleven years from the day the state was going to release me, the date we made in secret agreement to sew back some of the torn fabric of all that lost time. All the dread I felt coming wasn't for the time I still had left—it was for losing him. He didn't make it. Instead, he left a motionless body for me to talk to, in an impersonal room that smelled like death, with low ceilings and tacky fake plants and busy printed couches.

So I spoke to him. I told him that he was my best friend and that I was sorry for what I did to our lives. I told him I was sorry I wasted all this time. I told him he was the best man I had ever met and that I never deserved him. I spoke to the body and kissed his forehead, even though it didn't feel like he was in that body. Instead it felt like he was sitting on one of those couches watching me mumble what I was trying to say. It also felt like his dad, who had died when my dad was close to the age I am, was sitting next to him. My grandpa was *his* best friend before he had lost him so young. Now I imagined he was sitting next to him, had probably been getting reacquainted after the thirty years they had been apart. It could just be part of what my mind told me to get through it, but it felt like they were really there.

I sat down on the couch next to where I envisioned he was and looked over as though he were actually there, as though my grandfather was actually there, too, and watched how casual they were together, how happy they felt. It was something I was too young to see when they were both alive, and it made me happy, a complicated happy. I wanted to believe they were there, complicit in the notion that one day there would be a place for me too.

I went back to the body, just to see if there was anything I might have missed that I needed to take with me before it went into the furnace. I thought about keeping some of the hair from his mustache, but I felt weird trying to yank them from his face. There were so many things I wanted him to know I appreciated. I wanted to thank him for giving me a father, when so many others never got one, and for being the one he was. And how I was glad he and my mother had run away to that mountain and gave me a life no matter what it turned into. I wanted to thank him for working all those jobs that didn't value him the way they should have, but that he did anyway. I wanted to thank him for giving me baseball and letting me play softball with the team I was able to watch play my whole life, even though I really wasn't any good then.

I wanted to tell him how much I respected the time he socked me in the face when I was seventeen and jazzy as ever during dinner one summer night. I deserved it, and instead of treating me like a child, he showed me like a man, and I always respected him more after that. I also needed him to know how I had recognized the tears he had shed at my friend's funeral so many years before and that I loved him that much more after I saw them. I wanted to tell him how much I appreciated the months we lived alone in the house on Thirty-fifth Street after my parents separated. We both knew the metaphor of that house and that so much of our family was going away with it. There were so many things I needed to tell him, but I *didn't* want to tell him good-bye.

I wasn't sure how much time I had. The guards didn't sweat me; a time limit was never specified. There was only so long I could stay there by myself, and only so much I could remember to say to the empty vessel that used to be my father. Most of the stuff would come back in the ephemera of my memories. I thought about a future without his Sunday morning visits or his calm insight. I wished I could just get dropped off twenty blocks east and forget about the whole nightmare of what prison was, what it had done. But that wasn't real. And standing in a room with my father's dead body wasn't the same as standing in a room with my father. I felt like I was supposed to stay longer, but it would have to end sometime. I had said good-bye, had sat with him and my grandfather and all of the elders of my family, but it was time to leave. I told the guards I was ready to go, even though I felt like shit for not spending hours there, for not lying down on one of those couches and sleeping there until they moved me. I didn't know if I should have been praying or if I should have had some kind of ceremony, but really I just ended up by myself in a room a little misty-eyed but not ready for the great breakdown I had expected, still not ready to use the word *good-bye.*

They walked me back out through the back door and into the alley. I smelled the air, tried to taste it again so I would have another dimension to take with me. It tasted like I remembered, only a little bitter now, a little more acidic. I looked up and saw the same sky I looked at from inside the walls, blue and careful, but beneath me was a different piece of earth from which I was rooted. For a moment everything was still: so much of the neighborhood was the same, but I wasn't. It was the same city, but it didn't remember me anymore. We were past the point of staying the people we were. It didn't matter. The officers helped me back into the Blazer, my feet being lifted from the concrete of South Minneapolis one last time. I sat with my head rested against the window, my mind as blank and unmoving as it has ever been. And the city ran away from me again.

On that first day, when I was given the news from my mom, when everything was so hazy from the humidity that wrapped around everything, I went out and played softball. Really, I didn't have much else to do outside of thinking and absorbing the whole thing. I figured he would have done the same thing to keep his mind from drifting back to the ache of what just happened. We had become friends on a field like this, with gloves and a ball. He was so much younger then, and I barely existed yet. It was something primordial that existed between us that I could go out and play and that maybe he'd finally get to see me—maybe he'd get to see how good I'd become. I hoped he was on the bleachers. I envisioned that it was my grandfather who had brought him and that they sat together and smiled as they watched. I wanted to imagine my grandpa had been coming here to see me for years, but that was mostly just movie stuff, the enacted narrative I was using to soften the punches. I wanted to be able to tell my dad I was glad he came, and that I knew I was never as good as he ever was before he went walking back into the cornstalks.

And then I was in that tiny space again, ready to be shut in for another night—with at least one more piece of who I was gone. I wasn't sure I was ready to be this new person, with such an important part of my history gone. There were more pieces to pick up now, just like all the years of my life spent picking up scattered fragments of debris. All that time could've been spent doing something else, being someone else. There are just those skates rolling backwards, slipping deeper into the flickering obscurity.

The story is really written in the hearts we break, clearing space swinging the machete. We all get old, that's no secret. As the expectations change, the pain changes, bends, and shapes, shows nuance where shame and fear made the decisions. I wanted it to hurt, that stinging vibration on my nerves and on my heart as tribute to him. I wanted to be destroyed and weakened to an inactive state under my bunk, without the strength to come back out. I thought he deserved the declaration. I thought I deserved the pain. He was the man who silently came to love me more over all the years after I set off the bomb that wrecked our lives and changed the way we saw the world. He was one of the invisible forces standing somewhere in the way of the wilderness getting at me. I became someone

I would never be able to show him; I was nothing once, carried on his shoulders like royalty until he let me down to run around and be something.

Now I've lost this. And what happens next? Who's the next person this bid's going to eat? Am I so naïve to think there won't be more? It won't be the last explosion. There *will* be others, there has to be, because I've got too much time left. Maybe it will be me next time. Maybe those strange pains and all the things the doctors here dismiss as nothing might one day come get me before the last sprint to the door. All of the garbage that goes in and comes out some other kind of way, a poison. We don't all get sick—I did, though. All those years of being scared to death—being scared—all that viscous fear, and what happened? Death did. Now there are only ashes some-where, waiting for me to get out so I can take them from their container and sprinkle them along the first baseline at the field at Powderhorn Park, where at the same place, but in two sepa-rate universes, we both tried to grow up.

||||||||||||||||||||||||||||||

MOM THREW A PARTY to celebrate his life. All the people I looked up to as a kid showed up—older, much grayer, a little slower, a whole bunch of bad knees and back surgeries to go around. The generation that refused to get old was being eaten very realistically by life, but also in the lens of my experience, by the bid as well. There's no shaking what twenty years does: it makes the young less idealistic; it makes kids swimmers in the great ocean; and it makes the old who had so much at stake in the ideals of the young and the kids disappear. In the pictures, everyone had smiles, moving around amongst a lifetime of friends, understanding the abruptness of life but not letting it destroy them. They are the parts of ourselves that go away. I wished I could have been there just to be part of it one more time.

It was the convicts who showed up at my cell with con-dolences and cards. It was the tormented and discarded souls with lost decades and life sentences to show for most of their lives. They were the guys around every day, who weren't as young as they were when they came down for drive-by shootings during those hot summers in the middle of the '90s, or robberies that went bad where one of the great psycho-mirages of a Golden Gateway into a better life clouded over their eyes. One of my good friends unloaded schizophrenically into a vehicle; another killed his mom.

There were others, all much younger, all much more removed from the feelings that came to be their public definitions. There were those who robbed and cut throats, ones who woke up one person with a particular intention and an accident made them someone else, people who went out drinking one night and woke up monsters with bloodshot eyes blown-up full size on TV. These were the people with their own pain and hurt who signed cards and sent love over, pulled me aside in the hallway and offered their apologies.

There were prison guards and other staff from the joint, too, some I may have only spoken with sparingly over the years, who pulled me up to tell me how sorry they were. I wanted to believe they understood what it meant to lose relatives or a bit of sanity, a piece of yourself—or anything where there are winners and losers. It was universal and it was hard to accept I had been mostly insulated from this kind of blow for most of my life.

I was part of *this* family—the tiers rising into the sky, humidity floating, hovering through openings in these cell bars during summer. And my brothers here were the ones who offered support. They were brothers I sometimes hated for all the personal intricacies created by this place. I was afraid I would end up living under a blanket for a long time, or get myself high or drink myself numb. I didn't think I was ready for what this would make me. I was never good at managing grief or suffering. I had to figure out how to transform, just as this place has over the years, as places like this always do as seasons change and patterns are manipulated. But I had to try not to let it make me an angrier or less compassionate person, especially if I ever expected a woman to love me, or expected I could be a father with something worthwhile as a man to pass along to my children. I was all sorts of things, just like the prison was—a prison, an asylum, and catacombs all at the same time. I was a crook, crazy, and dead. The prison could also be a river that washes away the dirt on our souls. I had the sickness—I finally got it—without enough brawn, enough courage to fight it. I had to believe I could be washed clean, too.

Twenty-one

BOMBS
||||||||||||||||||||||||||||||||||||||||||

T HEY LOCKED US DOWN the same day somebody planted the bombs that went off at the Boston Marathon. We all knew it was coming. We usually did. We got our two lockdowns a year no matter what, and that was without the ones we got as a result of the chaos that kicked off when it did. Routine lockups were expected for months sometimes, with the gossip-mongers anticipating them at every count. Most people liked them. I used to love them. They were breaks for guys from their prison jobs as welders or machinists, with faces and clothes full of soot, or janitors wiping snot and shit from walls. They were breaks from all of the tension of maintaining aloof and indiffer-ent personas and hoping for some rest.

There is a certain spiritual strength it takes to get by through long stretches in the joint—that, or a certain ignorance that at times can seem like the same thing. I often used my days locked in my cell as a time of spiritual restoration. It gave guys a break from having to talk to each other about all the same stuff we talked about every day. I used to need a break from my time, and the trade-off came from the modest stress of getting your cell turned upside down. Now it seemed like we were con-stantly going on and coming off of lockdowns every few weeks. And if we weren't, we were constantly preparing for the next one. We just had one a few months before; I just didn't have patience for more of these kinds of disruptions.

This time we just hoped we'd get our canteen before they dropped the notice of the shakedown. The house was so dry, people were paying four times the cost for Ramen noodles and beef summer sausages. I didn't have any food in my canteen bag but a single noodle, a third of a roll of crackers, and a sealed pack of chicken. We were just a day from getting our commissary when they slipped the memo on our bars at 9:30 the night before. It was the usual memo with the presumption printed on it: *Thank you for your cooperation.* The news ignited the usual groans and guttural sounds in response to our never-ending string of disappointments. One guy screamed frustration until his voice went hoarse: "You are an evil person, Sgt. _____!" But it was mostly caught by the wind and carried away. Then there were those who used it to congratulate themselves: "I told you. Didn't I tell you they were going to do this?" I was surrounded on both sides by guys who didn't speak during lockdowns. The first night I got a "They're bogus for this" from my friend CF on my right. I didn't hear his voice much after that.

CF and I became close because we shared depressions. He was more manic; I was more depressive. Sometimes it made us hate each other. Sometimes we used our illnesses as our swords to fight with each other, a tit for tat at our varying levels of strength and weakness. Sometimes it would be the other way around and it would be my mania challenging his depression. When we were in sync, we shared a vision of an artist collective, a revival of all the things that seemed to emancipate the people who lived in these same cells a couple of generations before, who have now been ignored and forgotten from the history of this place. We also shared a sense of time and sanity, and how they both inevitably run out.

On my left was the old man China, who is really not an old Chinese man but a Laotian man only a couple of years older than I am who ran around South Minneapolis at the same time I did. He's twenty years of the way through his life sentence.

He wears an extra-scratchy personality on the outside, probably just to protect his sanity.

There was a whole cluster of us cloaked in our own cells with mountains on our backs, connected amidst the catacombs. On the other side of CF was J, who was fourteen when he got his life sentence, twenty-six when they gave it to him again. Next to J there was Preach, who was seventeen when he got his life sentence. Next to China was F—he was seventeen—and next to him another, seventeen as well. Below us was the twenty-year-old kid who was one of the first to get life without the possibility of parole, and next to him Yoda, also twenty years into his life stint. The sting of time had left marks on all of us. They all still liked lockdowns—called them vacations. It was easier when I was younger and didn't think I deserved very much. I was twenty-two once, and these bricks didn't know me yet. These guys considered me halfway out the door now, with only ten years left.

I kind of panicked. The timing was just bad and I wasn't prepared. I had hardly any food in my bag, and what they fed us was the lowest and vilest form of food they could find, frozen and stashed somewhere for weeks or months. All of my water bottles were empty, so I was consigned to the noxious chemical taste of unfiltered tap water from the old well, flowing through the hundred-year-old pipes. I had a bag of dirty laundry, hardly enough underwear to get me through the next few days. I was frustrated because I would lose typing days just weeks from a deadline. And I would miss poetry class on Wednesday night, one of the only nights in my week where I felt an ease from the strictures that held me in place.

I figured, though, that if they shook us down right away in the morning, I could spend those days writing and maybe finish the book I was reading. I was reading *Right to Be Hostile* about the public-schools-to-prison pipeline. It had taken me unusually long to read because I would get angry after a few pages and put it down. I might have the time now. It might keep me from obsessing over the food and the water and the treatment. I was better than this place, and I have proved it to myself over and over. I have told my family this so often they are tired of hearing about it.

I had been through so many of these during my prison bid, or bit, or stretch, or piece of whatever we call it. They were something that was ingrained in us. We used to cook meals in our hot pots and hand booze back and forth in the middle of the night. I had been through the fourteen-day lockdown when the old bruiser stomped that kid into a puddle. I had withstood a couple during the hottest weeks of summer. I'd had them where some wicked woman crouched down and counted our socks and dirty drawers and read letters from home, and when they brought dogs through, leaving paw prints on my blankets. I'd been in them during holidays and during prison softball championships. I was locked down on my thirty-second birthday and had a card signed by all of my friends, sent down the tier one cell at a time. I'd had visitors turned away without explanation because of them. Guys even used to talk about the month-long routines going back to the nineties. The guys in B-West broke dozens of windows with cartons of milk during their lockdown in '04. Then winter came. In 1983, they broke nine hundred of them. They could be tough, but we created stories from them—part of the communal endurance that made us know we could still be human. Hopefully, this one would be over in a few days and none of this would matter then.

But then there was always the *something* I knew I shouldn't have but thought I needed anyway—*something* that if they found it, I would have to reschedule the next year of my life. Most everyone has a *something* that could compromise them during these times. So I scrambled to hide things, just like I always did during the first night of all the lockdowns I'd ever been in. I was never sure what some brand-new young cop would try to book me with.

I have made a bid of staying reserved and cautious about the explosive elements of myself—a bomb of unexpressed knowledge and feeling regarding all I had seen about the way people are treated. I just didn't know how long before it exploded from me. I wanted to vent and yell something ignorant out my bars, but that would just make me sound like so many other guys shouting like they were children reacting to punishment from their parents. I am not a child—and they certainly aren't my parents. I couldn't waste the spiritual energy; I needed it all. It made me feel soft, though, or scared because I couldn't react the way my heart told me I should. I convinced myself I got past that scared shit a long time ago.

Day 1

I sat and watched TV. The same footage of the bombing continued to play in a loop. It reminded me a little of 9/11; I was in a cell for that, too. We waited in limbo as all the networks brought their "experts" aboard to shill their version of fear. We were supposed to be scared all over again. We were supposed to pull out our lists of usual suspects and choose one or two to be angry at; my list was different from theirs. I tried to stay as detached from the footage as I usually was, as though from a world of fiction where these things don't happen, where people didn't blow other people up. But I couldn't help but feel the drop, the tapping of footsteps on the other side of the future, the rattling vibration of another inert shifting of how we see our world. The fear might have even come from the knowledge that these shifts happened so often now.

But I watched anyway. I stayed up late, flipped between the NBA and continued shots of the bombings. There were scenarios everywhere: reports of a third bombing at the JFK Library that was later declared unrelated, possibilities of copycat bombings, and a fertilizer plant in West Texas that blew up in the night. During commercials I dug through my footlockers to make sure everything was hidden where I needed it to be, to make sure I had an accounting of all my extra T-shirts and drawers, and all the extra hygiene products I used for currency. I had way too many books; I was used to being told this, but most of the space was taken up by my notebooks, a collection that was mostly filled, growing larger with really no consolidation in sight.

Day 2

I already had a headache when I woke up to a guard stuffing a brown paper bag with cereal, milk, and two smashed boiled eggs between my bars. It was one of the feverish and debilitating headaches that have plagued me since I was a child and that I still got regularly. I took the two milks and flung them over the tier like bombs with no intended targets—simply to get the possibility of rotten milk stench as far from my cell as possible. I heard them smack against the floor, but I couldn't see where they landed. I had to drink my coffee with tepid water I got from the hot water button on my sink because I melted my hot pot a few weeks before. I tried to sleep, but I felt an urgency to get back up to rehide the things I'd already hidden. My first thoughts were about the *something* I had hidden that I knew would cause me the most consequence. Without getting it out of my mind, I would never be able to concentrate enough to read, let alone write. I went back and forth between throwing it off the tier, and manning up and dealing with it. The truth was it wasn't just mine to get rid of or keep: it belonged to a collective of us. It was one of those things that probably couldn't be replaced and affected all of the fellas, not just myself. I used the reflection of my toenail clipper to look back and forth on the galley for the police, hoping they would hurry up and shake us down.

I'm used to a cell. It has become natural to me. There is an inexplicable link between prisoner and cell. There are secrets it keeps without emotion attached to them. Being stuck in a cell can be like holding your breath. I never expected fifteen years would feel like this: the constant flux of open and close, the closing and crash of locking myself into a box over and over, inhale, exhale, until I'm complicit and even comfortable with it.

It is my space: the cell, the cage, my kennel, my box—six by eight by nine to the very back, with crisscrossing steel bars like Alcatraz or San Quentin that make checkered shadows in the rooms, connected by a break that opens at certain times of a day by a human being pulling an old steel lever. I essentially live in a bathroom stall. My head rests a foot and a half from my sink, two and a half feet from a stainless steel toilet. The doctor here told me once I had to piss all the time because I had to look at that toilet all day, every day. It is during these breaks when the cell and I get to know each other, become a part of the same history, connected to a whole block of cells anchored in a rectangular row of concrete that runs from hallway to showers in perfect rows four tiers high, its distance making it arc from one end to the other.

I like it dark when I am by myself. So I hung a sheet from wall to wall to completely block out my cell bars. When guards came by they asked me, "What are you doing back there?" I was really just reading or watching TV. I tried to meditate, but it always came back to hunger, then to hostility. In some ways the cell is the perfect enclosure for the single human being—alone with God. I often think maybe one day I might die in one of these.

CNN was still showing the bomb sequences. Day 2 brought all of the human-interest stories: the deaths, the paralysis. The experts were still spinning the likelihood that Al Qaeda or some other international group was lurking insidiously behind it all. While I drank my instant coffee, they were trying to draw connections between the bombings with the latest failed gun control bill in the House. ESPN streamed live tweets of reactions from professional athletes. Catchphrases started coming out like they always do: "Boston Strong." The hashtags #Bombings and #Go Sox!

I still had the headache when they brought lunch. It wouldn't go away; they never did, until they shook me down and the doors opened and my blood pressure dropped. Just hearing and smelling the food carts roll in made me a sick kind of anxious. A very tall African guard with a goofy smile on his face, who is always trying to carry on the silliest dialogues with inmates, tried to hand me a cardboard tray with some kind of rectangular patty, four tater tots, and about fifteen gray peas. I ate the bread and politely told him to keep the tray. My guy down the tier got mad at me for not giving it to him. Clueless, the guard asked me if I was all right. "Yeah, I'm fine."

Most moments during a bid are forgotten. It would be impossible to keep together all the scattered moments of hurt, or disappointment, or boredom, or indifference. Until they get so congested together at one time that they become the *Sickness*. I was already sick. I had been for so long. It is a different kind of sickness, though—a sickness that kills in slow motion. Rot. I spent most of the afternoon eating Ibuprofen and listening to my stomach grumble. I read two pages of *Right to Be Hostile*, but it was still hard to concentrate. I ate the food I did have and felt temporarily satiated. CNN cut in with news that an envelope with ricin, sent to some congressman, was intercepted. They broke in that another envelope had been snatched on its way to the President. I wanted to write, but my head hurt and I couldn't concentrate on anything other than the experts on TV spending hours explaining how the poison was made. I got a letter from my aunt, something abstract and separate from this place. Dinner came around again: meatballs. "Hey, Preach, take this garbage." I ate some more bread. By late afternoon they had somebody in custody for the ricin envelopes. It came with the news that Congress had struck down the new gun control bill. Lines attached to laundry bags with toilet paper and noodles in them zipped by my cell to someone down the tier.

That night the Ken Burns documentary about the Central Park Five came on PBS. It was the last thing I needed to see on this night—another dark example of how the justice system fucks and manipulates people, particularly poor young people. I watched an unrelenting public execute those boys through the media. Maybe it came from everything that was happening, but I cried for all of the years stolen from those boys. Maybe I was really crying about the years *I'd* lost. I was exhausted all over again. I was tired of being a slave. I tried to write a poem about it, but I could only get through one stanza:

> I can feel my own doom in those
> dark, distorting hours—just children
> bars on newfound hearts.

Nothing else came.

The nurse came by with my headache medication. When did I start taking medication anyway? I used to be so much stronger. Another documentary came afterwards, *The War Next Door,* about the lost war on drugs. I grit my teeth and let myself get dizzy. My hands got numb from clenching. I was tired of being sick.

I guess I was angry. I felt small under the forces I felt so suppressed by: the police, prosecutors, judges, the department of corrections, right on down to the people who made our food and the guards who dropped it off for us. It extended right on to a general public that has absorbed all of this as being just, so blind to understanding it could happen to them and their families as well. I'd always believed in a narrative of transformation and metamorphosis. In the beginning when I was still young to my bid, I read books written by men in prison who got out and went back to lives as artists and activists or started organizations. I saw myself as someone like this, stronger and incapable of being hurt by these years, instead fortified by the experience.

Lately, I'd started to see things differently. Especially on this night, I felt like maybe transforming and reemerging were really just terms meant for an earlier set of prisoners, before mass sentencing and before it became such a powerful industrial complex that stepped on those it captured. I thought maybe they should have just given us our OID numbers in the eighth grade so we wouldn't waste any more of that time dreaming.

I really needed them to shake us down in the morning so the pressure in my shoulders and the thump in my head might go away.

Day 3

But they didn't shake us down. I was awakened by the nurse bringing me my pills. My headache woke up with me. I was up again, checking my spots, contemplating to move the *something* around again. I decided not to—what will be will be. The coffee still tasted like fertilizer, a knot throbbed over my right eye, my mouth was dry, and I was still starving. I had decided I was done accepting this treatment. I would commit my life to the abolishment of prisons. The food carts came again: Salisbury steak patty. Are you fucking serious? The ricin envelope bomber was released and they were looking for his ex-wife now. They were already setting up vigils for the marathon victims.

I needed to write to fill these nervous days. When I'm working, I'm human. When I am not, I'm just a monkey that jumps up when a bell rings. Lockdowns used to be a time when I could work, when I could catch up on what I was reading or do homework. But I was sick; I was a monkey from eating next to nothing, and from carrying around the illness that grows up inside of us over all these years. Is this what fifteen years felt like? I took the tray and flung it through my bars out onto the tier. But most of it just hit the bars and left a mess on the floor and the inside of the room. I was too tired to clean it up. "Hey, Preach, you ain't getting this one." I lay down with a towel soaked in cold water wrapped around my head instead. I dreamt of sickness.

I woke up midafternoon in sweats, extrasensitive to the smell of trash and shit. Hefty bags tied to the outside of our cells, full of sitting milk cartons and festering trays. It is crazy how so many men get to shitting at the same time, toilets flushing in rhythm. I know I smelled, too. I caught myself with detergent and a scrub brush, washing socks and drawers in my sink. I couldn't help but look at myself in the mirror bolted to the wall. I splashed water over a face that got no cleaner.

When chow came again, I could feel my stomach sucking in. I knew I could eat it, but I also knew as soon as I bit into it I would be sicker, angrier. Maybe I wasn't really angry, maybe it was just fear that all that transcending shit about becoming something greater than this place I was spouting was fake. Maybe all of those extra years were really a trick to make me docile and weak. Maybe it didn't matter what a person did in that cell, maybe the force of everything you grow and do loses its power after so long. Maybe, I really had lost my spirit, my humanity. I was a caged animal, meant to eat like a beast.

I wanted to ask myself if I really had such a right to be so hostile. This *is* prison; it has been since I've known it, since it ever was. So why did it hurt so much now—the lockdown, the food? Was it because I was getting older? Or because I was afraid I had wasted it? Maybe I didn't have time to write the book I'd been trying to finish, or I would never have children. Or because I finally grew up. But it all came in here—living from lockdown to lockdown, scared they will take the last thing I really needed. Maybe it's because the clock never stops ticking, the future still comes in whatever form it chooses. Or was it because I was tired? Tired of being that passive slave in jailhouse oranges sleepwalking through years.

It is when I get to feeling like this that there is an inmate or a teacher or a guard who always feels he needs to tell me how much worse it is for prisoners in other places around the world. I tell them, "I know. Those are my people." We are all inextricably linked to each other through these cells, or maybe more so through time. The cell keeps us still; the time takes us to all the different places that change us, hopefully in ways beautiful, but most often in all the ugly ways. Prison has always been this way, I guess. I asked CF once, What if we had been born somewhere else—how do you think our lives would be different? "We'd probably just be in a cell somewhere else," he said, as though this was our natural state. "Some people are meant to be free. Most people aren't." It didn't make me any less tired, or scared, or crazy, though.

I turned the TV on again, and there was surveillance footage of the two alleged marathon bombers. They didn't look like terrorists. In the footage they had on cargo pants and bangs spilling out from under baseball caps and backpacks slung over their shoulders. They looked like high school or college students. They still walked like kids. We saw their blurry faces over and over—the same few shots—and whoever they were, they had to be somewhere watching, knowing it was almost over. It was their one chess move in life, and they blew up kids and parents, blew the legs off marathon runners. With all of the monsters and colliding monstrous forces in the world, and this was who they chose to expel their anger toward? These were the people we had to be afraid of? But I wasn't afraid of them. I was more afraid of going crazy in a cell after so many years. I just got the familiar nervous feeling I get whenever I see young people on the verge of inheriting a million years in a place like this. I felt a sorrow, not for these foolish youngsters who left irreparable damage behind them but for all of the foolish youngsters I've known. Soon we'll be linked to them too, whether we want to or not.

While I watched the National Guard with tanks, and an ocean of police assembled on every Boston street corner, guys were on the tier heatedly debating the existence of mermaids. They were watching something on a channel I didn't even know we had. "That shit is real." Another section of kids were rapping a Rick Ross song almost deliriously in unison. There was a guy on a tier below me practicing with his guitar, strumming the same chord over and over again. As much as I tried to separate myself from them, I couldn't—they were my people.

That night I watched the Central Park jogger documentary again, just for something to rage about. Yeah, I was tired of being a slave. But I was also tired of fighting. Nobody listened. By that evening they had two brothers identified as the marathon bombers. There was already a slew of family and friends in front of cameras for their own few minutes of fame. It was the way it has always been. Ask the Central Park kids about it.

Day 4

When I woke up again, cops were at my door, there to finally dig through my life. If what I had wasn't hidden well enough—well, then it was too late, I was fucked. The TV was on fire with the news that the older brother had died overnight. He'd been hit by the car the younger brother was driving to flee a gas station robbery. This was who they shut down an entire city for?

They strip-searched me and then brought me down the tier and handcuffed me to a railing next to CF and China and a couple of other guys I had done years and years alongside of. All of us with IDs clipped to our T-shirts with our OID numbers as testaments to how long we'd been in our cocoons. One of us considered that with the five of us gathered there, "we've probably been through two hundred lockdowns just between us." Yet there were rookies shaking our rooms down who had never participated in a lockdown before. It was crazy how after so many, I was still nervous. I was supposed to be tougher than this. *Why am I being so soft?* I probably could have asked China what *twenty* years felt like—or what he anticipated the next twenty might. He told me he needed a few more days of this. *Yeah, okay.*

One by one, guys were uncuffed and brought back to their cells, but I was still there as other prisoners came and were handcuffed next to me. There really wasn't time to be scared now. Several more prisoners were sent back to their cells before a skinny guard with a ridiculous blond mustache pulled up on me: they must have found *it*. I knew I messed up, I knew I overthought it. Instead, the guy had the nerve to tell me I had too many notebooks. I just shook my head and slammed the cell door behind me. I saw two seat marks side by side on my mattress. The TV channel had been changed to wrestling. The *something* was secure and safe where I had put it, at least until the next time.

With my headache still lingering, I watched an army hunt down the baby-faced little brother. They started to let the tiers out to take showers. The lockdown was almost over. I could wash the filth from my body and try to speak in sentences for the first time in a while. By the time I got back, they had the young bomber hiding in a boat in someone's backyard, full of bullet holes. They said he tried to blow himself up but couldn't. I wanted them to just let the kid die, so they could give us all some finality. By this point I wanted it *all* to be over. I needed my bid to be over, too.

But of course they didn't let the kid die; they pulled him in, saved him. There would be a trial now. I didn't want to have to choose between two sides like watching two basketball teams I hate. There would be more news coverage and all sorts of opportunities for others to jump forward and be heroes, but they wouldn't bring anybody back to life or undo any of what was broken. There would be more bombs hidden somewhere or falling from the sky.

It was over—but it wasn't really. There was still that deadline—for the story I was supposed to write, and the deadline that couldn't be pushed back. Our OIDs don't come with deadlines, though; they stay with us whether we get out, go crazy, or die. It doesn't matter *when* they give us our number, because we keep it the rest of our lives.

I would spend another night in my cell and it would tell me a secret. It would tell me: there *would* be a transformation. We *would* get transformed into something else, and that these moments would be written and remembered as an everlasting part of the metamorphosis. There would be no forgetting them. Everything would be obvious then. It would reaffirm my relationship to its fixed dimensions, and to CF and China and J and these other men pushed through the same pipeline, hoping to come out the other side transformed in any of the ways that didn't make us crazy. And tomorrow they would open these breaks: the cell door would open. I would have to exhale, I would have to talk to people again, but I would still be angry, and I would still be sick, and I would still be hungry.

Epilogue

THIS IS WHERE I AM

Soo THIS, THIS IS WHERE I AM. This is where I've been for the past seventeen years—it's where I was propelled from the blast. It's a steel fortress with a large entrance and a microscopic exit. When anybody asked where I was over that time and they were told I was somewhere else, with someone else's life—I was here. This is why I wasn't at Grandma A's or Papa Arno's funerals. Here I am—the prison, etched in myth. I used to think that maybe if I acted like it wasn't what it was, it might not be able to change me. If I acted like the walls didn't climb to outer space, or that my room wasn't really a cage that gets smaller every moment it stays locked, then maybe it wouldn't take everything from me. Maybe then the girl from Wisconsin wouldn't leave, my family wouldn't die, and I could walk back in time to South Minneapolis and start over.

I don't know if I still deserve to be here writing and speaking about my survival after some of the shit I've done. Maybe I don't. Maybe that's in the ether with my childhood and all of those secret packets of experience we carry around with ourselves, all of the garbage we do to live that we can't speak of or choose not to. The self-designed chaotic worlds we live in that change us into all of the things we become. I'm very sorry for the person I was. I wish I had done some things different.

I always wished I had been stronger and more able. I wish I was fearless, but I'm not, I never was, and that fear came out in ways I wish it hadn't. I fucked up—I didn't care enough about my life, I didn't care enough about the dreams and expectations my name and existence represented. I regret being so scared when I was young. There is something about the places where we are at our most miserable, most stepped on and deprived of all the sensory things and outlets of love and support, where people find ways to find themselves, to find God, where we often change our minds and decide to see and be different aspects of ourselves.

At one point, a combustion of a noxious mix of gases occurred in my life, rapid oxidation accompanied by heat and light. These explosions are part of the inevitable destruction the entire world gets, sometimes communally, sometimes individually. They blow out, come from within and expel matter into space. Sometimes communities explode—families and social circles. Something blows up and the pieces left scatter unpredictably. The parts of people that are left will have to pick up the charred pieces of their lives, forget about the parts pulverized by the blast, and start over without some of the things people thought they'd never have to live without. They propel shrapnel that cuts deep scars in families. They will make people admit their weakness; they can be the bruises that remind us we are still alive, or the boom that kills us—the sound and the fury of what Death becomes that hurts people it is not supposed to. Explosions are what happen after people lose control of the forces in their life. They are inevitable. They come back and steal dreams, give away hope as it spills out on pavement for nature to clean up. The myth was that we ever had control over the forces in our lives to begin with.

I am the leftover remnant of a lifetime of explosions—one great one that was unfortunate and carved scars in the hearts of people I never met and obliterated the constructions of my village and anything else I may have understood. It changed who I was several times, changed my dreams that were mostly dead by then anyway, changed my relationship to the world, in part made me ugly, and later made me invisible. My mom said during one of the hundreds of visits she made through snowstorms and torrential rains of personal moods and tragedy that she was worried that this place was going to make me somehow different. She said she was afraid prison was going to harden my heart and make someone bitter and broken from the poison. I told her I had no idea what it might do because it wasn't over yet.

IIIIIIIIIIIIIIIIIIIIIIIIIIIII

WE REPRESENT FAMILIES that don't necessarily have anything in common but to pack visiting room lobbies on any given Sunday to see and speak to the discarded, deceased, wayward, and resurrected fragments of their lives for an hour at a time.

That was my mom and my dad and my grandma. Just like so many families, my family as a unit has been fighting a lifetime of this tumult, and we won't all make it. Lives were sacrificed so that the worst from these groups might one day have lives, no matter how diminished they might end up.

Even Granny could only fight it for so long. She had protected me with those two cans of Raid, but they couldn't protect her from the hottest summer in the past hundred years. She sat in the house on Elliot without an air conditioner but with a spirit too stubborn to accept one, until the heat cooked her, and her letters finally stopped after thirteen years. She hung around for a few more years after that, but she was certainly not the same fearless woman in the yellow sundress. Even she couldn't beat this prison sentence.

IIIIIIIIIIIIIIIIIIIIIIIIIIIII

MOST OF US COME FROM all the unique dimensions of who we are. All of these individual human beings come to meet at the entrance to this: the joint. The system runs us through orientation and gives us a number. At that point we're not much different, just fresh faces seeing something for the first time. And then those individual bodies spread out again, start journeys outward, and especially inward. We are left to redesign our futures. But through all the revolutions, the magnetic forces of time will usually draw people back to the same place. It is the same place of the unfeeling gates that welcomed us in the beginning. It comes with the peace knowing that all the filigree that filled the blank spaces inside of us was only ornament we used to get through all the complicated workings of this alternate universe. But that who we were, no matter the decoration, came from the same isolation, the same loss and injury as all the others we met as we were coming through the gate.

I know my stories aren't unique. I don't pretend there is anything so special about any of the things that have happened in my life. They are nothing in relativity to some of the experiences of people in here. I've met people from all over the world who ran into their own exploding frontiers. We all met in the same place, the hurt aching in the same voids. I met a man who lost his father and uncles in the killing fields of Cambodia; he used to go with his brothers to dig through piles of bones looking for pieces of his relatives to take with them. Nobody in here is going to look at somebody else in here and express any astonishment at anything I've written. They aren't going to bring up anything about my deep-spooky depressions or about heartbreaks over someone not being able to love me anymore.

Stories about family members dying or the rigors of the justice system or how crazy Minneapolis was ever so long ago aren't anything interesting to most of the people in here because they went through it, too—sometimes much more vividly. It was a generation that had this sickness shared with them from the generation before, passing from cupped hands runneth over to anybody who came after us. There is little need to talk amongst ourselves about sleeping weeks away in the proverbial darkness; or about the people any of us cared an entire world about dying like exhausted matches; or about how their kids grew up without parents because their dads might've been pieces of shit, might still be, might be both pieces of shit and great people at the same time.

There were just too many of us trying to gather from what seemed like an endless well, but there was only so much water any of us could hold in our hands. It is the same pain that mothers and girlfriends, siblings and children have shared from the start of graft and the start of jail—life and death and a shortness of time. We thought it was money and opportunity we were competing for, but it was really time. Time is the water that we were all competing for, that we've always been competing for. We have had to say good-bye to so many things. I'm sure now there are other young, idealistic people out there who might think they have things all figured out, who are looking at the stars and declaring lives they can't possibly be prepared for, can't possibly understand the hurt they'll face. They won't grab on to the things they want because they're afraid of something. Nineteen ninety-five was twenty years ago, and soon after it will be nothing—forgotten, obscured, and abstracted. These new kids have their own life-and-death problems, they have their own boxed-in obfuscations to panic and blow up about. The scramble is shaped differently, but it's still the scramble.

In here the moment-to-moment push to stay comfortable tends to diminish our need to add meaning to our lives. It is this need that makes us want to think our lives are more important, that there are people out there who love us, and that the primal thirst that is killing us is killing them, too. There's hardly any work involved—a fifteen-minute phone call every once in a while, and it's like they did their part. They don't always understand the dull ache we feel of the world passing us by. Sometimes we are just hoping someone else is as tortured as we are by the way years hallucinate our sense over the actual. It usually doesn't do much but make us seem crazy, changed and broken, confused and out of touch.

At some point in my bid I started thinking about getting out and getting older, and the very real probability of going to funerals for the lifers who held me down for such a significant chunk of my life. Men who never got their chance to walk out the door. I had to start thinking about what that really meant. We're here and we make these friends, and the longer we are here the more they seem to supersede childhood friends and become like brothers. Whole lifetimes spent behind walls, children who grew up without parents, and life went on without them. And in this time when the cult of the individual carries so much value, accepting we weren't at the center of the universe often hurts the heart more than anything. And who will be at *my* funeral if everyone is gone and the entire world I've built is either dead or in prison?

There is not an exact formula to speak for the rehabilitative spirit. I wish there were, but there's not. There is only mostly just a vague and obscured set of precepts: education, job opportunities, drug treatment—it mostly depends on who's asking for the funding. There are all of these varying groups and programs competing for small chunks of funding to keep them relevant and afloat. There is no snap of the fingers or flash catharsis that magically transforms an individual. There are Character First mottoes and Restorative Justice phrases hung up on the walls to remind us to be better people, words scattered in collage form: *Honor, Meekness, Submission.* But the food still gets worse, is sometimes rotten, and the steel stays just as secure, just as shut as it ever was. The wall stays just as high, more layers of razor wire keep being added, sentences get longer, and more guilt but less redemption are laid on the shoulders of the men in blue shirts and concrete shoes. There are some who believe in these things, others who believe it's all a scam. It is like the redemption many of the people in here chase after for so many years. Some things just aren't redeemable.

It is a grueling process of self-realization, a weighing of facts and experience against other more textured factors and experiences that don't come or go through some dimensionless program set up by people who don't really have any longterm studies or evidence to back their claims for success. Rehabilitation is really an individual matter. It is the existentialist dilemma of choosing directions we hope bring us something meaningful. It is an individual understanding that we are captives and that we spread to everyone, that this isn't just a matter of human experience we are individually destined for: we are part of the machine, of one of the great complexes of our economy. Whips and chains don't make us a slave anymore:

gavels and keys do. And they are the same thing in the end. We have to find something to get us free from that, to figure out our new roles in the world.

And yet part of me understands how he has hurt people. Feeling rehabilitated doesn't take away someone else's hurt. I know I'm ready to go home. I know that any more time isn't going to make me any better—more than likely worse. But I'm not sure I really know how to love someone yet; I haven't had a chance to yet; or if I trust myself, the new self that grew from all of this, or if getting out really has anything at all to do with justice or righteousness; it probably doesn't. Either you get a chance or you don't. Either it is early, or it is later, or it's never— and how good a person you are, you were, or are going to be has nothing to do with it. And that's too bad because dirtbags leave real motherfuckers behind in the joint all the damn time, on their way to something wicked. And real motherfuckers stay here and build bridges and embrace another generation that got caught in these spider webs. I wanted to be a better person. I think I am, but if I'm not it wouldn't matter—a whole lot of folks go home worse. I wanted to be a better person, but I had to learn how, and it took good people to show me how to get there.

Standard prison narratives usually only take a few routes. There are those most often used clichés about the rotten souls. They are the young and completely misdirected who come into the joint, wild and out of control, and find themselves. These are the stories that are usually of redemption or meta-morphosis. There has always been a strength and power as-sociated with the metamorphosis from the concrete cocoon, the reemergence after going in as a heathen and coming out as legion: it is as old as the history of people itself, as Lazarus emerging from the ground. There are also those stories of kids who still had ideas, still believed they had life, still believed in themselves, who came here and got worse. They got dark and hateful, became perplexed, and went mad; tattooed all kinds of things on their souls that were meant to mean something; but only really ever said how much they hurt inside. The envi-ronment distorted that hope, smothered the dreams, and made those kids worse human beings. Because these places will do all of these things—there's no apology, just stone experience.

It becomes about merciless sentencing without reexamination. About people not understanding the complexities of something so volatile and important, so they disregard it and all the people it touches. It's about real people and real feelings, real disappointments for people who are genuine and decent, who have done exorbitant years, waiting to come home. It is about captors oftentimes becoming worse than the captives, letting the ugly and the sickness vomit out of them into the lives of other real human beings.

I'm not one or the other of those clichés; I was never that wild and I was equally never very idealistic. To suggest that one day something came into my life and redirected me to be something greater would be inaccurate. There wasn't something magic I discovered in a book or a sermon; life came to me from years and love—it was people giving a damn. My story isn't a piece about family waiting on an innocent man: it was more about blind justice throwing time indiscriminately at people and then expecting these people to be sane after decades in a degenerative world and inhumane environment that just are and never get better. Mostly it came from a family, like so many families, that mortgaged years of their own lives so that they could help support people they love, who the rest of the world already considered dead, so that hopefully there would be something for them outside the walls and that they *would* be sane when the doors opened for them.

I could say it was a pen and a notebook. It is romantic to say the written word changed my life. But that was something hard earned that didn't show its worth until long after I worked myself to death, sacrificed time I could have used learning something else. There were certain people who made me see something greater than I understood. Without people, I wouldn't have written anything.

⁞⁞⁞⁞⁞⁞⁞⁞⁞⁞⁞⁞⁞⁞⁞⁞⁞⁞⁞⁞⁞⁞⁞⁞

I GET TO THINKING about how we all started out: diluted images of being something better, bigger, more robust—some with a level of malice or their intention darker—more granulated than others, how the expulsion scattered us into our places. I read a book a friend of mine wrote about growing up in the city at around the same time I did. I remember feeling this awful anxiety as I read it, which came out as a sort of jealousy from not being there, not being able to write that book myself. It was something I tried hard to expel from inside me. But as it started to become clear to me, it was really anxiety over all the things I had missed: the actual world, not my own imagined scenarios from years of daydreaming—no, an actual world that went on and grew up while I was gone. The city moved on, my friends moved on. Then, what my mom told me when everything started to go wrong; she told me that I probably wasn't meant to have an easy life; it happens, and we get different things to endure. There is a new layer of grass, wildflowers, and trees; an entire generation and a new city have grown up out of what were the charred grounds we left. The book I was supposed to write was just different.

Instead, I've been here, waiting to get out. An old man trying to relate to people and the children who have grown up in the time I was gone. A forty-five-year-old kid fresh out of high school. The last time they saw me I smoked a half an ounce of weed a day and was sticking people up to pay the rent at a broken-down, old one-bedroom of a duplex. Getting out is supposed to offer this wonderful freedom, the culmination and awareness of who we are and the world as this great, big, all-encompassing whole. There is a sadness, though—because with it we know how much has been lost, and how so many have given their whole lives to the grind of that world.

Now I'm preparing myself to start jobs with Plexiglas ceilings a mile thick. I'll have to learn how to do basic things the rest of my generation has weathered through for the past twenty years. At some point, though, the realization comes: it's prison, and there are millions of other people throughout history who have faced this. Nobody has to care. I have to shut the fuck up because it's right. There are a lot of people who didn't get to be Superman in their worlds. There's always someone else who has been down longer and endured more. There are tragedies that exist everywhere that make me understand my own experience. Someone can always tell us to look at all the awful stuff that happens to people every day: cancerous tumors, and sick kids who never get to grow up and try to be what they want to be, who meant hope and renewal for their own families. There are parents who die and leave kids alone in a violent world. There are stories of pain and suffering all over the world. There are no points in our regular lives where we can stand on the mountaintop and watch everything burn without being scathed by the flash or the heat, or in the chaos of reconstruction in the aftermath of its destruction. I can think about my own friends sitting in the same institutions as I have, with forever. Plus forever.

This is where I am. I was the kid hidden behind an air conditioner who thought I had no other way out but death. But here I am, so many years later, prepared to indict that young version of myself for thinking erratically. I was the kid who every day trudged his way down Cedar and across Lake Street for a bottle of beer, loaded with the kind of despair only seen in a piece of literature, full of dread, full of desperation—feeling, but not understanding, the potential onslaught that was coming. I was the kid with a smile and a cardigan sweater posed in pictures behind the bars on Alcatraz Island, practicing for my future.

I was standing on the track in the yard of the Stillwater Correctional Facility when the swelling finally went down and my eyes opened. I could see myself as one of the infinite broken men who had passed through these gates and built these prisons. Generations of fractured promises shared by men who carved their names in the fresh concrete. We share a lineage of confinement that showed me who I was. So I took my pen and tried to write myself back together. I tried to write my father back to life and bring back the kid who was supposed to be the promise of a new life. These stories are my chance to tell the world I recognized part of what it was trying to do. I still don't completely know all it wants me to know.

These stories are my poem to the universe.

ACKNOWLEDGMENTS

Before all else, a most profound and necessary thank you to my editor at the University of Minnesota Press, Erik Anderson, who brought life to the project and etched a value in its content that I am forever grateful for. He helped me see this as a book rather than a manuscript of my gradual madness. He sat with me and helped me form what I wanted it to say over the course of our visits. Thanks also to everyone at the University of Minnesota Press I never got a chance to meet but who were working and reading and committed to my project, especially Laura, Louisa, and Rachel. I also acknowledge Todd Orjala for the interest he showed that originally made the project a thing; without his support this would never have been seen by anyone else at the Press. To Myrna Harper, who contributed hours of transcription and encouragement: your work was essential.

To all the friends and family who gave a piece of their lives to me or played a role over the course of this project. To Waleed, I know this isn't what we expected for our lives. To our friend Damon, who will probably never read this. To Judy, the first true and living artist I ever knew; Nancy and the kindness that never got its due. The Mortimer's and Leech Lake crews, Dale L., Linda S., Pat Myers and Al Smullin, my godparents Betty and George, Catiesha, Andrea, Wayne Haroldson, Alan

Foran, and Jan Palmer. To Strydio, Torsten, and Mike S., you guys visited when no one else would. To Jamie Haroldson, Little Dylan, Zach (New), Rachel P., Molly, Steve, Laura, and the Riverside Park kids, who aren't kids anymore. And to all the muses who came and went—I remember you.

Thank you to the people from the Minnesota Prison Writing Workshop, Deb, Jen, Elizabeth, Kristin, and all of the instructors who are too numerous to name but I recognize you, mentors, and contributors to a program we were so hungry for. To the MPWW, whose presence in the great literary community of Minnesota is so needed in our prison literary community.

To the Stillwater Writers Collective and Chris Cabrera, who understood the futility of trying to get people to write when there weren't people there to read your stuff—your moment is coming. To Kara, with thanks for your support of my writing and Bridge work.

To the fellas of the BRIDGE Trust: K. Reese, we won some games we thought we never could—just make layups. They can't stop the future. To Vina and our people at VOICES who saw real people when they came into these places. The Social and Community/Prisoner Disconnect is a real thing. I am so grateful to you and all of our partners for your understanding.

To PEN for creating a conduit for the voices of men and women in the different layers of oppression, marginalization, and persecution. We just have to figure out what we're saying, or just start speaking. Your prison writing contest has given volume to some great voices and granted validation to my own work in the eyes of plenty of people who had catalogued me a certain way.

To Joyce Carol Oates for selecting my submission in *Prison Noir*—it was one of the great honors of my life.

To the original Stillwater Poetry Group: Dopp, Pauline Geraci for championing it, Desdamona, and Rachel Raimist.

To my early writing teachers, George Schell from South High School, and Celia Swanson, who made me promise her I would give her an acknowledgment in my first book. To all of the educators I have encountered during my incarceration, especially John Schmidt, Mark Stoltenburg, and the ed. directors who supported the arts.

To the men who have shared these spaces with me, who have their own losses and burdens: Tone, Zim, China, Johnny H., Barry, Dallas, Bino, Aaron M., Ghost, Vell, Slugs, Kou, Prime, Aguila, The Outlaws, especially Little Outlaw, Kiz, Tay, Eli, Ben A., 5-5, Florida, Woe, Jerry, Fong, Moeller—and there are far too many others to be named. And to the whole diaspora. We've all shared the sickness at some point. RIP Cav.

Finally, and most important, to my tri-part shield of protection that saved my life so many times. To my father, for sharing baseball, and his friends, and his park, and his neighborhood. You are South Minneapolis to me. To Granny: for years your letters reminded me I was still alive. You deserved so much more from us. To Dad and Granny, I thought you would both live forever. I hope you are watching and that I have done right by you both.

And to Mom: it all goes to you. You have kept our family alive through all the losses. You know a book could never offer the redemption we would all love, but who needs redemption when you are loved like you have loved me over the thirty-eight years of my life? Period.

Zeke Caligiuri is a writer of fiction, nonfiction, and poetry who grew up in the Powderhorn Park neighborhood of South Minneapolis. His short story "There Will Be Seeds for Next Year" is in the collection *Prison Noir*, edited by Joyce Carol Oates, and his writing was also published in *From Education to Incarceration: Dismantling the School-to-Prison Pipeline* and *From the Inside Out: Letters to Young Men and Other Writings*. His articles have been featured in the Minnesota *Spokesman-Recorder*, and he has won awards through the PEN Prison Writing Contest, including two first prizes for "The Last Visit from the Girl in the Willow Tree" and "Bombs," which was published in the 2016 PEN America journal *Hauntings*. He also works as a prison justice advocate.